D1561274

MELANCHTHON AND PATRISTIC THOUGHT

STUDIES IN THE HISTORY
OF
CHRISTIAN THOUGHT

EDITED BY

HEIKO A. OBERMAN, Tübingen

IN COOPERATION WITH

HENRY CHADWICK, Cambridge
JAROSLAV PELIKAN, New Haven, Conn.
BRIAN TIERNEY, Ithaca, N.Y.
E. DAVID WILLIS, Princeton, N.J.

VOLUME XXXII

E. P. MEIJERING

MELANCHTHON AND PATRISTIC THOUGHT

LEIDEN
E. J. BRILL
1983

MELANCHTHON AND PATRISTIC THOUGHT

The doctrines of Christ and Grace, the Trinity and the Creation

BY

E. P. MEIJERING

LEIDEN
E. J. BRILL
1983

ISBN 90 04 06974 7

CONTENTS

Preface IX

Introduction 1

  I. The Attack on Speculative Theology 4

  II. Melanchthon as a Patristic Scholar 19

III. Continuity and Discontinuity in the Thought of Melanchthon 109

IV. Conclusions and some Final Observations 138

Bibliography 145

Indices 148

PREFACE

There are historical studies and systematic studies. Historical studies can be reliable, if they have been correctly carried out, systematic studies can be interesting, if the right questions have been asked and answered. But reliable historical studies still can be of no interest, and interesting systematic studies can often be unreliable, if they lack foundation in history. The present book is both historical and systematic, but we cannot promise to offer "the best of both worlds": The presentation of the Patristic material in Melanchthon is not exhaustive, two aspects have in fact deliberately been left out, *viz.*, the material in connection with ethics and with the eucharist, partly because these have been dealt with by others and partly because these would require a broader treatment than could have been given within the scope of this book. We confine ourselves to the doctrines of the Trinity, christology and creation, i.e. to the subjects which are largely ignored by the young Reformer Melanchthon since he regards them as speculative, and which are later on treated extensively by him. The systematic question asked in this study (the element of continuity and discontinuity in the thought of Melanchthon in connection with theological speculation) has been asked before, and the answer given by us will not take many readers by surprise. But if we cannot promise to offer "the best of both worlds", we certainly hope that the reader will not feel presented with "the worst of both worlds".

I want to thank the "Netherlands Organization for the Advancement of Pure Research" for providing a subsidy, E. J. Brill's for publishing the book, and Professor H. A. Oberman for accepting it in the series "Studies in the History of Christian Thought".

I am most grateful to my nephew Mr F. N. Marshall, London, for correcting my English.

The book has been dedicated to Prof. H. J. Heering, Leyden. It is almost twenty years ago that I was his assistant at the University of Leyden. Ever since those years I have learned from him that theological liberalism at its best does not imply hostility towards the broad tradition of Christian thought.

June 1982
Oranjelaan 11
Oegstgeest/The Netherlands   E.P.M.

INTRODUCTION

The young Reformer Melanchthon attacks in the first edition of his *Loci communes* speculations about the Trinity, the incarnation and creation. This attack is well known and often quoted. Almost equally well known is the fact that later on Melanchthon was a strong defender of the Patristic doctrine of the Trinity and of the Patristic doctrine of Christ, and that he agreed with the death sentence passed on the anti-trinitarian Servet.

Several questions have been raised in this context. Was Melanchthon's original attack on speculative theology caused by humanistic scepticism about man's ability to penetrate into the mystery of God's being or by reverence for God's revelation given in Scripture which man should adore rather than seek to comprehend? This reverence would be typical of a Reformer.[1] Can we trace continuity between the young Reformer Melanchthon who attacks speculations about the Trinity and the doctrine of Christ and the somewhat older Melanchthon who strongly defends the Patristic doctrine about Christ and God, or is it clear that Melanchthon changed his mind and later on did himself what he had attacked with youthful zeal?[2]

These two key questions have been answered by most modern scholars in the sense that the original attack on speculative theology is caused by reverence for Scriptural revelation rather than by scepticism, and that there is more continuity than discontinuity in Melanchthon's thought. We should like to look again at these questions from the angle of Melanchthon's relationship to Patristic theology. Was Melanchthon's original attack on speculative theology directed not only against Medieval scholastics, but also against the Fathers of the church? Did Melanchthon's appraisal of the Fathers change in the course of his life?

Melanchthon's relationship with the Fathers can be described from various points of view. One can—as P. Fraenkel did in an excellent study[3]—ask in which contexts Melanchthon used to refer to the Fathers as authorities which must back up his doctrinal statements, and which judgements he passed on the Fathers. Since this approach has been

---

[1] See W. Maurer, Melanchthon, *Die Religion in Geschichte und Gegenwart*, Dritte Auflage, IV, p. 835, and further *infra* 16, note 95.

[2] H. Engelland in the Preface to his edition of the *Loci communes* from 1521, in R. Stupperich's *Studienausgabe* (= St.A.), II, p. 3, and *infra*, 138, note 4.

[3] See P. Fraenkel, *Testimonia Patrum. The Function of the Patristic Argument in the Theology of Philip Melanchthon*, Geneva 1961.

followed by Fraenkel in a very fruitful way for the understanding of the structure of Melanchthon's theology, we want to deal with this matter somewhat differently. Melanchthon's relation to Patristic theology can be described primarily from the point of view of a Reformation scholar and primarily from the point of view of a Patristic scholar. The former is done in Fraenkel's book, the latter is attempted in the present study. We want to ask which Fathers Melanchthon knew, which editions of their works he had or may have had at his disposal, what are the most important quotations he gives and what he wants to prove with these quotations. We shall also ask how precisely he quotes his sources.

Our approach will be both systematic and historical. The historical question: What knowledge did Melanchthon have of the Fathers, and how did he use his knowledge, should give an answer to the systematic question: What was Melanchthon's attitude towards speculative theology in the various periods of his life? If Melanchthon changed his mind on the authority of the Fathers, then he may have had different views on speculative theology as well, if he did not, then his attitude towards speculation may have remained basically the same as well.

We shall first try to analyse his views on speculation from a formal point of view: How did Melanchthon draw the line between useful knowledge and futile speculation? Even if he never changed his mind in this respect, it could still be asked whether he later on sometimes treated as useful knowledge that he had at first rejected as futile speculation. The Reformers regarded what went beyond Scripture as speculation. One can maintain this principle throughout one's life and nevertheless treat certain questions as speculative in one period of one's life and as perfectly Scriptural in another period. Melanchthon's attitude towards Patristic theology could give an answer to the question of whether he was not only formally but also materially consistent in his attitude towards speculative theology. Therefore the analysis of Melanchthon's views on speculation will be followed by an analysis of his knowledge of and use of the Fathers of the church. Once this has become clear, it can be asked what the function of the Fathers is when he later on deals with those questions which he deliberately ignores in the first edition of the *Loci communes*: the Trinity, the doctrine of Christ, the doctrine of the creation, and what their function is in the all important theme of his whole life as a theologian: the doctrine of grace and redemption. In this context the continuity and discontinuity in the thought of Melanchthon in connection with theological speculation will be discussed. We feel entitled to confine ourselves to the doctrines of the Trinity, of the person of Christ and the creation, since these are the subjects which were largely ignored by the young Reformer Melanchthon and which were later on treated extensively by him. So the question of how far there is continuity and discontinuity in the thought of Melanchthon circles around these subjects. In determining the use which Melanchthon makes of the Fathers in connection with these subjects we may be able to find out how far Melanchthon's Patristic studies influenced his development as a theologian, and how far Melanchthon became a more speculative theologian in this development.

Finally we want to deal briefly with the question of how far Melanchthon's use of the theology of the Fathers is justified by Patristic theology itself, and what the function of tradition could be in theology.

CHAPTER ONE

THE ATTACK ON SPECULATIVE THEOLOGY

When Melanchthon, in the beginning of the *Loci communes* of 1521 attacks futile speculations about the Trinity, the natures of Christ, the ways of the incarnation, and the creation, he contrasts these speculations with useful knowledge about why Christ took upon Himself human flesh.[1] He makes the same distinction repeatedly.[2] Those whom Melanchthon finds guilty of curiosity and speculation are, of course, the Scholastic theologians who follow metaphysical philosophers. Their interest focuses on such questions as the unity, intellect, will and simplicity of God.[3] They show a futile interest in God's being, against which Melanchthon stresses that knowledge of God in not knowledge of His being, but of His will.[4] The divine mysteries of the Trinity, of Providence and of the incarnation ought to be adored rather than scrutinized.[5] In this

---

[1] *Loci communes* (1521) (St.A. II), p. 7: ...hoc est Christum cognoscere beneficia eius cognoscere, non, quod isti docent, eius naturas, modos incarnationis contueri. Ni scias, in quem usum carnem induerit et cruci affixus sit Christus, quid proderit eius historiam novisse? Cf. H. Stege, Beneficia Christi. Das Zeugnis der Reformation in den *Loci communes* Philip Melanchthons, *Evangelische Theologie* (21), 1961, pp. 264ff., S. Wiedenhofer, *Formalstrukturen humanistischer und reformatorischer Theologie bei Philipp Melanchthon*, Bern/Frankfurt a.M./München 1976, pp. 316ff., A. Schirmer, *Das Paulusverständnis Melanchthons*, Wiesbaden 1967, pp. 80f.

[2] See e.g. his commentary on *Genesis* (CR 13, 783) where he talks about questions which are more curious than useful, and his commentary on the gospel according to St. John (CR 15, 265).

[3] See his treatise, dating from 1521, *Didymi Faventini adversus Thomam Placentinum pro Martino Luthero theologo oratio* (St.A. I), p. 75: De Deo, de iis quae Deo tribuuntur ab hominibus, de unitate, de intellectu, de voluntate, de simplicitate disserunt metaphysici, quos vocant, quam partem Theologia scholastica sibi totam vindicavit. — For the difference between Melanchthon's faith and the Scholastic one cf. H. Römer, *Die Entwicklung des Glaubensbegriffs bei Melanchthon nach dessen dogmatischen Schriften*, Bonn 1902, pp. 9ff., see also H. Maier, Philip Melanchthon als Philosoph, *An der Grenze der Philosophie*, Tübingen 1909, pp. 38f.

[4] *Nova Scholia in Proverbia Salomonis* (St.A. IV, p. 318: quod nosse Deum sit nosse voluntatem eius erga nos ... Nec est nosse Deum subtiliter de natura divina disputare, cf. p. 408, *Scholia in Epistolam Pauli ad Colossenses* (St.A. IV), p. 285, *Commentarii in Epistolam Pauli ad Romanos* (St.A. V), p. 72: Neque vero notitia Dei intelligi debet de speculationibus, in quibus quaeritur de essentia Dei, sed notitia Dei est notitia voluntatis Dei erga nos. — In his fight against the anti-trinitarians he will modify his position in this respect, see *infra*, 119f.

[5] See apart from the famous words in the opening chapter of the *Loci communes* (1521), pp. 6f.: Mysteria divinitatis rectius adoraverimus quam vestigaverimus, also p. 43, and *Declamatiuncula in Divi Pauli doctrinam*, dating from 1520 (St.A. I), p. 40: Si quidem Christum scire non est aeternae generationis aut admirandae incarnationis modos

rejection of speculations Melanchthon hardly changed his mind. When he later on defends the doctrine of the Trinity against the anti-trinitarians he still insists that idle speculations about the Trinity ought to be avoided.[6] In this context Melanchthon also opposes speculations about God's will behind God's predestination, especially about the causes of God's predestinating will.[7] What Melanchthon particularly criticizes in all these speculations is that they go beyond the revelation given in Scripture. In all the periods of his life he stresses that man should not try to go beyond Scriptural revelation, since in doing so he becomes guilty of curiosity.[8]

The clear implication of what Melanchthon says about speculative theology and in contrast a theology which is based on God's revelation is that there must be a sharp difference between the doctrine given in the Bible and philosophy. It seems to us that there is a development in Melanchthon's attitude towards philosophy, but that he essentially did

scrutari, sed beneficia ... agnoscere, *Did. Fav. adv. Th. Placentinum*, dating from 1521, p. 87: Adorari et credi volunt sublimia de trinitate de providentina, de incarnatione verbi mysteria, rationibus humanis penetrari non volunt, p. 95: Neque enim ex re Christiana fuit, sublimia illa mysteria divinitatis ad rationis methodos vocare, *Annotationes in Evangelium Matthaei*, dating from 1523 (St.A. IV), p. 185: Humana opinio de Christo contemplatur de illius natura et maiestate, divinitus inspirata utitur Christo, vivitque Christum, *Annotationes et conciones in Evangelium Joannis*, dating from 1523 (CR 14), p. 1062.

[6] See the final edition of the *Loci communes* (1559) (St.A. II), p. 176: Ita primum de essentia Dei iudicat (sc. ecclesia) non ex humanis imaginationibus, sed ex verbo Dei certis testimoniis traditio. Deinde de voluntate certo scimus Filium Dei constitutum esse mirabili et inenarrabili consilio ... His discriminibus initio consideratis ... rectius intelligetur quomodo quaerendus, agnoscendus et invocandus sit Deus, quam ex otiosis speculationibus, quas multi cumularunt sine modo in commentariis Longobardi. — In the *Enarratio Symboli Nicaeni*, dating from 1550 (CR 23), p. 229 it says: Etsi autem testimonia de essentia (sc. Filii) etiam passim sparsa sunt, tamen saepius de beneficiis dicitur. This remark is made in the part written by C. Cruciger (see O. Ritschl, *Dogmengeschichte des Protestantismus*, Leipzig 1908, p. 115, note 6. Melanchthon's text begins on p. 254), but it fully reflects Melanchthon's views; cf. H. Römer, *op. cit.*, p. 33: "Ein spekulativer Theologe ist nun Melanchthon auch später nie gewesen".

[7] *Comm. in ep. ... ad Rom.* (St.A. V), p. 251: ...hic non resistit humana curiositas, sed incipit quaerere causas electionis, quod nihil opus est. Quorsum enim nobis opus est de Dei consilio disputare? Cf. pp. 280f., *Loci communes* (1559) (St.A. II), p. 661, and his commentary on the epistle to the Romans, dating from 1540 (CR 15), pp. 505f. and his commentary on this epistle dating from 1556 (CR 15), pp. 978ff., 998.

[8] See e.g. *Nova Scholia in Prov. Sal.* (St.A. IV), p. 408: Credant igitur omnes et hanc revelatam voluntatem amplectantur et amittant quaerere arcana quae non sunt revelata, quia Deus non potest cognosci, nisi quatenus revelat se per verbum suum, p. 444, p. 459, *Responsiones ad articulos Bavaricae inquisitionis*, dating from 1558 (St.A. VI), p. 308, the letter to the Senate of Venice (CR 3), p. 750 (dating from 1539), *Enarratio brevis concionum libri Salomonis, cui titulus est Ecclesiastes*, dating from 1550 (CR 14), p. 120, *Conciones explicantes evangelium Matthaei*, dating from 1558 (CR 14), pp. 561f., p. 903, *Enarratio epistulae prioris ad Timotheum*, dating from 1550 (CR 15), p. 1298 and furthermore the passages referred to in the previous note.

not change his mind in this respect:[9] In his little treatise *Unterschidt zwischen weltlicher und christlicher Fromkeyt*, dating from 1521 or 1522,[10] he concedes that human mind does know that there is one God who punishes the evil, but says that it is not really afraid of Him and that it certainly does not understand that God forgives sins, this latter notion being revealed in the gospel. In a letter to Nicolaus von Amsdorff, dating from 1520, he is very critical of philosophy which comes forward with futile speculations.[11] The remark made in the letter of dedication of the *Loci communes* of 1521, that the intends to make a clear difference between the doctrine of Christ and Aristotelian subtleties, is indicative of the same view.[12] But at the same time he stresses that Luther does not reject all philosophy, but only that metaphysical part of it which speculates about God,—natural sciences are not rejected by him.[13] But, possibly *inter alia* as a reaction against the Anabaptists,[14] he speaks more favourably about philosophy a few years later in explaining *Col.* 2:8.[15] But what he says then is an elaboration of what he had said before. The usefulness of natural sciences is stressed,[16] man does have some positive ideas about morality.[17] But the human mind errs when it makes statements about God's will, although it does have a vague idea about the existence of one God. The most important aspect of God's will is that God wants to justify

---

[9] Cf. for the following: Cl. Bauer, Die Naturrechtsvorstellungen des jüngeren Melanchthon, *Festschrift für Gerhard Ritter zu seinem 60. Geburtstag*, Tübingen 1950, pp. 244ff. (in which it is stressed that the iustitia of natural man is the iustitia of the *homo carnalis*) and Q. Breen, *Christianity and Humanism. Studies in the History of Ideas*, Grand Rapids 1968, pp. 80ff., H.-G. Geyer, *Von der Geburt des wahren Menschen. Probleme aus den Anfängen der Theologie Melanchthons*, Neukirchen 1965, pp. 63ff.

[10] See St.A. I, pp. 171ff.

[11] See CR 1, pp. 273ff.

[12] See St.A. II, p. 4: ...indicantur hic christianae disciplinae praecipui loci, ut intelligat iuventus ... quam foede hallucinati sint ubique in re theologica, qui nobis pro Christi doctrina Aristotelicas argutias prodidere. Cf. A. Brüls, *Die Entwicklung der Gotteslehre beim jungen Melanchthon, 1518-1535*, Bielefeld 1975, pp. 44ff.

[13] *Did. Fav. adv. Th. Plac.* (St.A. I), p. 72, pp. 86f.

[14] See the letter of dedication preceding the *Loci communes* (1535), CR 2, p. 926, cf. R. Stupperich's general observation: "Beim Magister Philippus überwogen so stark intellektuelle Neigungen und lehrmässige Interessen, dass er jeder gefühlsbetonten, enthusiastischen Art, die er an einigen Vertretern des Täufertums von Anfang an kennenlernte, abhold sein musste." *Kerygma und Dogma* (3) 1957, p. 151.

[15] See *Scholia in Epistulam Pauli ad Colossenses*, dating from 1527 (St.A. IV), pp. 230ff.

[16] p. 230.

[17] p. 230. This seems to contradict what he had taught earlier, *viz.*, that philosophical morality is incompatible with the gospel, see *Annotationes in Epistolas Pauli ad Corinthios*, dating from 1522 (St.A. IV), p. 20: Philosophia omnia tribuit nostris viribus et operibus, evangelium omnia adimit docens non aliud esse iustificationem nisi credere in Christum, and *Annotationes in Evangelium Matthaei*, dating from 1523 (St.A. IV), pp. 150f. But the positive things philosophy says about morality refer to outward actions, not to spiritual life, which is a gift of God's grace,—on this distinction see *infra*, 133.

the sinner through Christ. It is constantly stressed by Melanchthon that here we find the difference between philosophy, which teaches that man can be just through his virtues, and the gospel which teaches that man is justified by God through His grace in Christ.[18] Man does have a vague knowledge about the existence of one good and just God. Repeatedly Melanchthon refers with qualified approval to Plato's definition of God, the qualification being that Plato does not know that this God is the triune God and that He forgives sins.[19] The vague knowledge about God and the philosophical knowledge about what man should do are useful to restrain natural man.[20]

So Melanchthon criticizes the Scholastics for focusing their attention on something which is at its best a mere preparation for Christian faith, viz., the philosophical knowledge of God's being and of moral virtues.[21] The core of Christian faith is not, however, found by philosophical speculations, but is found in the revelation given in Scripture. The Fathers of the Church have a certain authority, but their authority is sub-

---

[18] See e.g. *Praefatio in officia Ciceronis*, dating from 1534 (St.A. III), pp. 85f., *Philosophiae moralis epitomes libri duo*, dating from 1546 (St.A. III), pp. 157ff., his letter of dedication to the *Enarratio aliquot librorum ethicorum Aristotelis*, dating from 1536 (CR 2), pp. 851f., *Disputatio de discrimine Evangelii et Philosophiae* (CR 12), pp. 689ff., *Enarratio epistulae Pauli ad Colossenses*, dating from 1559 (CR 15), pp. 1247 ff., *Explicatio Sententiarum Theognidis* (CR 19), p. 58.

[19] *Loci communes*, (1559) (St.A. II), p. 176: Platonica (sc. descriptio dei) haec est: Deus est mens aeterna, causa boni in natura. This definition often returns (not always with Plato's name), see e.g. p. 652, *Definitiones multarum appellationum, quarum in Ecclesia usus est*, dating from 1552/'53 (St.A. II), p. 782, p. 806, *Initia doctrinae physicae*, dating from 1549 (CR 13), p. 199, *Explicatio Proverbiorum Salomonis*, dating from 1557 (CR 14), p. 80, *Explicatio Symboli Nicaeni*, dating from 1557 (CR 23), pp. 496f., the reference is to Plato, *Philebus* 22C and *Politeia* II 379C, 380B. The definition is in an amplified way also ascribed to Xenophon, see the letter of dedication to *Georg. Purbachii Theoreticae novae Planetarum*, dating from 1535 (CR 2), p. 816, *Explic. Symb. Nic.*, p. 356, without Xenophon's name this definition also appears e.g. in *Liber de anima*, dating from 1553 (St.A. III), pp. 317, 334, 341. On Melanchthon's use of philosophy in the doctrine of God see H. Maier, Melanchthon als Philosoph, *Archiv für Geschichte der Philosophie* (11) 1898, pp. 233ff. Maier points out that Melanchthon's major source for knowledge of philosophy was Cicero, see *op. cit.*, pp. 88ff. and his paper, Philip Melanchthon als Philosoph, *An der Grenze der Philosophie*, Tübingen 1909, pp. 54ff., see also W. Maurer, Melanchthons *Loci communes* von 1521 als wissenschaftliche Programmschrift, *Luther-Jahrbuch 1960*, Berlin 1960, pp. 28ff. On the influence of Ciceronian scepticism on the various editions of the *Loci communes* see C. B. Schmitt, *Cicero Scepticus: A Study of the Influence of the Academia in the Renaissance*, The Hague 1972, pp. 59-62; on Aristotle's influence on Melanchthon see P. Petersen, Aristotelisches in der Theologie Melanchthons, *Zeitschrift für Philosophie und philosophische Kritik* (164) 1917, pp. 149ff.

[20] See *Scholia in epist. Pauli ad Colossenses* (1527) (St.A. IV), pp. 232ff.

[21] This means that according to Melanchthon metaphysical speculation and moralism go together, — the same view is held by Luther, see Th. Harnack, *Luthers Theologie* I, p. 58; for Melanchthon's rejection of moralism and speculation see also *Disputationes* (CR 12), p. 522, *Chronicon Carionis* (CR 12), pp. 1016f., and *infra*, 119ff.

jected to that of Scripture and dependent on the question of whether their doctrine is in line with Scriptural doctrine. This is Melanchthon's view in the years around the first edition of the *Loci communes*. In 1519 he writes against Eck that when the Fathers disagree with each other they must be judged after Scripture.[22] In the *Loci communes* of 1521 he briefly dismisses Augustin's early ideas about free will[23] and says that he has nothing to do with what Origen teaches, but only with Scriptural doctrine.[24] In the defence against Eck he explicitly says that the Fathers can give faulty explanations of Biblical texts.[25] Where he believes the Fathers it is because he believes Scripture.[26] In his treatise *De ecclesia et de autoritate verbi Dei*,[27] which appeared in 1539, at a time when he already defended the doctrine of the Trinity against the anti-trinitarians, he still maintains the same view. He believes Augustin's doctrine about original sin not because of Augustin but because of Scripture,[28] various tenets of Tertullian are only accepted in so far as they are in line with Scripture.[29] He in fact is in this treatise fairly critical of the Fathers, so critical that he feels obliged to state that his only object is to prove those who admire the Fathers to such a degree that they regard them as faultless err themselves. Although the Fathers can sometimes teach us, they have to be judged after the Word of God.[30] And even in his fairly traditional interpretation of the Nicene Creed he subjects the Fathers to Scripture.[31]

---

[22] *Defensio Phil. Melanchthonis contra Joh. Eckium* (St.A. I), p. 17: Deinde puto non temere fieri, sicubi sententiis S. patres variant, quemadmodum solet, ut iudice scriptura recipiantur. See also *Did. Fav. adv. Th. Placentinum* ... (St.A. I), p. 107: Etenim Chrysostomo, aut Ignatio aut quibusvis auctorum non credam, nisi quatenus permittit scriptura, *Adv. furiosum Parris. Theol. decretum Phil. Melanchthonis pro Luthero apologia* (St.A. I), p. 148.
[23] See p. 8.
[24] See p. 39.
[25] See St.A. I, p. 18: ...immo ausim et hoc dicere nonnumquam sensu quodam S. patres interpretatos esse scripturas ... quem ... nos homunculi ad literam quadrare non videmus...
[26] *Def. contra Joh. Eckium*, p. 19: Patribus enim credo, quia Scripturae credo, *Loci communes* of 1521, p. 61: De divinitate filii credo Nicaeno concilio, quia scripturae credo.
[27] On the background and interpretation of this piece of writing see J. N. Bakhuizen van den Brink, Melanchthon: De ecclesia et de autoritate Verbi Dei (1539) und dessen Gegner, *Reformation und Humanismus. Robert Stupperich zum 65. Geburtstag*, Herausgegeben von M. Greschat und F. G. Goeters, Witten 1969, pp. 91ff.
[28] St.A. I, p. 338: credimus articulum non propter Augustinum, sed propter verbum Dei.
[29] St.A. I, p. 350: Sed eius enarrationes et disputationes non recipiantur tanquam dogmata, nisi quatenus consentiunt cum Apostolica scriptura.
[30] St.A. I, p. 369: ...tantum recensere errata volui, ut appareat falli eos, qui sic admirantur Patres, tanquam fuerint ἀναμάρτητοι, et nusquam dissentiant a scripturis divinis manifestis. Etsi igitur aliquid monent interdum eruditiores Patres, tamen de eis iudicandum est ex verbo Dei.
[31] *Explicatio Symb. Nic.* (CR 23), p. 363: In his disputationibus illustrata sunt dicta Prophetica et Apostolica de tribus personis, et editae sunt confessiones Sanctorum, qui affir-

In 1521 he says explicitly that in the Fathers we find futile speculations about the divine mysteries, but on a much smaller scale than in the Scholastics.[32] In the first edition of the *Loci communes* he says that immediately after the beginning of the Church the Christian doctrine was robbed of its Scriptural foundation through Platonic philosophy.[33] In 1538 he still condemns the contamination of the Gospel and the (misunderstood) philosophy of Plato which took place in the days of Origen.[34] Melanchthon felt free during the whole of his life to make such criticism of the Fathers, but since the fight against the anti-trinitarians had begun such criticism was seldom directed against their doctrine of the

---

mabant se doctrinam ab Apostolorum discipulis accepisse. — Cruciger's words in the *En. Symb. Nic.* (CR 23), p. 200, are entirely in line with Melanchthon's views: Synodi non gignunt nova dogmata, sed tantum profitentur sententias prius in scriptis Propheticis et Apostolicis traditas. A. Sperl, who traces a development in Melanchthon's thought on tradition, nevertheless states that even the later Melanchthon subjects the Nicene Creed to Scripture as far as its contents is concerned, although he believes that *methodologically* the Creed is to be preferred, since it puts the Scriptural doctrine into clear words, see *Melanchthon zwischen Humanismus und Reformation. Eine Untersuchung über den Wandel des Traditionsverständnisses bei Melanchthon und die damit zusammenhängenden Grundfragen seiner Theologie*, München 1959, pp. 91ff., cf. W.-D. Hausschild, Die Confessio Augustana und die altkirchliche Tradition, *Kerygma und Dogma* (26) 1980, p. 157: "Sie (sc. die Tradition) tritt nicht nur auslegend verstärkend, sondern auch ergänzend zur Schrift hinzu, ohne indessen eine komplementäre Quelle der Wahrheitserkenntnis zu werden. Vielmehr ist sie ein wesentlicher Teil der kontinuierlichen Geschichte reiner Lehre. Sie hat als solche zwar keine konstitutive, wohl aber eine regulative Funktion für die Theologie, weil die in ihr entfalteten Anfänge von Kirche und Lehre eine besondere Nähe zur offenbarten Wahrheit haben." See also the detailed expositions given by K. Haendler in his monumental study *Wort und Glaube bei Melanchthon. Eine Untersuchung über die Voraussetzungen und Grundlagen des melanchthonischen Kirchenbegriffs*, Gütersloh 1968, pp. 73ff., 199ff., 218ff.

[32] *Did. Fav. adv. Th. Placentium* (St.A. I), p. 77: Non ignoro autem, esse aliquod apud patres exemplum talium disputationum, quo se tueri fortasse inimici queant, sed et illos optarim divina purius tractasse, quanquam, bone deus, quanto parcius quam isti philosophantur?

[33] *Loci communes* (1521) (St.A. II), p. 8: ...statim post ecclesiae auspicia per Platonicam philosophiam christiana doctrina labefactata est. Cf. W. Maurer, Melanchthon als Humanist, *Philip Melanchthon. Forschungsbeiträge zur vierhundertsten Wiederkehr seines Todestages dargeboten in Wittenberg*, herausgegeben von W. Elliger, Göttingen 1960, p. 125, and R. Friedler, Zum Verhältnis Luthers und Melanchthons zu Platon, *Das Altertum* (13) 1967, p. 225.

[34] See his *Declamatio de Platone* (CR 11), p. 425: Quare prudentia adhibenda est in discernendis doctrinarum generibus et explodendi sunt inepti illi, qui offendunt caliginem Evangelio, imo obruunt ac delent Evangelium, cum transformant in Platonicam Philosophiam. Magis etiam taxandi sunt, qui ne Platonem quidem intelligentes, eius figuris depravatis, monstrosas opiniones genuerunt, easque in Ecclesiam sparserunt, ut Origenes et post eum alii multi fecerunt; flagitiose enim contaminata est doctrina Christiana veteribus illis temporibus, inepte admixta Platonica Philosophia. Here Melanchthon reproduces an ancient argument: Christian heretics adopt philosophical tenets and in doing so distort these tenets, see e.g. Irenaeus, *Adv. Haer.* 2, 18, 1; 2, 8, 2; 3, 39, 41, Tertullian, *Adv. Marc.* 1, 13, 3, *De anima* 23, 5, Athanasius, *De Decretis Nic. Syn.* 28, Hilary, *De Trinitate* 7, 1ff.

Trinity, but against their ethics in connection with the doctrine of grace.[35]—Some contradiction can here be detected in Melanchthon. On the one hand he subjects the Fathers to the Bible and says that one cannot speak of "the theology of the Fathers", since they differ from each other,[36] on the other hand he sometimes claims to be in line with the *consensus* of the Catholic Church as clearly expressed by the early Church and the Fathers.[37]

Melanchthon's views on the authority of the councils are closely connected with his views on the authority of the Fathers and are identical with these. In his letter about the Leipzig Disputation (1519) he says that councils have no right to establish new dogmas.[38] This means that no new doctrine after the revelation given in the Bible is acceptable. The authority of the councils is surpassed by that of Scripture.[39] In the treatise *De ecclesia et de autoritate verbi Dei* (1539) he defends decisions taken at various councils about the Trinity and christology, but feels free to criticize them on other matters.[40] Towards the end of his life he still holds the same view as appears from his treatise *Responsiones scriptae ad impios articulos Bavaricae inquisitionis*, dating from 1558.[41]

Melanchthon has rightly been called a traditionalist.[42] But from the

---

[35] See *infra*, 33, 72. We agree with P. Fraenkel that there is no difference between the young and the old Melanchthon in his evaluation of Patristic theology, see his paper, Revelation and Tradition, *Studia Theologica*, 1959, pp. 125ff. For mild criticism of the Fathers in connection with the doctrine of the Trinity see *infra*, 118f.

[36] See *De ecclesia et de autoritate verbi Dei* (St.A. I), p. 362: Cum Patres citantur, quae dicta patrum sunt consentanea divinae voci (sc. considerent lectores). Est enim magna dissimilitudo patrum, and p. 376: Scio ex veteribus excerpi posse multa pugnantia cum nostris sententiis ... Non provoco ad omnes Scriptores, sed ad meliores, Ambrosium, Augustinum, et quatenus alii cum his consentiunt, qui cum ipsi interdum pugnantia dixerint, veniam nobis dabunt, si quaedam reprehendemus.

[37] *De recusatione concilii*, dating from 1537 (CR 3), p. 317: Nam haec pura Evangelii doctrina, quam amplexi sumus est haud dubie consensus catholicae Ecclesiae Christi, sicut testimonia veteris Ecclesiae et S. patrum perspicue docent. Non enim recepimus aut approbamus ullas opiniones absurdas et pugnantes cum consensu sanctorum patrum. K. Haendler exaggerates when he says that Melanchthon always objected to the idea of the *consensus quinquesaecularis, op. cit.*, pp. 203f., cf. L. C. Green, The Influence of Erasmus upon Melanchthon, Luther and the Formula of Concord in the Doctrine of Justification, *Church History* (43) 1974, p. 200.

[38] St.A. I, p. 9, cf. for the following: S. Wiedenhofer, *Formalstrukturen humanistischer und reformatorischer Theologie bei Philipp Melanchthon*, pp. 137ff.

[39] *Declamatiuncula in Divi Pauli doctrinam*, dating from 1520 (St.A. I), p. 44: Deinde conciliorum autoritatem scripturae autoritate vinci, cf. p. 50.

[40] St.A. I, pp. 340ff.

[41] St.A. VI, p. 291: Fides autem, qua amplectimur symbola, nititur non autoritate aut mandatis Ecclesiae, sed perspicuo verbo Dei, cf. F. W. Kantzenbach, *Das Ringen um die Einheit der Kirche im Jahrhundert der Reformation*, Stuttgart 1957, p. 108.

[42] O. Ritschl, *Dogmengeschichte des Protestantismus* I, pp. 276ff. Interesting is W. Maurer's interpretation of Melanchthon's traditionalism: the root of it is Neo-Platonic universalism with which Melanchthon became acquainted via the Florentine Academy,

formal point of view he has always been a Biblicist traditionalist who rejected any doctrine which might add something new to what is revealed in the Bible.[43] As was not unusual[44] Melanchthon sometimes connects curiosity with the love of novelty and as such rejects it.[45] This means that if councils had the right to make new dogmas, that would open the door to curiosity.

Melanchthon's views on curiosity and futile speculation stand in a long tradition, as he was aware himself. He knows that the words used for curiosity in ancient Greek were περιεργία and πολυπραγμοσύνη.[46] Both in ancient philosophy and in Christian theology curiosity played an important part. In Christian theology it always was an important question where the line ought to be drawn between useful knowledge and futile curiosity.[47] For his view that this line is the revelation given in Scripture Melanchthon can find support in the writings of the Fathers, as may appear from the following examples:

Irenaeus[48] calls Scripture perfect, since it is inspired by God.[49] Pious knowledge is the knowledge of what God has clearly revealed in Scrip-

---

see Maurer's paper, Die geschichtliche Wurzel von Melanchthons Traditionsverständnis, *Zur Auferbauung des Leibes Christi* (Festgabe Peter Brunner), herausgegeben von E. Schlink und A. Peters, Kassel 1965, pp. 166ff.

[43] Cf. H. Engelland, *Melanchthon, Glauben und Handeln*, München 1931, pp. 1ff., 185ff., J. N. Bakhuizen van den Brink, Traditio in de Reformatie en in het Katholicisme in de zestiende eeuw (*Mededelingen der Koninklijke Nederlandse Academie van Wetenschappen*, Afd. Lett., N.R. 2, Amsterdam 1952), pp. 41ff. (15ff.), J. A. B. van den Brink, Bible and Biblical Theology in the Early Reformation, *Scottish Journal of Theology* (14) 1961, pp. 346ff., W. Pauck, Luther und Melanchthon, *Luther und Melanchthon, Referate des zweiten internationalen Lutherkongresses*, Göttingen 1961, p. 18, A. Sperl, *op. cit.*, pp. 91ff.

[44] See *infra*, 12ff.

[45] See *Confessio Saxonica*, dating from 1551 (St.A. VI), p. 164: Ostendit autem res ipsa nos non curiositate novas aut argutas disputationes quaesivisse, *In Danielem Prophetam Commentarius*, dating from 1543 (CR 13), p. 867: Graecorum ingeniorum mira fuit in experiundis novis rebus, artibus et consiliis curiositas, Letter to Prince Ernestus, dating from 1537 (CR 3), p. 443: Ita dedit mundus poenas spreti Evangelii, et curiositatis, qua sibi quisque immani audacia fingebat novas opiniones.

[46] For references to περιεργία see e.g. *Did. Fav. adv. Th. Placentinum* (St.A. I), p. 74, *De studiis adolescentum* (CR 11), p. 181, to πολυπραγμοσύνη *Loci communes* (1559) (St.A. II), p. 306 and p. 722, *Nova Scholia in Proverbia Salomonis* (St.A. IV), p. 446, the letter to Burcard Mithobius, dating from 1539 (CR 3), p. 629, *Enarratio in Evang.* (CR 15), p. 289; περιεργία has more the meaning of intellectual curiosity, πολυπραγμοσύνη is more related to activities to which one is not entitled.

[47] Cf. for the following: H. A. Oberman, *Contra vanam curiositatem. Ein Kapitel der Theologie zwischen Seelenwinkel und Weltall*, Zürich 1974, E. P. Meijering, *Calvin wider die Neugierde. Ein Beitrag zum Vergleich zwischen reformatorischem und patristischem Denken*, Nieuwkoop 1980, in which the author tries to analyse the thoughts of Irenaeus, Tertullian and Augustin on curiosity.

[48] For the use Melanchthon makes of Irenaeus see *infra*, 67ff.

[49] *Adv. Haer.* 2, 41, 1: ...Scripturae quidem perfectae sunt, quippe a Verbo Dei et Spiritu eius dictae.

ture.[50] When the young Reformer Melanchthon rejects speculations about creation and Christ's eternal generation he is in line with Irenaeus, who refuses to answer the question what God did before He created the world, since Scripture reveals nothing about this,[51] equally Scripture is silent about how God created the world.[52] The generation of the Son also transcends human knowledge.[53]

In the Arian controversy some of the orthodox Fathers explicitly reject intellectual curiosity and insist that human speech about the Father, Son and Holy Ghost should not go further than Scriptural revelation. Athanasius[54] says that when the disciples heard the commandment of the Lord to baptize in the name of the Father, Son and Holy Ghost, they did not ask curious questions about the Trinity, but believed as they heard.[55] He opposes the temerity which tries to think of new words which deviate from Scripture to explain the Trinity.[56] He advises the Arians to stop asking curious questions about the Trinity and simply believe in it.[57]—Hilary of Poitiers[58] stresses that the commandment to baptize in the name of the Trinity ought to have been enough to the believers.[59] Time and again Hilary states that man should not go beyond the revelation given in Scripture.[60] Scripture sets clear bounds to the *libertas intellegentiae*, uninhibited speculation.[61] Curious questions about why God created the universe as He did are rejected by Hilary.[62]—Basil[63] stresses

---

[50] *Adv. Haer.* 2, 40, 1: Sensus autem sanus ... et religiosus ... quae quidem dedit in hominum potestatem Deus, et subdidit nostrae scientiae, haec prompte meditabitur ... Sunt autem haec ... quaecumque aperte, et sine ambiguo ipsis dictionibus posita sunt in Scripturis.

[51] *Adv. Haer.* 2, 41, 4: Ut puta, si quis interrogat, Antequam mundum faceret Deus, quid agebat? dicimus quoniam ista responsio subiacet Deo. Quoniam autem mundus hic factus est apotelesticos a Deo, temporale initium accipiens, Scripturae nos docent: quid autem ante hoc Deus sit operatus, nulla Scriptura manifestat.

[52] *Adv. Haer.* 2, 42, 2, cf. G. C. Stead, *Divine Substance*, Oxford 1977, pp. 195ff.

[53] *Adv. Haer.* 2, 42, 3-4.

[54] For the use Melanchthon makes of Athanasius see *infra*, 34ff.

[55] See *Ad Serapionem* 4, 5: οἱ γοῦν μαθηταὶ ἀκούσαντες, βαπτίζοντες αὐτοὺς εἰς τὸ ὄνομα τοῦ Πατρὸς καὶ τοῦ Υἱοῦ καὶ τοῦ ἁγίου Πνεύματος, οὐ περιειργάσαντο διὰ τί δεύτερον ὁ Υἱὸς καὶ τρίτον τὸ Πνεῦμα ἢ διὰ τί ὅλως Τριὰς ἀλλ' ὡς ἤκουσαν ἐπίστευσαν (Melanchthon knew Athanasius' letters to Serapion, see *infra*, 37f.).

[56] *Ad Ser.* 1, 17.

[57] *Ad Ser.* 1, 18: ῏Ω ἀνόητοι πάντα τολμηροί, διὰ τί μὴ μᾶλλον ἐπὶ τῆς ἁγίας Τριάδος παύεσθε περιεργαζόμενοι καὶ μόνον πιστεύετε ὅτι ἔστιν; cf. also *Contra Arianos* 3, 1 and 2, 36.

[58] For the use Melanchthon makes of Hilary see *infra*, 65ff.

[59] *De Trin.* 2, 1: Sufficiebat credentibus Dei sermo ... cum dicit Dominus: Euntes nunc docete omnes gentes, baptizantes ... (Melanchthon refers to another sentence from *De Trin.* 2, 1, see *infra*, 65).

[60] See *De Trin.* 4, 14; 9, 44; 11, 1; 12, 26, *In Matth.* 20, 10, *In Ps.* I 3.

[61] *De Trin.* 9, 42: Concludit autem audacissimum impietatis tuae furorem apostolica fides, ne quo licentia liberae intellegentiae evageris, cf. *De Trin.* 7, 16; 11, 1.

[62] *De Trin.* 12, 53.

[63] On Melanchthon's use of Basil see *infra*, 39ff.

that faith in the Trinity is dependent on the formula used in baptism.[64]—
Tertullian[65] is also strongly opposed to curiosity,[66] but to him the barrier
against speculation is not Scripture, but the *regula fidei*.[67] Tertullian
explicitly rejects (at least in theory) what Melanchthon and the other
Reformers warmly advocate: refuting the heretics with Biblical texts.[68]—
Of great importance is, of course, Augustin, for whom Melanchthon and
the Reformers had a great admiration because of his doctrine of grace.[69]
Augustin cannot be called a (formal) Biblicist as e.g. Irenaeus and Hilary
wanted to be, in the sense that they claimed only to come forward with
what was plainly taught in the Bible. Augustin wants to seek the hidden
meaning behind the surface of Biblical texts. God must reveal the true
meaning of the texts, and this true meaning of the texts need not be identical with the original intention of a Biblical writer.[70] Augustin explicitly
wants to speculate about the meaning of God's creative activities.[71]
These speculations should not, however, exceed the boundaries of Christian faith.[72] God reveals His truth in the interior of man,[73] and this
revelation can even transcend Scriptural revelation, in the sense that he
who receives this revelation no longer needs the explication of Biblical
texts.[74]

When Melanchthon opposes uninhibited speculation and points
towards the Bible as the only authority for a Christian theologian, and
furthermore states that the Fathers speculated much less than the
Scholastics, he is (as he is aware himself)[75] backed up by statements made

[64] *Liber de spiritu sancto* 67 (Migne 32, 193A): ...ὡς βαπτιζόμεθα οὕτω καὶ πιστεύειν ὀφείλ-
οντες. Melanchthon refers to this statement, see *infra*, 88.

[65] On Melanchthon's use of Tertullian see *infra*, 79ff.

[66] See on this subject J. H. Waszink's edition of *De anima*, Amsterdam 1947, pp. 113f.
and J.-C. Fredouille, *Tertullien et la conversation de la culture antique*, Paris 1972, pp. 412-442.

[67] See the famous statement in *De praescr. haer.* 14, 5: Cedat curiositas fidei ... adversus
regulam nihil scire omnia scire est.

[68] *De praescr.* 16, 2 and 19, 1. Tertullian is not consistent in this respect, he often does
fight the heretics with Biblical texts. Melanchthon refers to Tertullian's tenet that the old
is true and the new false, Melanchthon here either does not realize the difference between
himself and Tertullian to whom the true and old is the *regula fidei*, or he ignores the difference, cf. *infra*, 93.

[69] For Melanchthon's use of Augustin see *infra*, 20ff.

[70] *Conf.* 12, 18, 27: dum ergo quisque conatur id sentire in scripturis sanctis, quod in
eis sensit ille qui scripsit, quid mali est, si hoc sentiat, quod tu, lux omnium veridicarum
mentium, ostendis verum esse, etiamsi non hoc sensit ille, quem legit, cum et ille verum
nec tamen hoc sensit? Cf. also 12, 23, 32 and 12, 25, 35.

[71] See *Conf.* 11, 3, 5ff. Melanchthon is acquainted with Augustin's speculations in the
eleventh book of the *Confessiones*, see *infra*, 130.

[72] *Conf.* 12, 1, 1, *De Gen. lib. imp.* 1, 1, *De Gen. ad litt.* 1, 19, 38, 39; 1, 20, 40; 7, 1, 1;
12, 1, 1.

[73] *Conf.* 11, 3, 5.

[74] See e.g. *Conf.* 13, 22, 32.

[75] See *infra*, 86ff.

by Irenaeus, Athanasius, Hilary and Basil, but much less by Augustin. In itself this says little about how close he was in his actual theological thought to those Fathers, since one may agree that the Bible is the only authority but still disagree on the question of what is in fact Biblical faith and what is not.[76]

Before turning to Luther and Erasmus as the background of Melanchthon's ideas on speculative theology we want, in the wake of Oberman,[77] draw attention to the fact that late Medieval nominalism was strongly opposed to intellectual curiosity in Christian theology as well. We choose as an example J. Gerson, whom Melanchthon knew and of whom he had a favourable opinion.[78] He who is curious, says J. Gerson, dismisses what is useful and turns to what is less useful and what cannot be attained.[79] True theology should not constantly seek something new but confine itself to the revelation given in Scripture.[80] In such matters as the doctrine of the Trinity theologians should not come forward with lengthy expositions but state their views briefly.[81]

Erasmus draws a distinction between pious and impious curiosity.[82] The pious curiosity wants to know what can be known.[83] What Erasmus

---

[76] How close Melanchthon was to those Fathers will be discussed in chapter III, see *infra*, 109ff.

[77] See H. A. Oberman, *op. cit.*, pp. 33ff. and *Werden und Wertung der Reformation*, Tübingen 1977, p. 54 and pp. 124f.

[78] Cf. *Adv. furios. Parris. Theol. decr.* (St.A. I), p. 142, where he calls Gerson "plenum Christiani spiritus", p. 144 where he calls him a man "great in all respects". The main reason of this praise is that Gerson opposes human traditions which become an intolerable burden to human consciences, see e.g. *Loci communes*, dating from 1521 (St.A. II), p. 63, *Loci communes*, dating from 1559 (St.A. II), p. 745 (here Gerson is mildly criticized), *Confessio Augustana* (Variata) (St.A. VI), p. 52, *Confessio Saxonica* (St.A. VI), p. 151 (here Gerson is again mildly criticized), Letter to King Franciscus of France and King Henry VIII of England (CR 2), p. 472, Letter to King Henry VIII (CR 3), p. 682, *Enarratio Epist. Pauli ad Col.*, dating from 1559 (CR 15), p. 1258, Preface to the second volume of Luther's works, dating from 1546 (CR 6), p. 159, — see on the subject of Gerson and the Luteran Reformation further W. Dress, Gerson und Luther, *Zeitschrift für Kirchengeschichte* (52) 1933, pp. 122ff., and on Gerson's thoughts on tradition G. H. M. Posthumus Meyjes, *Jean Gerson. Zijn kerkpolitiek en ecclesiologie*, The Hague 1963, pp. 264ff.

[79] See his treatise *Contra curiositatem studentium*, in: *Oeuvres complètes, Introduction, texte et notes par Mgr Glorieux*, Tournai 1962, p. 230: Curiositas est vitium, quo dimissis utilioribus homo convertit studium suum ad minus utilia vel inattingiblia sibi vel noxia.

[80] On the rejection of striving after novelty see p. 238 and 244, on the confinement to Scriptural revelation see p. 233: Constat enim quod doctrina fidei quamvis philosophiam superet habet terminos suos praedefinitos in sacris litteris nobis revelatis, ultra quos nihil audendum esse definire vel tradere beatus Dionysius expressit... But Gerson makes it clear in the same context that ecclesiastical tradition can help to understand Scripture, cf. G. H. M. Posthumus Meyjes, *op. cit.*, pp. 252-274.

[81] *Op. cit.*, p. 244.

[82] A similar distinction already occurs in Tertullian, *De anima* 58, 9: there is a iusta ac necessaria and an enormis et otiosa curiositas. On Erasmus' views on curiosity see also S. Wiedenhofer, *op. cit.*, pp. 63ff.

[83] See *Paraclesis* (ed. Holborn), p. 141.

rejects is impious curiosity. Instead of keeping oneself busy with futile questions one should cling to Christ's doctrine.[84] A confinement to what is said in Scripture is a remedy against curious speculation.[85] Erasmus does not want to be sceptical about what is said in the Bible.[86] Another remedy against curiosity can be found in the writings of the Fathers who are reliable exegetes. Erasmus contrasts the theology of the Fathers with the speculations of the Scholastics.[87] In two interesting passages Erasmus gives an enumeration of what he regards as futile questions.[88] Quite a few are in connection with the doctrine of the Trinity,[89] and some of these curious questions are not only dealt with by Medieval Scholastics, but also by the Fathers, a fact which was undoubtedly known to Erasmus. We give a few examples of such questions: Could God have created man in such a way that he could not have sinned? This is a question raised by the Gnostics, Marcionites and Manicheans, but Irenaeus, Tertullian and Augustin discuss it seriously and extensively.[90] Can God reverse past events and so e.g. make a prostitute into a virgin? This question is answered e.g. by Cyril of Alexandria.[91] Can God command evil? This question was raised by the Marcionites in connection with God's commandment to the Hebrews to rob the Egyptians of gold and silver, and it was answered extensively by Irenaeus and Tertullian.[92] Was the Son

---

[84] See e.g. *Enarratio Symboli* (ed. J. N. Bakhuizen van den Brink in: *Opera omnia Des. Erasmi Rot.* V, 1, N.H.P.C. Amsterdam-Oxford 1977), p. 237, *Paraclesis*, pp. 145f.: Neque enim ob id, opinor, quisquam sibi Christianus esse videatur, si spinosa molesteque verborum perplexitate de instantibus, de relationibus, de quidditatibus ac formalitatibus disputet, sed si quod Christus docuit et exhibuit, id teneat exprimatque, cf. *Methodus* (ed. Holborn), p. 151, *Ratio* (ed. Holborn), p. 180: Quod datur videre, pronus exosculare, quod non datur, tamen opertum quicquid est adora simplici fide proculque venerare, absit impia curiositas, *Enarratio Symboli*, p. 224, cf. F. W. Kantzenbach, *Das Ringen um die Einheit der Kirche im Jahrhundert der Reformation*, pp. 77f.

[85] See e.g. *Modus orandi Deum* (ed. J. N. Bakhuizen van den Brink in *Opera omnia Des. Erasmi Rot.*), p. 146: Et fortassis haec est bona pars christianae religionis in rebus divinis venerari omnia, nihil autem affirmare praeter id quod in sacris literis palam expressum est, *Ad censuras Facultatis Theologiae Parisiensis* (*Des. Erasmi opera omnia*, ed. J. Clericus, t. IX, p. 921: Necessarias ac sobrias de divina natura quaestiones non improbo, praesertim si iuxta Scripturarum oracula cum tremore peraguntur. Curiosas ac supervacaneas noto.

[86] *Hyperaspistae diatribes liber I* (*Des. Erasmi opera omnia*, ed. J. Clericus, t. X), p. 1258.

[87] *Enchiridion* (ed. Holborn), p. 33, *Methodus* (ed. Holborn), pp. 160ff., *Ratio* (ed. Holborn), pp. 189ff.

[88] See *Ratio* (ed. Holborn), pp. 297ff. and his Commentary on the First Epistle to Timothy (*Des. Erasmi opera omnia*, ed. J. Clericus, t. VI), pp. 926ff.

[89] For Erasmus' views on the doctrine of the Trinity see *infra*, 120ff.

[90] See Irenaeus, *Adv. Haer.* 4, 61ff., Tertullian, *Adv. Marcionem* 2, 5ff., Augustin, *De Genesi at litteram* 11, 4, 6ff.

[91] See *Adv. Anthropomorphitas* 13 (Migne PG 76, 1100A).

[92] See Irenaeus, *Adv. Haereses* 4, 46 and Tertullian, *Adversus Marcionem* 2, 20. The question whether God's omnipotence implies that God can want and do evil is raised by Celsus and discussed by Origen, see *Contra Celsum* 3, 70, cf. 5, 23 and the notes given by H. Chadwick, *Origen: Contra Celsum, Translated with an Introduction and Notes*, Cambridge 1963[2], pp. 175 and 281.

generated by nature or by free will? This question is dealt with by Athanasius.[93]—It is hardly conceivable that Erasmus was not aware of the fact that some of the questions which he opposes as futile curiosity were treated seriously by the Fathers. He obviously had the idea that the Fathers speculated much less than the later Scholastics and that the fact that sometimes they did speculate showed that they were not infallible, as he insists that they were not in their exegesis of Biblical texts.[94]

Erasmus' opposition to curiosity shows clear similarity with Melanchthon's attack on speculative theology. But the difference ought not to be overlooked. It can be stated in the following way:[95] Erasmus advocated a return to antiquity and regarded the Fathers as the most reliable exegetes of the Bible, because they were the closest in time to the Apostles. This traditionalism is different from Melanchthon's traditionalism which regards the Bible as the only authority. Erasmus read the New Testament with the eyes of the Fathers, Melanchthon wanted to read and judge the Fathers with Biblical eyes.—Both Erasmus and Melanchthon have a practical scope with their opposition against speculation, but the *praxis* they envisage differs: Melanchthon is interested in Christian faith which believes in the forgiveness of sins, Erasmus is interested in Christian life which lives after Christ's commandments. A nice illustration of Erasmus' moralism in this matter can be found in his catalogue of futile questions. Instead of asking questions about the nature of sin the Christian theologian should make all people hate sin. Instead of asking whether the grace with which God loves us is the same as the one with which we love God, we should live in such a way that God regards us worthy of this gift. Instead of asking how the material hellfire can burn the incorporeal souls of the unbelievers we should live in such a way that that hellfire, however it is constituted, finds nothing in us to burn.[96]

---

[93] See *Oratio contra Arianos* 3, 59-67, cf. *infra*, 61, 100.

[94] See *Ratio* (ed. Holborn), p. 295: Homines erant, quaedam ignorabant, in nonnullis halucinati sunt, and *De ratione concionandi*, 1 III (*Des. Erasmi opera omnia*, ed. J. Clericus, t. V), pp. 1026ff.

[95] Cf. W. Maurer, *Der junge Melanchthon zwischen Humanismus und Reformation II*, Göttingen 1969, pp. 60 and 163, and his paper, Der Einfluss Augustins auf Melanchthons theologische Entwicklung, *Kerygma und Dogma* (9) 1959, p. 188. We do not agree with J. S. Oyer, *Lutheran Reformers against Anabaptists. Luther, Melanchthon and Menius and the Anabaptists of Central Germany*, The Hague 1964, when he says, p. 148: "Scripture of Melanchthon was more than the 'plain Scripture' to the Anabaptists. For Melanchthon it meant also as the fathers in general interpreted it." This applies to Erasmus, not to Melanchthon.

[96] See the passage from the Commentary on the First Epistle to Timothy quoted in note 88, p. 926: Quorsum enim attinet decertare, quot modis accipiatur peccatum, privacio duntaxat sit, an macula inhaerens animae? Hoc potius agat Theologus, ut omnes horreant oderintque peccatum. Totis seculis disputamus, an gratia, qua Deus nos diligit ac trahit, et qua nos illum vicissim diligimus, eadem sit gratia ... Illud potius agamus, puris precibus, innocentia vitae, piis factis, ut eo munere nos dignetur deus ... Disputamus qui

In a letter to Erasmus in 1536 Melanchthon says that he has always been sceptical about doctrines which go beyond Scriptural revelation and that he believes that Erasmus' attitude was the same in this respect.[97] This is not a correct interpretation of Erasmus' views, certainly not of his views after he had attacked the Reformation. It would perhaps be more correct to say that Erasmus was sceptical about doctrines which are not revealed by Scripture and clearly elaborated by the Fathers, and that he was sceptical about lengthy speculations about Scriptural and Patristic doctrines, without doubting these doctrines in themselves.[98]

When the young Reformer Melanchthon vigorously attacks speculative theology he must have had the feeling that he had the full backing of Luther in this matter.[99] In 1521 Melanchthon writes that Luther condemned philosophy and the dregs of philosophy, *viz.*, Scholastic theology.[100] Luther was strongly opposed to a theology which starts from above, at the majesty of God's being, instead of from below, in the incarnate Son of God.[101] He rejected curiosity which wants to read the thoughts of God.[102] The only authority for theology is the Word of God, the Bible, the authority of synods and councils is only valid in so far as it is confirmed by Scripture. Luther had a high regard for the first four ecumenical councils, especially the Nicene council, although he had some reservations about the word *homoousios*.[103]

Melanchthon's attack on futile, speculative theology stands in a long tradition. For as long as there has been Christian theology the question

---

fieri possit, ut ignis, quo cruciabuntur impiorum animae, cum sit materialis, agat in rem incorpoream. Quanto magis referebat, huc totis viribus eniti, ne quid in nobis reperiet ignis ille, qualis qualis est, quod exurat? On this statement about speculations on the Trinity see *infra*, 122.

[97] See CR 3, p. 69: In articulis fidei, in promissionibus et comminationibus require certam assensionem, in quibus tu quoque requiris. Si quae sunt disputationes extra Scripturam, in illis et mihi placet ἐπέχειν more Academicorum. Hic quid pugnet cum tua sententia, ne nunc quidem video.

[98] See *infra*, 122.

[99] Cf. for the following: Th. Harnack, *Luthers Theologie mit besonderer Beziehung auf seine Versöhnungs- und Erlösungslehre*, I (Neue Ausgabe), 1927, pp. 33ff., Q. Breen, *Christianity and Humanism*, pp. 76ff. and H. A. Oberman, *Contra vanam curiositatem*, pp. 39ff.

[100] See *Did. Fav. adv. Th. Placentinum* (1521) (St.A. I), p. 86: Obiter perstrinximus argumenta quaedam sententiae Lutheri, cur is et philosophiam et philosophorum fecem, Theologiam scholasticam, damnet...

[101] See the quotations given by Th. Harnack, *op. cit.*, pp. 41ff. and *Luthers Theologie*, II, pp. 100ff.

[102] See the quotations given by H. A. Oberman, *op. cit.*, p. 46.

[103] On his reservations about the word *homousios* see Th. Harnack, *Luthers Theologie* II, p. 147, on Luther's view on the council of Nicaea see his *Von den Conciliis und Kirchen* (W.A. 50), pp. 548ff., cf. C. Tecklenburg Johns, *Luthers Konzilsidee in ihrer historischen Bedingtheit und ihrem reformatorischen Neuansatz*, Berlin 1966, pp. 43ff.

has been asked where the line ought to be drawn between useless curiosity and useful knowledge. Christians always opposed curiosity, but they
were divided on the question of where curiosity began and of what were
the criteria with which it could be detected. The attack on speculation
was renewed by late Medieval nominalism, and in the sixteenth century
both the Reformation and Humanism were strongly opposed to it. The
difference between these two was that the Reformation wanted to attack
it with the clear doctrine of the Bible, whilst e.g. Erasmus wanted to
liberate the minds from futile, Scholastic curiosity by returning to the
simplicity of the doctrine of the Bible and the Fathers.

The young Reformer Melanchthon attacks Scholastic theology with
the authority of Scripture and rarely with explicit quotations from the
Fathers. Later on the constantly takes his arguments from Scripture and
the Fathers. We have seen that this cannot mean that he moved from the
Reformation view to the humanistic position, since in his later years, too,
he subjects the Fathers to the authority of Scripture and only produces
arguments from the Fathers since he regards them as Scriptural. Furthermore it is, at least at the face of it, not entirely clear whether the attack on
speculative theology in the first edition of the *Loci communes* was only
directed against Scholastic theology or also against Patristic theology.
Whether he also attacked the latter one depends on the question of
whether he attacked only speculations about the Trinity, the natures of
Christ and the creation, or whether he also dismissed these doctrines as
such as unimportant. If we try to determine the continuity and discontinuity in the thought of Melanchthon from the point of view of his relation to Patristic theology, we shall have to make an effort to find out
which part Patristic theology played in the first edition of the *Loci communes* and whether this part could be greater than the relatively few
quotations suggest. But first we should try to give a picture of Melanchthon as a Patristic scholar. Having determined what kind of knowledge
he had of the Fathers we may be able to see mote clearly which use he
made of their doctrines.

CHAPTER TWO

MELANCHTHON AS A PATRISTIC SCHOLAR

In the present chapter[1] we shall try to determine from which writings of which Fathers Melanchthon quotes when he refers to the Fathers as supporters of his own doctrines, or when he criticizes the Fathers. Since Melanchthon seldom gives exact references when he quotes it seems useful to register the passages quoted by him. In this field the work done by the editors of the *Studienausgabe* has been of great help, although in a minority of cases the reader will notice that we propose other places in the writings of the Fathers than given in the *Studienausgabe*. In the *Corpus Reformatorum* no references to the sources are provided. Since the bulk of Melanchthon's works can still only be found in the *Corpus Reformatorum* our list may be the more useful. We do not claim to provide an exhaustive presentation of all the traditional material available in Melanchthon, but shall confine ourselves to the subjects on which the continuity and discontinuity in Melanchthon will be illustrated, *viz.*, the doctrines of Christ and grace, the Trinity and the creation. Clear quotations will be distinguished from references or possible references. If possible it will be shown which editions Melanchthon used. Melanchthon's evaluation of the various Fathers will, if possible, be compared with Luther's and Erasmus' evaluation. It will also be asked whether Melanchthon's general opinion of a Father influenced the way in which he uses him.

We shall begin with Augustin, since he is obviously Melanchthon's most important Patristic source. After him the Fathers will be discussed in alphabetical order, whereby their degree of importance will become clear from the way in which and the frequency with which Melanchthon makes use of their writings. This alphabetical order need not conceal Melanchthon's development as a Patristic scholar. We shall give the dates (provided in the *Studienausgabe* and the *Corpus Reformatorum*) of the various writings in which the quotations from the Fathers appear. These dates and the subjects on which the Fathers are referred to show when Melanchthon was interested in which aspects of Patristic theology. The well known development of Melanchthon's theological thought from a concentration on the doctrine of grace, sin and justification to a broader presentation of all articles of faith will be illustrated by the quotations from the Fathers: first these are in the context of the doctrine of grace, sin and justification, later on also of the Trinity, christology and creation.

---

[1] Cf. for the following: P. Fraenkel, *Testimonia Patrum*, pp. 15ff.

Augustin

In 1519 Melanchthon claims to have a better knowledge of Augustin, Jerome and Ambrose than Eck has of Aristotle.[2] He had a high esteem of Augustin, although not always for same reasons.

The doctrine of Christ and grace

As far as the person of Christ is concerned Augustin is sometimes quoted as one of the representatives of the orthodox doctrine: Augustin makes a clear distinction between the act of the incarnation and Christ's descent into the hearts of the believers. A quotation is given in the following way:[3]

> Augustinus IV De Trinitate inquit: Quotidie mitti Filium in corda sanctorum. Et ait: Aliter mittitur ut sit homo, aliter ut sit cum homine.

This quotation is repeated with small variations.[4] The reference is fairly exact and the quotation is almost literal. In *De Trin.* 4, 20, 27 Augustin says:

> Aliter mittitur ut sit cum homine aliter missa est ut ipsa sit homo (sc. sapientia).

In connection with the question of why the Son and not the Father or the Holy Ghost became man Melanchthon refers to a reason which according to him is given by Augustin: If the Father had assumed human nature, He would have been Father and Son at the same time, if the Holy Ghost had assumed human nature, there would have been two Sons. So in order that there might be one Son, He assumed human nature who also in the divine nature in the Son:[5]

> ...Si pater assumeret humanam naturam, tum esset et pater et filius, si spiritus sanctus, essent duo filii. Ut igitur sit unus fillius, assumit humanam naturam, qui in divina quoque natura est filius.

---

[2] *Def. Phil. Melanchthonis contra Joh. Eckium* (St.A. I), p. 19: Quaeso: quoties lapsus est Hieronymus, quoties Augustinus, quoties Ambrosius? Nec enim tam ignoti mihi sunt, ut non hoc libere ausim dicere, immo fortasse notiores aliquanto sunt mihi, quam Eckio suus Aristoteles.

[3] See his letter to Strigelius, dating from 1552 (CR 7), p. 1057.

[4] See his letter to Werner, dating from 1556 (CR 8), p. 925: Nec reiicio Augustini dictum de filio: quotidie mittitur sapientia, ut sit cum homine, and *Quaestio Academica*, dating from 1555 (CR 10), p. 849: Et Augustinus inquit, Quotidie mitti sapientiam, scilicet Filium, ut sit nobiscum, Letter to Strigelius, dating from 1553 (CR 8), p. 191, Letter to Hardenbergius, dating from 1552 (CR 7), p. 1149.

[5] *Postilla Melanchthoniana* (CR 24), p. 77.

We could not trace this argument in the writings of Augustin. Something similar does, however, appear in the *Sententiae* of Petrus Lombardus, and what Melanchthon says could be a combination of the answers to two questions raised by Petrus Lombardus. The first question is why it says of the Holy Ghost that He procedes and not that He is generated.[6] Quoting Augustin as his authority Petrus Lombardus says that if the Holy Ghost were generated, He would be the Son of the Father and the Son, which is absurd.[7] The second question is why the Son and not the Father or the Holy Ghost assumed nature, the answer which is given comes very close to the quotation ascribed by Melanchthon to Augustin: He became son of man who in divinity is the Son. The Holy Ghost did not assume flesh, lest there were a difference between the Son in divinity and the Son in humanity, and the Father was not born from a human being lest He be the Father and the Son at the same time.[8]

In connection with the two natures of Christ Melanchthon quotes Augustin as saying that Christ died as God through what He was as man and that He was raised again as man through what He was as God:[9]

> Per illud, quod homo erat, mortuus est Deus, et per illud quod Deus erat, homo exuscitatus est et resurrexit.

This is an almost literal quotation from *Enarrationes in Psalmos* 130, 10:

> Per id ergo quod homo erat, mortuus est Deus, et per id quod Deus erat, ecitatus est homo et resurrexit...

Melanchthon criticizes Augustin for saying that he found the Christian doctrine in the Platonists with one exception, *viz.*, the incarnation of the Word:[10]

---

[6] Melanchthon deals with this question in *Explic. Symb. Nic.* (CR 23), p. 500 and *Postilla Melanchthoniana* (CR 24), p. 871 (cf. *infra*, 116).

[7] *Sent.* I, dist. xiii, cap. 1, the section quoted from Augustin is *De Trin.* 15, 26, 47. But Augustin does not say that a generation of the Holy Ghost would imply two sons, but that it would imply that He would be the Son of the Father and the Son.

[8] *Sent.* III, dist. i, cap. 1, 3: Quod ideo factum est, ut qui erat in divinitate Dei Filius, in humanitate fieret hominis filius. Non Pater vel Spiritus Sanctus carnem induit, ne alius in divinitate esset Filius, alius in humanitate, et ne idem esset pater et filius, si Deus Pater de homine nasceretur. — The fact that Petrus Lombardus does not produce a quotation from Augustin in this context is an indication that Augustin did not say this. On the other hand the appearance of this argument in Petrus Lombardus is a clear indication that it was generally known in later scholasticism. If our assumption is right, then Melanchthon ascribes a Scholastic argument to Augustin, cf. *infra*, 122.

[9] *Explic. Symb. Nic.* (CR 23), p. 510.

[10] *Disputationes Ph. Mel.* (CR 12), p. 690. But in the *Declamatio de vita Augustini*, dating from 1539, Melanchthon says that according to Augustin the Platonists imitated and astutely twisted the words of the evangelist in order to make them look like their own words and to lessen the authority of the Christian doctrine, see CR 11, p. 451: Narrat (sc. Augustinus) se tunc in Plotini libros incidisse, in quibus fuerint quaedam de natura Dei et

> Ineptit etiam Augustinus qui dicit se Christianorum doctrinam in Platonicis reperisse, praeter hunc unum articulum: Verbum caro factum est.

This is a clear reference to Augustin, *Confessiones* 7, 9, 13-15, especially 14:

> Item legi ibi, quia verbum, deus, non ex carne, non ex sanguine, non ex voluntate viri neque ex voluntate carnis, sed ex deo natur est; sed quia verbum caro factum est et habitavit in nobis, non ibi legi.

Luther criticizes Augustin for the same reason, adding that Augustin was deceived by a book written by Hermegistus.[11]

It is in connection with *the doctrine of God's grace in Christ* that Melanchthon produces the greatest number of quotations from Augustin.

A few times he gives the quotation that men are saved by the precious blood of Christ:[12]

> Augustinus inquit: Totius fiduciae certitudo esse debet in pretioso sanguine Christi.

This is a quotation from (Ps.-) Augustin, *Liber Meditationum* 14.

Man's total dependence on God's grace is also expressed in the following quotation from *Confessiones* 9, 13, 34:[13]

> (Sic enim inquit Augustinus ... lib. IX Confess.) Vae hominum vitae quantumcumque laudabili, si remota misericordia iudicetur.

---

de verbo aeterno, quae imitati sunt Philosophi, et astute transtulerunt ad sese, ut Christianae doctrinae autoritas extenuaretur. — According to Melanchthon Augustin discovered this fraud and then threw away the books: Sed tamen Augustinus ait se deprehensa fraude eos libros abiecisse. This statement by Melanchthon finds no support in Augustin's own words.

[11] This is in a disputation held in 1536, see W.A. 39, I, pp. 179f., cf. H. A. Oberman, *Contra vanam curiositatem*, p. 43, n. 84.

[12] *Enarr. Epist. Pauli ad Romanos* (CR 15), p. 877, *Responsiones ad articulos Bavaricae inquisitionis* (St.A. VI), p. 327, Letter to Pfauser, dating from 1556 (CR 8), p. 711, *Explic. Symb. Nic.* (CR 23), p. 492 (with a reference to *Liber Meditationum*), of special interest is *Postilla Melanchthoniana* (CR 25), p. 424, where he says that Augustin's doctrine of grace and faith may not always have been completely right, but that this statement shows that his intention was right: ... bene, vel saltem melius quam caeteri (tractat) doctrinam de gratia et fide, de iustitia fidei. Etiamsi interdum minus commode loquitur, tamen hoc vult quod dicit: Totius fiduciae certitudo est nobis in sanguine Christi. Ibi docet nos confidere merito Domini nostri Jesu Christi, non novitate nostra. For his criticism of Augustin's doctrine of grace (which has to do with the 'novitas nostra'), see *infra*, 28.

[13] *Apol. Conf. Aug.* B (CR 27), p. 505. Augustin's words are: et vae etiam laudabili vitae hominum, si remota misericordia discutias eam. This quotation already played a role at the *Leipzig Disputation*, see O. Seitz, *Der authentische Text der Leipziger Disputation*, Berlin 1903, p. 233, p. 237. This section from the Confessiones is treated with some caution in *De ecclesia et de autoritate verbi Dei* (St.A. I), p. 365, since the following words have according to Melanchthon been distorted by the Romans in order to support the doctrine of the Purgatory: Inspira, Domine, servis tuis, ut ad altare meminerint matris meae et patris.

Augustin gives the right interpretation of the Sermon on the Mount by declaring that Jesus gives precepts and not merely counsels. This is said repeatedly in 1521.[14] The references are to *De sermone Domini in monte* I 19, 56-57 and the letter to Marcellinus (*Epistola* CXXXIX). But Melanchthon is at the same time also critical of the fact that Augustin gives as the only reason why the Old Testament law was abrogated, that it is a ceremonial law. According to Melanchthon the law was abrogated, because it could not justify and only showed human sin.[15]

In the first edition of the *Loci communes* he refers to Augustin's *De gratia Christi et de peccato originali contra Pelagium ad Coelestium* as a learned refutation of the Pelagian doctrine.[16] Augustin is referred to as a supporter of Luther's doctrine of grace and justification.[17] Throughout his life Melanchthon referred to Augustin's Anti-Pelagian writings as support for his doctrine of grace:[18]

In his *Adv. furiosum Parris. Theol. decr.* he gives the following almost literal quotation from *De spiritu et littera* 4, 6:[19]

> sed ubi sanctus non adiuvat spiritus, inspirans pro concupiscentia mala concupiscentiam bonam, hoc est, charitatem diffundens in cordibus nostris, profecto lex illa, Non concupisces, quamvis bona, auget prohibendo desiderium malum.

In the *Confessio Augustana* (Variata) art. XX the following literal quotation is given from *De spiritu et littera*:[20]

> Quandoquidem per legem ostendit homini infirmitatem suam, ut ad eius misericordiam per fidem confugiens sanaretur.

In the *Loci communes* of 1559 he gives the following fairly literal quotations from Augustin's same piece of writing:[21]

> Ex lege timemus Deum, fide confugimus ad misericordiam. Item, Fides dicit, Sana animam meam, quia peccavi tibi.

---

[14] *Adv. furiosum Parris. Theol. decr.* ... (St.A. I), p. 148 and *Loci communes* (1521) (St.A. II), p. 51.

[15] *Loci communes* (1521), p. 134, the reference is to *Contra Faustum Manichaeum* 19, 10.

[16] *Loci communes* (1521), p. 19.

[17] *Adv. furiosum Parris. Theol. decr.* ... (St.A. I), pp. 147ff., *Loci communes* (1521), p. 130.

[18] See the list of Augustin's anti-Pelagian writings which Melanchthon gives in *De Erasmo et Luthero elogion, Ratio discendi, et quo iudicio Augustinus, Ambrosius, Origenes ac reliqui doctores legendi sint*, dating from 1522 (CR 20), p. 705.

[19] (St.A. I), p. 159, cf. H. O. Günther, *Die Entwicklung der Willenslehre Melanchthons in der Auseinandersetzung mit Luther und Erasmus* (Diss. Erlangen) 1963, p. 30, W.-D. Hausschild, *op. cit.*, pp. 150f.

[20] (St.A. VI), p. 30, see *De spiritu et littera* 9, 15.

[21] (St.A. II), p. 368, see *De spiritu et littera* 29, 50: Ex lege timemus Deum ... per fidem confugiat (sc. anima laborans) ad misericordiam Dei, 30, 52: Fides dicit: Sana animam meam, quoniam peccavi tibi.

In the *De ecclesia et de autoritate verbi Dei*, from 1539, there are general references to the *De spiritu et littera*: When Paul says that man is justified without the works of law he does not mean ceremonial law, but the law which prescribes moral acts.[22] Melanchthon had a very high esteem of the *De spiritu et littera* as appears from the Preface to an edition of this book which came out im Wittemberg in 1545, in which he declares that in the Lutheran church the doctrine given in this book is preached, and that it has been studied in Wittenberg for many years.[23]

Other Anti-Pelagian writings from which Melanchthon quotes are *De peccatorum meritis et remissione*, *Contra Julianum*, *De gestis Pelagii*, *De gratia et libero arbitrio*, and (Ps.-Augustin) *De praedestinatione et gratia*, and these quotations appear in the context of the doctrine of original sin, grace and infant baptism: The *De peccatorum meritis et remissione* is in general referred to as a testimony of infant baptism.[24] *De pecc. mer. et rem.* 3, 6, 12 is referred to in the defence of the doctrine of original sin: Augustin testifies that he cannot remember anyone in the Church who denies original sin.[25]—*De pecc. mer. et rem.* II 5 is referred to when Melanchthon denies that *Sach.* 1:3: "Convertimini ad me et ego convertar ad vos" means that the beginning of penitence lies in man:

> ... "Convertimini ad me et ego convertar ad vos", non efficit poenitentiae initium in nobis esse positum. Excussit autem hanc sententiam Augustinus non uno loco...[26]

Augustin's words are:

> Cum ergo nobis iubet dicens: "Convertimini ad me, et convertar ad vos" ... quid aliud dicimus quam: Da quod iubes?

The *Contra Julianum* is in general referred to as a testimony of infant baptism.[27] *Contra Julianum* 2, 4, 8 is freely quoted:[28]

---

[22] (St.A. I), pp. 359f. See, however, his criticism of Augustin quoted *supra*.

[23] (CR 5), p. 804: Hunc autem Augustini commentarium ideo nunc edimus, quia multo ante constitutum est in hac Academia, ut interdum hic liber proponatur ac enarretur, ut studiosi conferant aetates et scriptores, et quaesita una perpetua et catholica Ecclesiae dei sententia, videant in hac nostra ecclesia vere sonare, retineri et propagari illam unicam puram perpetuam verae ecclesiae dei sententiam ...

[24] *Adversus Anabaptistas iudicium* (St.A. I), p. 281.

[25] See *Nova Scholia in Prov. Salomonis* (St.A. IV), p. 431. It should be noted that Augustin adds the restriction: amongst those who accept both the Old and the New Testament.

[26] *Loci communes* (1521) (St.A. II), p. 36.

[27] *Adv. Anab. iud.* (St.A. I), p. 281.

[28] See *Apol. Conf. Aug. Prior* (CR 27), pp. 277f., the first part of the quotation is repeated in *Apol. Conf. Aug. Altera* (CR 27), p. 426, a reference is also possibly given in the Colloquium at Worms (CR 4), p. 42: Lege peccati quod licet iam remissum est, in vetustate tamen carnis manet.

Peccatum remittitur in baptismo, non ut non sit, sed ut non imputetur. Item. Lex peccati, quae in membris corporis est, remissa est regeneratione spirituali, et manet in carne mortali, remissa, quia reatus solutus est in sacramento quo renascuntur fideles.

Augustin's words are:

Lex itaque peccati repugnans legi mentis, quae in tanti quoque apostoli membris erat, remittitur in Baptismate, non finitur ... reatus eiusdem mali ... sicut generatione contrahitur, ita nisi regeneratione non solvitur.

So the word 'imputare' which is very important to Melanchthon does not appear in what Augustin actually says here.—The following litteral quotation is given from *Contra Julianum* 5, 3, 8:[29]

Concupiscentia carnis adversus quam bonus concupiscit Spiritus, et peccatum est, quia inest illi inobedientia contra dominatum mentis, et poena peccati est, quia reddita est meritis inobedientis, et causa peccati est, defectione consentientis, vel contagione nascentis.

A sentence from (Ps.-Augustin) *De Praedestinatione et gratia* 9, 10 is quoted in the following way:[30]

Eos qui vocationis munus congrua pietate susceperunt, et, quantum in homine est, Dei in se dona servantes adiuvat (sc. Deus).

Here God's grace does not exclude man's free will. In this context a statement made in (Ps.-Augustin) *Hypognosticon* III 4, 5 (Migne PL 45, 1623) is quoted in order to show that man does have a free will in outward actions, but not in actions which affect his relationship with God:[31]

Esse fatemur liberum arbitrium omnibus hominibus, habens quidem iudicium rationis, non per quod sit idoneum in iis quae ad Deum pertinent, sine Deo aut inchoare aut certe peragere, sed tantum in operibus vitae praesentis, tam bonis, quam malis. Bonis dico, quae de bono naturae oriuntur, id est, velle laborare in agro, velle manducare et bibere, velle habere amicum, velle habere indumenta, velle fabricare domum, uxorem velle ducere, pecora nutrire, artem discere diversarum rerum bonarum, vel quicquid bonum ad praesentem pertinet vitam. Quae omnia non sine divina gubernatione subsistunt, imo ex Deo et per ipsum sunt et esse coeperunt. Malis vero dico, ut est, velle idolum colere, velle homicidium etc.

---

[29] See the Colloquium at Worms (CR 4), p. 41, cf. *Commentarii in Epist. Pauli ad Romanos*, dating from 1532 (St.A. V), p. 172.

[30] *Loci communes*, dating from 1559 (St.A. II), p. 599, cf. *Comm. in Epist. Pauli ad Rom.* (St.A. V), p. 254, *Postilla Melanchthoniana* (CR 24), p. 390, see also P. Fraenkel, *Testimonia patrum*, p. 300, n. 58.

[31] *Conf. Aug.*, art. xviii, *Conf. Aug.* (Variata) (St.A. VI), p. 24. On Augustin's influence on Melanchthon's doctrine of predestination and free will see also H.-G. Geyer, Zur Rolle der Prädestinationslehre Augustins beim jungen Melanchthon, *Studien zur Geschichte und Theologie der Reformation*. Festschrift für Ernst Bizer, herausgegeben von Luise Abramowski und J. F. Gerhard Goeters, Neukirchen 1969, pp. 175ff.

In the same context Augustin's exegesis of *Eccl.* 15:17 ("Deus reliquit hominem in manu consilii sui. Si voles servabis mandata, posuit coram te aquam et ignem, ut ad utrum voles extendito manum") is repeatedly referred to with approval. These quotations differ from each other, none of them is literal.[32] In his most extensive quotation Melanchthon claims that Augustin in his exegesis refutes both Stoic determinism and the Manichean's dualistic phantasies:[33]

> (Augustinus breviter et recte respondet:) Ad utrum voles extendito manum. Voluntas potest per sese extendere manum ad malum, quia certissimum est, ruentes contra conscientiam non cogi, ut labantur, sed libere et volentes labi, ac refutat illo ipso loco Syracides furores eorum, qui dicunt Deum esse causam peccati. Damnat igitur Stoicam necessitatem et Manichaea portenta. Deinde de bono etiam recte dicitur, Voluntas extendit manum. Sed adiuvatur a Spiritu sancto.

This is a free quotation from (and explanation of) *De gestis Pelagii* 3, 7:

> Manifestum est quod, si ad ignem manum mittit et malum ac mors ei placet, voluntas id hominis operatur, si autem bonum et vitam diligit, non solum voluntas id agit, sed divinitus adiuvatur.

A sentence from the *De sermone Domini in monte* is (very freely) quoted in order to show that the Christian remains a sinner:[34]

> Etsi deleta est iniquitas, nondum tamen finita est infirmitas. Adhuc dices, Dimitte nobis debita nostra.

It seems as if Melanchthon here ascribes a sentence from *Tract. in Joann.* XLI 10 to Augustin's exegesis of "Forgive us our trespasses":

> Numquid quia deleta est tota iniquitas, nulla remansit infirmitas?

There is a clear quotation from *Tract. in Joann.* XLI 12 in the same context:[35]

> Non regnet peccatum in nostro mortali corpore, Non dicit, non sit, sed non regnet. Quam diu vivis peccata necesse est esse in membris tuis. Saltem illi regnum auferatur, non fiat quod iubet.

---

[32] See *En. Symb. Nic.* (CR 23), pp. 288f., *Explic. Symb. Nic.* (CR 23), pp. 439ff., 545. This text was already debated at the *Leipzig Disputation*, see O. Seitz, *Der authentische Text der Leipziger Disputation*, pp. 15ff.

[33] *Explic. Symb. Nic.* (CR 23), pp. 439f.

[34] See the Colloquium at Worms (CR 4), p. 42 and the *Disputatio de peccato reliquo in renatis* (CR 12), p. 442, this quotation can only be a free reference to *De serm. Dom. in monte* II 10, 37: Et peccata nunc nobis dimittuntur,et nunc dimittimus ... tunc autem nulla erit venia peccatorum, quia nulla peccata.

[35] (CR 4), p. 41. Only the word 'vivis' seems to have been added by Melanchthon.

In connection with his definition of faith as trust to receive the forgiveness of sins Melanchthon quotes almost literally *En. in Ps.* XXXI ii 7:[36]

> Qui sunt beati? non illi in quibus non inveniet peccatum, nam in omnibus invenit. Omnes enim peccaverunt et egent gloria Dei. Si ergo in omnibus peccata inveniuntur, remanet, ut non sint beati, nisi quorum remissa sunt peccata. Hoc ergo Apostolus sic commendavit: Credidit Abraham Deo, et imputatum est ei ad iustitiam.

In the same context a long quotation is given from *En. in Ps.* XXX ii sermo i 6:[37]

> In tua iustitia erue me, nam si attendas ad iustitiam meam, damnas me. In tua iustitia me erue. Est enim iustitia Dei, quae et nostra fit, cum donatur nobis. Ideo autem Dei iustitia dicitur, ne homo sese putet a seipso habere iustitiam, sicut enim dicit Apostolus Paulus: Credenti in eum, qui iustificat impium, id est qui ex impio facit iustum, Si agat tanquam ex regula legis proposita, damnandus est peccator. Hac regula, si ageret, quem liberaret? Omnes enim peccatores invenit. Hoc ait Apostolus, "Omnes peccaverunt et egent gloria Dei." Quid est, egent gloria Dei? Ut ipse liberet, non tu. Quia tu non potes liberare, indiges liberatore, Quid est, quod te iactas? quid est, quod de lege et iustitia praesumis? Non vides, quid intus tecum pugnet? Non audis decertantem et confitentem et adiutorium in pugna desiderantem: "Miser ego homo" etc.

The following brief quotation is given repeatedly from *Epistula* CLXXXVI 3, 10:[38]

> Praeeunte gratia, comitante voluntate

This is a brief summary of the following words:

> ... non gratiam Dei aliquid meriti praecedit humani, sed ipsa gratia meretur augeri ... comitante, non ducente pedissequa, non praevia voluntate.

---

[36] See *Loci communes*, dating from 1559 (St.A. II), p. 368. Melanchthon's conclusion from the quotation is: Hic certe Augustinus fidem intelligit fiduciam, quae accipit remissionem peccatorum, see also *De ecclesia et de autoritate verbi Dei* (St.A. I), pp. 363f.

[37] *Conf. Aug.* (Variata) (St.A. VI), pp. 32f. The quotation is given fairly literally, whereby Melanchthon reproduces what he regards as the most important sentences in this section.

[38] *Disputatio de bonis operibus* (CR 12), p. 672. The same quotation (without Augustin's name) is given in *Philosophiae moralis epitomes I* (St.A. III), p. 187, *En. Symb. Nic.* (CR 23), p. 285, *Postilla Melanchthoniana* (CR 24), p. 364, p. 391, *Examen ordin.* (CR 23), p. 15, cf. K. Haendler, *op. cit.*, pp. 543f., see also *Explicatio Sententiarum Theognidis* (CR 19), p. 131, where there is also a quotation from Aeschylus (*Persae* 742), which is believed to say something similar: Ἀλλ' ὅταν σπεύδει τις αὐτὸς καὶ θεὸς συνάπτεται, and *Enarratio libri II. Ethicorum Aristotelis* (CR 10), p. 330.

Eternal life is a gift of God's grace and cannot be earned by man, this statement of Augustin is, of course, quoted with approval by Melanchthon:[39]

> (Et Augustinus inquit:) Vita aeterna nullis humanis meritis redditur, sed Dei donantis gratia largiente donatur.

Melanchthon here obviously has in mind *De gratia et libero arbitrio* 9, 21:[40]

> Gratia autem Dei vita aeterna: ut hinc intelligeremus, non pro meritis nostris Deum nos ad vitam aeternam, sed pro sua miseratione perducere.

It is because of his doctrine of grace and sin that Augustin is highly praised by Melanchthon. He sees the Lutheran doctrine of grace and justification confirmed by Augustin.[41] When he lists Augustin amongst the true proclaimers of the Gospel, as he often does, then it is because of Augustin's doctrine of grace.[42] But Melanchthon is also in this respect not entirely uncritical of Augustin. In his commentary on the Epistle to the Romans, dating from 1532, he opposes the doctrine that the justification implies the beginning of man's renewal and concedes that this doctrine finds some support in Augustin.[43] This is a view which Melanchthon opposed throughout his life. In the *Loci communes* dating from 1559 we read:[44]

> ... quoties de liberatione a Lege dicitur, intelligatur non tantum auxilium, ut Augustinus plerumque enarrat, sed etiam gratuita imputatio iustitiae. Augustinus plerumque sic loquitur: Liberati sumus a Lege, id est, donato Spiritu sancto iuvamur, ut Legi obediamus, nec iam frustra nitimur coacti a Lege ...

---

[39] See e.g. *Annotationes in Epist. Pauli ad Rom.* (CR 15), p. 668, cf. p. 541. For opposition against the theory that eternal life is given as a reward see also *Comm. in Epist. Pauli ad Rom.* (St.A. V), p. 44, p. 51, p. 52.

[40] *De gratia et libero arbitrio* 9, 21 is quoted in *Apol. Conf. Aug.* (CR 27), p. 278 and *Apol. Conf. Aug.* B (CR 26), p. 505.

[41] *Adv. furiosum Parris. Theol. decr.* ... (1521) (St.A. I), pp. 147ff., *Loci communes* (1521) (St.A. II), p. 130, his letter to G. Pontanus, dating from 1543 (CR 5), p. 234.

[42] See e.g. *De restituendis scholis*, dating from 1540 (St.A. III), p. 113, Colloquium at Worms (1541) (CR 4), p. 38, *De ecclesia et de autoritate verbi Dei* (St.A. I), p. 376. Augustin surpasses all other Fathers, *Brevis discendae theologiae ratio* (CR 2), p. 459, even Athanasius, Chrysostomus and Basil, see *Postilla Melanchthoniana* (CR 25), p. 425.

[43] (St.A. V), p. 100: Repudianda est et imaginatio aliorum, qui adeo putant nos fide iustificari, quia fides sit initium renovationis. Hi fingunt nos iustos esse propter nostram novitatem et qualitatem. Ac propemodum ex Augustino hanc persuasionem hauriunt. Similar mild criticism is expressed on pp. 121, 266, 327, 33f., 45f., see R. Schäfer's note on p. 100. Melanchthon may here have in mind *De spiritu et littera* 29, 50ff.; cf. *Enarratio Epist. Pauli ad Rom.* (CR 15), pp. 882f. On Melanchthon's use of and criticism of Augustin's doctrine of grace see S. Wiedenhofer, *op. cit.*, pp. 213ff.

[44] (St.A. II), pp. 765f. (This criticism is expressed in a similar way in the edition of 1535 (CR 21), p. 459.)

He also opposes Augustin's view that all sin, including original sin, is voluntary sin. According to Melanchthon this holds true of actual social sins, not of original sin.[45]

The doctrine of the Trinity

Augustin's doctrine of the *vestigium trinitatis* was criticized by the young Reformer Melanchthon. In the commentary on the First Epistle to the Corinthians, dating from 1522, he says that Augustin's doctrine that man is created in God's image appears from memory, intelligence and will in the soul, which represent the Father, Son and Holy Ghost, that this doctrine lacks Scriptural and rational support.[46] In his commentary on the Epistle to the Colossians, dating from 1527, he refers to this doctrine in more extensive expositions and gives it a guarded approval:[47]

> Quidam imaginem Dei in ratione posuerunt et in veteri homine quod sit quaedam trinitatis effigies in nostra mente, quia memoria gignat intelectionem. Memoriam atque intellectionem comitetur velle, ut pater filium gignit. Vocatur enim ideo filius verbum, quia sicut in cogitando rei, de qua cogitamus, simulacrum concipimus, ita substantialis imago patris filius est, sic in epistula ad Hebraeos scriptum est: "Character substantiae eius." Porro Spiritui sancto tribuitur agitatio et varietas donorum. Ideo voluntati Spiritus sanctus comparatur. Sic imaginem trinitatis in humana mente esse scripserunt. Hanc ego cogitationem non reprehendo.

A few times Melanchthon says that the Father generated the Son as an Image through looking into Himself. This statement is made in the con-

---

[45] *Loci communes* (1559) (St.A. II), p. 266: Nunc admonendus est lector de quibusdam dictis: Nihil est peccatum, nisi sit voluntarium. Haec sententia de civilibus delictis tradita est. Nam iudicio forensi puniuntur tantum voluntaria delicta ... Sed non transferendum est hoc dictum ad doctrinam Evangelii de peccato et ad iudicium Dei. Augustinus argute inquit et peccatum originis voluntarium esse, quia de eo delectamur. Sed haec interpretatio arguta longius recedit ab illa praetoria sententia. This is a reference to *Retractationes* I 13, 5 where Augustin discusses a statement he made in *De vera religione* 14, 27. This is a misinterpretation of Augustin, who believed only Adam's and Eve's sin to be voluntary, not the sin of our own, cf. P. Fraenkel, *Testimonia patrum*, p. 38, n. 156.

[46] (St.A. IV), p. 56: Augustinus ideo censet hominem imaginem esse Dei, quia sicut in anima memoria, intelligentia, et voluntas, quae tria repraesentent personas divinas, patrem, filium, et Spiritum sanctum. Sed hoc commentum non modo sine auctoritate scripturae, sed etiam sine ratione confictum est.

[47] (St.A. IV), p. 285. This description of the *vestigium trinitatis* reoccurs in the *Liber de anima* (St.A. III), p. 362, *En. Symb. Nic.* (CR 23), pp. 255f., *Explic. Symb. Nic.* (CR 23), pp. 399f. — These are not quotations but an interpretation of Augustin's doctrine of the *vestigium trinitatis* which is memoria, intellectus and voluntas, see book X of the *De Trinitate*.

text of Augustin's doctrine of the *vestigium trinitatis* and is therefore a reference to Augustin's idea of the self-knowledge of God.[48]

In connection with the *doctrine of the creation* there seems to be no direct reference to Augustin. In his commentary on Genesis, dating from 1523, he opposes the idea that "the beginning" in which God created heaven and earth was the Son.[49]

In his high esteem of Augustin because of his doctrine of sin and grace Melanchthon is to close to Luther and differs from Erasmus, who—at least for a time—placed Jerome above Augustin.[50]

AMBROSE

As early as 1519 Melanchthon claims to have a good knowledge of Ambrose.[51] Ambrose certainly can be regarded as one of those Fathers to whom Melanchthon's attitude was very favourable.

The doctrine of Christ and grace:

The later Melanchthon gives some quotations from Ambrose as a corroboration of his doctrine of Christ as God and man. In his response to Stancarus he quotes Ambrose almost literally in connection with the two natures of Christ as the Mediator:[52]

---

[48] *Liber de anima* (St.A. III), p. 362: Nam pater aeternus intuens se, et cogitans gignit verbum, quod est imago aeterni patris, see further *Explic. Symb. Nic.* (CR 23), p. 360 (in this latter case not in the context of the doctrine of the *vestigium trinitatis*). Melanchthon could have in mind here *De Trin.* 14, 6, 8: Mens igitur quando cogitatione se conspicit, intelligit se et recognoscit: gignit ergo hunc intellectum et cogitationem suam. — For Melanchthon's reference to the classical doctrine "Opera trinitatis ad extra sunt indivisa" see *infra*, 114.

[49] *Commentarius in Genesin* (CR 13), p. 763: De principio multa fabulati sunt, et pro eo quod est in principio, quidam in Filio legerunt, — this interpretation is given by Augustin, see e.g. *Conf.* 11, 9, 11.

[50] This was certainly the case at the time when Erasmus edited the works of Jerome in 1516, at the time of his edition of Augustin he regards Augustin as one of the great Fathers, and at the time of the second edition of Jerome in 1524 he does not detract from the praise of Jerome expressed in the Introduction to the first edition. Luther saw his own evaluation of Augustin, in which he placed Augustin above Jerome, as a clear dissent from Erasmus, see H. A. Oberman, *Werden und Wertung der Reformation*, see, however, also C. Béné, *Erasme et Saint Augustin ou l'influence de Saint Augustin sur l'humanisme*, Geneva 1969, who traces Augustin's influence on Erasmus during all periods of Erasmus' life. — On Luther's use of Augustin's writings see further E. Schäfer, *Luther als Kirchenhistoriker*, Gütersloh 1897, pp. 184ff.

[51] See the quotation given *supra*, 20.

[52] See *Responsio Phil. Mel. de controversiis Stancari*, dating from 1553 (St.A. VI), p. 274. The reference is to Ambrose, *Commentarius in Epistulam 1 ad Timotheum* (Migne PL 17), 493.

Ut mediator Dei et hominum esset, homo Christus Jesus, non sine divinitate, quia in Deo homo erat, et Deus in homine, ut ex utroque esset Mediator.

With approval Ambrose is quoted when Melanchthon says that Christ died in His human nature and not in His divine nature:[53]

Ambriosius de incarnatione verbi: Ergo moriebatur secundum naturae nostrae susceptionem, et non moriebatur secundum aeternae vitae substantiam.

There is a general reference to Ambrose's (and Hilary's) doctrine that Christ appeared in the theophanies testified in the Old Testament.[54]

From (Ps.-Ambrose) *De vocatione gentium* about which Melanchthon in 1521 expresses doubts as to whether it was written by Ambrose,[55] but which he later regards as authentic, he gives the following quotation:[56]

Vilesceret redemptio sanguinis Christi, nec misericordiae Dei humanorum operum praerogativa succumberet, si iustificatio, quae fit per gratiam, meritis praecedentibus deberetur, ut non munus largientis, sed merces esset operantis.

And from the same piece of writing he quotes:[57]

Fides bonae voluntatis et iustae actionis genetrix est.

The following quotation is given repeatedly:[58]

(... extat apud Ambrosium memorabilis et insignis sententia, his verbis:) Hoc constitutum est a Deo, ut qui credit in Christum salvus sit, sine opere, sola fide, gratis accipiens remissionem peccatorum.

This is a literal quotation from *Comm. in Pauli Epist. ad Cor. I* (Migne PL 17) 195.

---

[53] *Explicatio Symb. Nic.* (CR 23), p. 510. This is a fairly literal quotation from the *Liber de incarnatione* 5, 37 (Migne PL 16), 863, cf. also *De spiritu sancto* 1, 9, 107 and *Commentarius in Epistulam I ad Corinthios* (Migne PL 17), 205.

[54] *Annotationes in Evangelia*, dating from 1544 (CR 14), p. 177: Et Ambrosius et Hilarius dicunt Filium cum patribus locutum esse, — see e.g. Ambrose, *De fide* 2, 13, 83.

[55] See *Adv. furiosum Parris. Theol. decr. ...* (St.A. I), p. 148. In 1539 he refers to this piece of writing without doubting its authenticity, see *De ecclesia et de autoritate verbi Dei* (St.A. I), p. 357.

[56] *Conf. Aug.*, art. xx (CR 26), p. 286, *Conf. Aug.* (Variata), dating from 1540 (St.A. VI), pp. 29f. This is a literal quotation from *De vocatione gentium* 17 (Migne PL 51), 669, cf. W. Maurer, *Historischer Kommentar zur Confessio Augustana. Band 2. Theologische Probleme*, Gütersloh 1978, pp. 135f.

[57] *Conf. Aug.*, art. xx (CR 26), p. 288, *Conf. Aug.* (Variata) (St.A. VI), p. 31, see *De voc. gentium* 23 (Migne PL 51), 676.

[58] See e.g. *Conf. Aug.*, art. vi (CR 26), p. 276, *Conf. Aug.* (Variata) (St.A. VI), p. 15.

Melanchthon finds his doctrine of justification confirmed in the following passage from *Epist.* LXXIII 10f. which he quotes almost literally:[59]

> (Ambrosius enim inquit in epistola ad Irenaeum quendam:) Subditus autem mundus eo per legem factus est, quia ex praescripto legis omnes conveniuntur, et ex operibus legis nemo iustificatur, id est, quia per legem peccatum cognoscitur, sed culpa non relaxatur. Videbatur lex nocuisse, quae omnes fecerat peccatores, sed veniens Dominus Jesus peccatum omnibus quod nemo poterat evitare, donavit, et chirographum nostrum sui sanguinis effusione delevit. Hoc est quod ait: Abundavit peccatum per legem, Superabundavit autem gratia per Jesum. Quia postquam totus mundus subditus factus est, totius mundi peccatum abstulit, sicut testificatus est Joannes dicens: Ecce agnus Dei, ecce qui tollit peccatum mundi. Et ideo nemo glorietur in operibus, quia nemo factis suis iustificatur. Sed qui iustus est, donatum habet, quia post lavacrum iustificatus est. Fides ergo est, quae liberat per sanguinem Christi quia beatus ille cui peccatum remittitur, et venia donatur.

Also the following brief quotation is meant as a confirmation of the doctrine of grace and justification:[60]

> (Et praeclare hic inquit Ambrosius) Agnoscenda est gratia, sed non ignoranda natura.

This is a quotation from *Expositio in Lucam* VIII 32:

> Non te praeferas, quia filius Dei diceris: agnoscenda gratia, sed non ignoranda natura.

The following quotation from *De poenitentia* II 9, 80 must prove the same:[61]

> (Ideo praeclare ait Ambrosius de poenitentia:) Ergo et agendam poenitentiam, et tribuendam veniam credere nos convenit, ut veniam tamen tamquam ex fide speremus, tamquam ex syngrapha fides impetrat.

There is also an interesting quotation from the letter to Demetrias, which Melanchthon ascribes to Ambrose (but which was written by Pelagius):[62]

> Nec ob aliud datur praeceptum, nisi ut quaeratur praecipientis auxilium.

---

[59] *Apol. Conf. Aug.* B (CR 27), p. 445. The last sentence of the quotation is perhaps referred to in *Apol. Conf. Aug.* B (CR 27), p. 553: Item fides est quae peccata nostra cooperit. Part of the first sentence is quoted in *De ecclesia et autoritate verbi Dei* (St.A. I), p. 356.

[60] *Apol. Conf. Aug.* B (CR 27), p. 508.

[61] *Apol. Conf. Aug.* B (CR 27), p. 553. Between 'speremus' and 'tanquam' Melanchthon leaves out: non tanquam ex debito, aliud est enim mereri, aliud praesumere.

[62] *De ecclesia et autoritate verbi Dei* (St.A. I), p. 357. The closest parallell we could find is *Epistula ad Demetriam* 3 (Migne PL 30), 19: vide quid Christiani facere possunt, quorum in melius per Christum natura et vita instructa est: et qui divinae quoque gratiae iuvantur auxilio.

But Melanchthon also expresses criticism of Ambrose, especially of his ethics (which, of course, implies criticism of his doctrine of grace). He explicitly disapproves of Ambrose's statement that fasting is compulsory in Lent and that it is voluntary in the rest of the year:[63]

> Is tamen inquit de ieiunio quadragesimae: Caetera ieiunia sunt voluntatis, hoc necessitatis est.

Despite criticism which he makes every now and then[64] (and which he sometimes turns into praise by saying that even great men can fail[65]) Melanchthon had a very high esteem of Ambrose. He claims to be in line with his doctrine of grace (though not completely).[66] Ambrose belongs with Augustin to the *scriptores meliores*,[67] and his name appears in the list of the *scriptores puriores*.[68] The reason why he views Ambrose so favourably is

---

[63] *De ecclesia et autoritate verbi Dei* (St.A. I), p. 332 (Melanchthon is opposed to compulsory fasting, since this contradicts the doctrine of grace, see e.g. *Commentarii in Epist. Pauli ad Rom.* (1532) (St.A. V), pp. 340ff. and *Conf. Aug.* (Variata) (St.A. VI), pp. 51ff.), cf. Ambrose, *Sermo* xxiii 3 (Migne PL 17), 671: Nam sicut reliquo anno ieiunare praemium est, ita in Quadragesima non ieiunare peccatum est, illa enim voluntaria sunt ieiunia, ista necessaria.

[64] Apart from the criticism just noticed Melanchthon is critical of Ambrose's allegorical exegesis in which he detects the influence of Origen, see the letter of dedication to the *Loci communes* (1521) (St.A. II), pp. 4f.: Ex Origene si tollas inconcinnas allegorias et philosophicarum sententiarum silvam, quantulum erit reliquum? Et tamen hunc auctorem magno consensu sequuntur Graeci et ex Latinis, qui videntur esse calumnae, Ambrosius et Hieronymus, cf. *De Erasmo et Luthero elogion* etc., (CR 20), p. 705: Origenem, Ambrosium, Hieronymum cum iudicio lege. — In his letter to Spalatinus dating from February 6th 1522 he says that Ambrose followed the Greek Fathers (CR 1), p. 547, — the influence of Basil on Ambrose is supposed by Melanchthon in his *Encomium formicarum* (CR 11), p. 150 in connection with the exegesis of *Genesis* 1, the *Hexaemeron*, and in his long *Declamatio de Ambrosio* (CR 11), p. 570.

[65] See *Annotationes et conciones in Evang. Matthaei* (CR 14), p. 880: Having referred to the apostles' original error in connection with the ceremonial law Melanchthon adds: Discamus igitur ex hoc exemplo quod non sit mirum, in Augustino, Ambrosio et similibus fuisse etiam aliquos errores, — *Postilla Melanchthoniana* (CR 25), p. 320: here he makes a distinction between an apostle who received his words directly from God and a bishop who is called by God through men and has to follow the words of the apostle. Such men are fallible: Possunt autem tales errare, sicut sunt errata etiam in optimorum scriptorum scriptis: ut errata non pauca sunt in Ambrosio at Augustino.

[66] See the letter to Pontanus, dating from 1543 (CR 5), p. 234, where he counters the Roman claim that Luther dissented from the church of all ages in connection with the doctrine of justification by saying *inter alia*: De scriptoribus Ambrosio et Augustino non dubium est eos nobiscum sentire, sed non semper satis commode loquuntur. — Ambrose and Augustin are better exegetes of Paul than Origen, see *Decl. de dono interpretationis* (CR 11), p. 646. — In his *Responsiones ad articulos Bavaricae inquistionis*, dating from 1558 (St.A. VI), p. 291 he claims to be in line with Irenaeus, Ambrose and Augustin.

[67] See the quotations given *supra*, 28.

[68] See *De restituendis scholis*, dating from 1540 (St.A. III), p. 113 and the Colloquium at Worms (1541) (CR 4), p. 38.

that he found in him the correct doctrine about the person of Christ and about justification and grace.[69] Melanchthon is here in line with Luther, who praises Ambrose for his doctrine of grace.[70] Luther says that from Augustin, Jerome, Hilary and Ambrose it appears that the church of those days believed in Jesus Christ (which, of course, means that it believed in God's saving grace which appeared in Christ).[71] Ambrose, Hilary and Augustin restored the Word of God which later on was again oppressed.[72] Erasmus, too, has a high esteem of Ambrose, but for different reasons. He lists him with Origen, Jerome and Augustin amongst the best exegetes of the Bible, because he does not give a literal interpretation.[73]

ATHANASIUS (and ARIUS)

The doctrine of Christ

Melanchthon repeatedly quotes from the *De Incarnatione Verbi*. Although there is an occasional reference to a page, we were unable to determine of which edition of Athanasius he made use.[74]

In connection with the assumption of a mortal body by the immortal Word of God Melanchthon quotes Athanasius as saying:

> Cum non esset possible ipsum mori verbum, quippe immortalem patris filium, corpus sibi quod mori possit assumsit.

---

[69] See *De ecclesia et de autoritate verbi Dei* (St.A. I), p. 356: Multas causas attingit Ambrosius, videlicet de Trinitate, contra Novatianos, de iustificatione ... perspicuum est est eius longioribus disputationibus sensisse eum de gratia et de iustificatione quôd nos docemus.

[70] See *Tischreden* I (dating from 1531), p. 18: Ambrosius simplex fidei est assertor contra fiduciam operum.

[71] *Tischreden* I (dating from the same period of time), p. 435.

[72] *Tischreden* IV (dating from 1538), p. 150: Deinde Ambrosius, Hilarius, Augustinus iterum verbum restaurarunt, postea iterum extinctum est. See further E. Schäfer, *op. cit.*, pp. 180f.

[73] *Enchiridion* (*Erasmi opera omnia*, t. V, ed. J. Clericus), p. 8: Ex interpretibus Divinae Scripturae eos potissimum delige, qui a littera quam maxime recedunt. Cuiusmodi sunt in primis post Paulum Origenes, Ambrosius, Hieronymus, Augustinus, cf. *Ratio verae theologiae* (*Erasmi opera omnia*, t. V), p. 133 where he lists him among the great interpreters of the Bible after Origen (cf. p. 83), see Ch. Béné, *op. cit.*, p. 275. See also Erasmus' introduction to the edition of Ambrose which came out in 1538: Inter priscos ecclesiae doctores Latinos, vix alium arbitror esse digniorem, cuius extent integrae lucubrationes quam divum Ambrosium.

[74] See *Refutatio erroris Serveti et Anabaptistarum* (St.A. VI), p. 374, *Explic. Symb. Nic.* (CR 23), p. 508. The reference is to p. 28. This page does *not* correspond with the edition of a Latin translation of Athanasius' works (with a Preface by Erasmus) which came out in Paris in 1519. For other editions cf. E. Schäfer, *op. cit.*, p. 173.

This quotation is given repeatedly either with small variations[75] or with the addition that this assumption took place in order to placate the wrath of God:[76]

> Corpus assumsit quod mori posset, quia morte placanda erat ira aeterni Patris.

This is a reference to *De Inc. Verbi* 9:

> Οὐχ οἷόν τε δὲ ἦν τὸν Λόγον ἀποθανεῖν ἀθάνατον ὄντα καὶ τοῦ Πατρὸς Υἱόν, τούτου ἕνεκεν τὸ δυνάμενον ἀποθανεῖν ἑαυτῷ λαμβάνει σῶμα.

The addition that this took place in order to placate the wrath of God is an interpretation given by Melanchthon: Athanasius wants to make it clear that God had to be consistent in his threat that man would die if he sinned and that in His goodness He could not let man die after He had created Him.[77]

In the same doctrinal context occurs the following quotation from *De Incarnatione Verbi*:[78]

> Congruebat Filium assumere humanam naturam, ut haec persona, quae est substantialis imago aeterni patris, restitueret imaginem Dei in nobis.

This quotation is given repeatedly with considerable freedom.[79] Athanasius' text which is freely quoted here runs as follows:

> ὅθεν ὁ τοῦ Θεοῦ Λόγος δι᾽ ἑαυτοῦ παρεγένετο, ἵνα ὡς εἰκὼν τοῦ Πατρὸς τὸν κατ᾽ εἰκόνα ἄνθρωπον ἀνακτίσαι δυνηθῇ.

Melanchthon refers to Athanasius as his authority when he compares the union of the two natures of Christ with the union of the human soul and the human body:[80]

> (Et quaesitae sunt qualescunque umbrae ad huius mirandi foederis declarationem, ut, an sit qualiscunque similitudo, copulatio animae et corporis,

---

[75] See *Refutatio erroris Serveti*, p. 374, *Explic. Symb. Nic.*, p. 371, *Chronicon Carionis* (CR 12), p. 1029.

[76] *Explic. Symb. Nic.*, p. 508.

[77] See *De Incarnatione Verbi* 6ff.

[78] *Explic. Symb. Nic.*, p. 370, see *De Inc. Verbi* 13.

[79] *Postilla Melanchthoniana* (CR 24), pp. 77f.: Congruebat, ut illa persona assumeret humanam naturam quae et propriissime et quidem substantialis imago Dei ut in nobis quoque restitueret Dei imaginem. This variation can have been caused by the fact that Melanchthon here explains why the Son and not the Father or the Holy Ghost became man. Almost in the same way and in the same context this sentence is quoted in an oration, dating from 1553 (CR 10), p. 961. In the *Enarratio Ep. Pauli ad Col.*, dating from 1559 (CR 15), p. 1239 the quotation is given in the following way: Congruebat filium assumere naturam humanam, ut per imaginem Dei essentialem homo restitueretur, conditus ut esset imago Dei creata. Quia per verbum, quo divinitas patefecit, restituitur imago.

[80] *Enarratio Symb. Nic.* (CR 23), p. 340.

qua similitudine usus est) Athanasius, inquiens, Sicut anima rationalis et caro unus est homo, ita Deus et homo unus est Christus.

Melanchthon says quite often that Athanasius uses this analogy.[81] This seems to be one of the examples that Melanchthon not infrequently quotes his sources rather carelessly. Athanasius produces the union of the soul and the body as an illustration of the union of the Word and His human body, but then rejects this illustration by saying that the Word was not tied to the human body in the way in which the soul is tied to the body.[82] Melanchthon elsewhere explicitly quotes this passage from *De Inc. Verbi*:[83]

> Λόγος non colligatus est corpori, sed ipse corpus continet, ut et in eo sit, et extra omnia, et in sinu patris, neque cum sit in omnibus, fit pars in aliorum, sed omnia vitam, sustentationemque ab ipso accipiunt.

It should be noted that the other analogies for the union of Christ's two natures which Melanchthon ascribes to Athanasius do not appear in Athanasius' writings, *viz.*, branch and trunk, the potency of mixed seeds in plants, water heat.[84]

In connection with the incarnation Melanchthon quotes Athanasius as saying of Christ's body:[85]

> ἅμα σάρξ, ἅμα λόγου σάρξ.

---

[81] *Explic. Symb. Nic.* (CR 23), p. 369, p. 510, *Postilla Melanchthonianan* (CR 24), p. 560, *Disputationes* (CR 12), p. 593, p. 616, p. 649 (always together with Cyril of Alexandria and Ps.-Justin).

[82] *De Inc. Verbi* 17: Ψυχῆς μὲν οὖν ἔργον ἐστὶ θεωρεῖν μὲν καὶ τὰ ἔξω τοῦ ἰδίου σώματος τοῖς λογισμοῖς, οὐ μὴν καὶ ἔξωθεν τοῦ ἰδίου σώματος ἐνεργεῖν, ἢ τὰ τούτου μακρὰ τῇ παρουσίᾳ κινεῖν ... οὐ δὴ τοιοῦτος ἦν ὁ τοῦ Θεοῦ Λόγος ἐν τῷ ἀνθρώπῳ· οὐ γὰρ συνεδέδετο τῷ σώματι, ἀλλὰ μᾶλλον αὐτὸς ἐκράτει τοῦτο, ὥστε καὶ ἐν τούτῳ ἦν καὶ ἐν τοῖς πᾶσιν ἐτύγχανε, καὶ ἔξω τῶν ὄντων ἦν, καὶ ἐν μόνῳ τῷ Πατρὶ ἀνεπαύετο. — Athanasius does compare the ruling presence of the Logos in the world with the human soul which rules the body, see *Contra Gentes* 38.

[83] *Enarratio in Epist. Pauli ad Col.* (CR 15), p. 1271. The latter part of the sentence seems to be drawn from what Athanasius says about the Logos a few sentences earlier than the one quoted in the previous note: ... καὶ ἕκαστον καὶ πάντα ὁμοῦ ζωοποιῶν, περιέχων τὰ ὅλα ... Melanchthon gives the same quotation in *Postilla Melanchthoniana* (CR 24), p. 861.

[84] See *Enarratio Symb. Nic.* (CR 23), p. 340: Item, an qualiscumque similitudo sit, ramus insitus trunco. Item, mixtorum seminum vis in rebus natis, aut subiectum sustentans accidentia, ut aqua calorem. Perhaps Melanchthon had in mind the quotation Athanasius gives from Dionysius of Alexandria, *De Decr. Nic. Syn.* 25: καὶ γὰρ φυτὸν εἶπον ἀπὸ σπέρματος ἢ ἀπὸ ῥίζης ἀνελθὸν ἕτερον εἶναι τοῦ ὅθεν ἐβλάστησε, καὶ πάντως ἐκείνῳ καθέστηκεν ὁμοφυές, *De Sententia Dionysii* 18, — this quotation is repeated in ch. 19 and 22 (Athanasius approves of this image). (Didymus of Alexandria does use the image of branch and root, which Melanchthon ascribes to Athanasius, see *De Trin.* 1, 30).

[85] See *Postilla Melanchthoniana* (CR 24), p. 131. The closest parallel we could find is (Ps.-) Athanasius, *De incarnatione Domini nostri Jesu Christi contra Apollinarium*, I 4: ἡ γὰρ τῆς σαρκὸς ἕνωσις πρὸς τὴν τοῦ Λόγου θεότητα ἐκ μήτρας γέγονεν.

Athanasius is also quoted as an authority when Melanchthon says that Christ suffered and died in His human nature:[86]

(Saepe sic loquitur Athanasius, ut in libro cui titulus est "De assumptione hominis" inquit:) Nonne haec omnia secundum humanam naturam sustinuit?

This seems to be a free reference to *De Incarnatione Verbi* 18:

῞Οταν τοίνυν ἐσθίοντα καὶ πίνοντα καὶ τικτόμενον αὐτὸν λέγωσιν οἱ περὶ τούτου θεολόγοι, γίνωσκε ὅτι τὸ μὲν σῶμα, ὡς σῶμα, ἐτίκτετο καὶ καταλλήλοις ἐτρέφετο τροφαῖς, αὐτὸς δὲ ὁ συνὼν τῷ σώματι Θεὸς Λόγος τὰ πάντα διακοσμῶν, καὶ δι' ὧν εἰργάζετο ἐν τῷ σώματι οὐκ ἄνθρωπον ἑαυτόν, ἀλλὰ Θεὸν Λόγον ἐγνώριζε. λέγεται δὲ περὶ αὐτοῦ ταῦτα, ἐπειδὴ καὶ τὸ σῶμα ἐσθίον καὶ τικτόμενον καὶ πάσχον, οὐχ ἑτέρου τινός, ἀλλὰ τοῦ Κυρίου ἦν.

The doctrine of the Trinity

There are four quotations from Athanasius with which Melanchthon tries to corroborate his doctrine of the Trinity:

(Et Athanasius inquit:) Patefecit se pater hominibus per imaginem in qua ipse lucet.[87]

This seems to be quoted from *Oratio contra Arionos* I 16:

καὶ τοῦτό ἐστιν αὐτοῦ τὸ ἀπαύγασμα ἐν ᾧ τὰ πάντα φωτίζει, καὶ ἀποκαλύπτεται οἷς ἐὰν θέλῃ.

The most important quotation in this context is given very often and once with a clear reference to the edition Melanchthon used:[88]

(Athanasius expresse dicit): Quandocumque dicitur in aliquo esse Spiritus, intelligitur in eo esse Verbum dans Spiritum.

This must be meant as a translation of *Ad Serapionem* I 30:

Καὶ τοῦ Πνεύματος δὲ ὄντος ἐν ἡμῖν, καὶ ὁ Λόγος ὁ τοῦτο διδούς ἐστιν ἐν ἡμῖν (καὶ ἐν τῷ Λόγῳ ἐστὶν ὁ Πατήρ).

---

[86] *Responsio de controversiis Stancari* (St.A. VI), p. 263.

[87] *Refutatio erroris Serveti* (St.A. VI), p. 373.

[88] The reference to page 54 of the edition is in the *Commentarii in Psalmos*, dating from 1553 (CR 13), p. 1228. The quotation we give is from the letter to Strigelius (dating from 1552) (CR 7), p. 1057, see further: the letter to Hardenbergius, dating from 1552 (CR 7), p. 1149, letter to Strigelius, dating from 1553 (CR 8), p. 191, letter to Praetorius (dating from 1556 (CR 8), pp. 667f. (an abbreviation), *Disputationes* (CR 12), p. 613, *Enarratio in Epist. Pauli ad Rom.* (CR 15), p. 951, *Explic. Symb. Nic.* (CR 23), p. 462, p. 500, p. 524 (here the quotation is also ascribed to Cyril of Alexandria), *Postilla Melanchthoniana* (CR 24), p. 750, p. 874, *Postilla Melanchthoniana* (CR 25), p. 20, *Examen ordinandorum* (CR 23), p. 4. The abbreviated quotation is (with minor variations): Ubicumque est Spiritus sanctus, est ibi per Verbum).

The third quotation in this contest is:

Pater per Verbum Spiritu operatur.

According to Melanchthon Athanasius often said this.[89] He probably has in mind *Ad Serapionem* III 5:

Αὐτὸς γὰρ ὁ Πατὴρ διὰ τοῦ Λόγου ἐν τῷ Πνεύματι ἐνεργεῖ (καὶ δίδωσι τὰ πάντα).

The fourth quotation in this context is:[90]

Non extra Verbum Spiritus est.

This, too, is probably quoted from *Ad Serapionem* III 5:

Οὐ γὰρ ἐκτός ἐστι τοῦ Λόγου τὸ Πνεῦμα.

The support Melanchthon believes he receives from Athanasius in his doctrine of Christ and the Trinity leads him to a very high esteem of Athanasius which is expressed in frequent praise: He lists him amongst the most important ecclesiastical writers,[91] he is named with Ambrose and Augustin as an important defender of orthodoxy against the heretics,[92] he belongs to those Fathers whose faith Melanchthon wants to preserve.

As Melanchthon is positive about Athanasius, he is negative in his judgement of Arius. Just like Paul of Samosata and Pelagius Arius draws his doctrine from human *ratio*, not from Scripture.[93] His doctrine can easily be refuted with Scriptural testimonies.[94] The anti-trinitarian movement certainly made Melanchthon believe that the heresy of Arius (and the one of Paul of Samosata) was a very dangerous heresy which ought to be recognized and refuted.[95] Melanchthon was uncompromising in his rejection of Arianism, as clearly appears from his very negative judgement of the Semi-Arian synod at Rimini.[96]

---

[89] *Commentarii in Psalmos* (CR 13), p. 1228.

[90] *Commentarii in Psalmos*, p. 1228.

[91] Colloquium at Worms (CR 4), p. 38.

[92] *Declamatio de Ambrosio* (CR 11), p. 571.

[93] *De ecclesia et de autoritate verbi Dei* (St.A. I), p. 335: Saepe autem accidit in Ecclesia, ut impii, excellentes ingeniis, sumant impetus constituendi religionem humana sapientia, qui cum non moveantur verbo Dei, sed ducantur rationis imaginatione et quaerant concinnas opiniones, gignunt impia dogmata, sicut Samosatenus, Arius, Pelagius, cf. *Loci communes* (1559) (St.A. II), p. 482.

[94] *Loci communes* (1559) (St.A. II), pp. 194ff.

[95] In the anti-trinitarian movement of his time Melanchthon saw a resurgence of the doctrines of Arius and Paul of Samosata, see *infra*, 64, 80.

[96] See e.g. *Quaestiones Academicae* (CR 10), p. 735, *Decl. de odio sophistices* (CR 11), p. 546, *Declamatio de iudiciis ecclesiae* (CR 12), p. 141, *Disputationes* (CR 12), p. 661, *Chronicon Carionis* II (CR 12), p. 986, *Annotationes et Conciones in Evang. Matthaei* (CR 14), p. 576, *Enarratio Epist. prior. ad Tim.* (CR 15), p. 1350. According to Melanchthon the Semi-Arian substitution of the ὁμοούσιος by ὅμοιος was a fraud. As early as 1521 Melanchthon (indirectly) opposes the Synod at Rimini, see the quotation given *infra*, 109.

Melanchthon's high esteem of Athanasius and his rejection of Arianism was in line with both Luther and Erasmus, albeit partly for different reasons. Luther, too, was completely opposed to the Arian doctrine[97] and so was Erasmus. It is true that Erasmus sometimes spoke about the Arians in more favourable terms, but then he wanted to show that they were more orthodox than their opponents believed, in this context Erasmus referred to the Semi-Arian synod at Rimini.[98] But Erasmus certainly had no sympathy for the doctrine that Christ was a creature.[99]

BASIL

As early as 1522 Melanchthon was in the possession of writings of Basil,[100] and he quotes him in the first edition of the *Loci communes*.[101]

The doctrine of grace

(The quotations from Basil in relation to the person of Christ will be discussed under the heading of the doctrine of the Trinity.) In connection with the doctrine of grace Basil is both praised and criticized by Melanchthon.

Melanchthon finds his doctrine of justification confirmed by the following words of Basil:

Dicit autem Apostolus: "Qui gloriatur, in Domino glorietur", dicens quod "Christus nobis factus sit sapientia a Deo, iustitia, sanctificatio et redemp-

---

[97] See e.g. Luther's Preface to Bugenhagen's edition *Athanasii libri contra idolatriam* (1532) (W.A. 30, 3), pp. 530f. (for the praise of Athanasius) and his rejection of Arianism in the sermon of Dec. 29th 1538 (W.A. 46), pp. 531ff. On Luther and Athanasius see also E. Schäfer, *op. cit.*, pp. 172ff.

[98] Erasmus lists Athanasius among the best interpreters of the Bible, *Ratio verae theologiae* (*Erasmi opera omnia*, t. V, ed. J. Clericus), p. 133. According to Erasmus the Arians tried to beat Athanasius by imagining crimes committed by him when they saw that they could not refute him with Scriptural arguments, *De amabili ecclesiae concordia* (*Erasmi opera omnia*, t. V), p. 475. On the rejection of Arianism see e.g. his Commentary on the Gospel according to St. John (*Erasmi opera omnia*, t. VI, ed. J. Clericus), p. 337. Erasmus does insist that the Arian doctrine can be refuted by correct exegesis of Biblical texts, he rejects opposition against Arianism which scraps Biblical texts, see his Commentary on the Gospel according to St. Matthew (*Erasmi opera omnia*, t. VI), p. 127. (See further his views on the Trinity, *infra*, 120ff.) It is true that Erasmus sometimes speaks out in defence of the (Semi-) Arians, but then he says that the Semi-Arians at Rimini were more orthodox than their opponents thought and that they did not deny the divinity of Christ, see J. D. Tracy, *Erasmus, The Growth of a Mind*, Geneva 1972, pp. 154f. Melanchthon feels obliged to dissociate himself from Erasmus' more differentiated views on Arianism, see his letter to Camerarius (1529) (CR 1), pp. 1083f., cf. A. Sperl, *Melanchthon zwischen Humanismus und Reformation*, p. 183.

[99] See *infra*, 120ff.

[100] See his letter to Spalatinus (CR 1), p. 547, see also his *Annotationes in Epistulas Pauli ad Corinthios*, dating from 1522 (St.A. IV), p. 97 where a quotation from Basil is given.

[101] (St.A. II), p. 154, see *infra*, 41, note 110.

tio, ut sicut scriptum est, gloriaturus in Domino glorietur.'' Haec est enim perfecta et integra gloriatio in Deo, quando ne quidem propter iustitiam suam aliquis effertur, sed agnoscit sibi deesse veram iustitiam, fide autem sola in Christum iustificari, et gloriatur Paulus se despicere suam iustitiam, quaerere autem fide per Christum iustitiam quae ex Deo est.

This quotation is given time and again,[102] once with a clear reference to the edition Melanchthon used.[103] It is an almost literal quotation from Basil's *Homilia de humilitate* (Migne PG 31, 529):

Λέγει δὲ Ἀπόστολος· Ὁ καυχώμενος, ἐν Κυρίῳ καυχάσθω, λέγων ὅτι Χριστὸς ἡμῖν ἐγενήθη σοφία ἀπὸ Θεοῦ, δικαιοσύνη τε καὶ ἁγιασμὸς καὶ ἀπολύτρωσις· ἵνα καθὼς γέγραπται, Ὁ καυχώμενος, ἐν Κυρίῳ καυχάσθω. Αὕτη γὰρ δὴ ἡ τελεία καὶ ὁλόκληρος καύχησις ἐν Θεῷ, ὅτε μήτε ἐπὶ δικαιοσύνῃ τις ἐπαίρεται τῇ ἑαυτοῦ, ἀλλ' ἔγνω μὲν ἐνδεῆ ὄντα ἑαυτὸν δικαιοσύνης ἀληθοῦς, πίστει δὲ μόνῃ τῇ εἰς Χριστὸν δεδικαιωμένον. Καὶ καυχᾶται Παῦλος ἐπὶ τῷ καταφρονῆσαι τῆς ἑαυτοῦ δικαιοσύνης, ζητεῖν δὲ τὴν διὰ Χριστοῦ, τὴν ἐκ Θεοῦ δικαιοσύνην ἐπὶ τῇ πίστει ...

An interesting observation can be made about the Latin translation which Melanchthon produces: The word δεδικαιωμένον has been translated by Melanchthon with 'iustificari', 'iustificatum esse' would have been more literal and correct, but would less have suited Melanchthon, for whom justification did not take place once, but takes place daily.[104]

When he tries to determine the relationship between God's sovereign grace and man's free will Melanchthon time and again[105] gives the following quotation from (Ps.-) Basil:

---

[102] The quotation given by us is from *De ecclesia et de autoritate verbi Dei* (St.A. I), p. 353, see further *Loci communes* (1559) (St.A. II), pp. 368f., *Confessio Saxonica* (St.A. VI), p. 102, *Responsiones ad articulos Bavaricas inquisitionis* (St.A. VI), p. 327, the piece of writing to the Academici of Wittenberg dating from 1558 (CR 9), p. 442 (where the quotation is given in Greek), *Declamatio de Basilio episcopo*, dating from 1545 (CR 11), p. 683, *Disputationes* (CR 12), p. 532 (where the quotation is again given in Greek), *Postilla Melanchthoniana* (CR 24), p. 363, cf. P. Fraenkel, *Testimonia Patrum*, p. 296.

[103] See the *Enarratio Epistulae Pauli ad Romanos*, dating from 1556 (CR 15), pp. 877f., the reference is to p. 388 of the edition which came out (with a Preface by Erasmus) in 1532 in Basle (Froben).

[104] Melanchthon, who had an excellent knowledge of Greek, must, of course, have known that δεδικαιωμένον ought to be translated with *iustificatum* instead of *iustificari*, and in another context he provides this correct translation of δεδικαιωμένον, see *Postilla Melanchthoniana* (CR 25), p. 342: Et hoc est δεδικαιωμένον id est, iustificatum esse.

[105] See his letter to Calvin, dating from May 1543 (CR 5), p. 109, his letter to students, dating from January 1548 (CR 6), p. 783, *Declamatio de precatione* (CR 11), p. 988, *Disputationes* (CR 12), p. 491, *Annotationes in Evangelia* (CR 14), p. 311 (here the quotation is given in Latin: Tantum velis, et Deus praeoccurrit), *Ethicae doctriane elementa* (CR 16), p. 193 and p. 240, *Explic. Symb. Nic.* (CR 23), p. 436 and p. 544, *Postilla Melanchthoniana* (CR 25), p. 74 (quotation given in Latin with the variation of the future tense 'praeoccurret'), *Loci communes*, dating from 1559 (St.A. II), p. 244 (the quotation already appears in the edition of the *Loci communes*, dating from 1535 (CR 21), p. 376, *Enarratio libri II. Ethicorum Aristotelis* (CR 16), p. 328 and p. 330, cf. K. Haendler, *op. cit.*, pp. 543f.

Μόνον θέλησον καὶ θεὸς προαπαντᾷ.

As appears from the reference he twice makes to "The sermon on the prodigal son"[106] Melanchthon must here have in mind (Ps.-) Basil's sermon "On Penitence" in which (Ps.-) Basil talks about man's will to be saved and God's willingness to save man and refers to the parable of the prodigal son as an illustration and says (*De paen.* 3, Migne PG 31, 1480f.):

Μόνον θέλησον, καὶ αὐτὸς προαπαντᾷ.

The quotation is almost literal, but the reference is incorrect, since in the edition used by Melanchthon the sermon has the title Περὶ μετανοίας. In connection with God's help and the assent of man's will the following further quotations from Basil are given with approval:

οὐδὲ γὰρ ἡ περὶ τὰ καλὰ τῶν ἀνθρώπων ἐγχείρησις δίχα τῆς ἄνωθεν βοηθείας τελειωθήσεται, οὐδὲ ἡ ἄνωθεν χάρις νοῦν τὸν μὴ σπουδάζοντα παραγένοιτο ἄν.[107]

and:

πᾶσα κατόρθωσις παρὰ θεοῦ ἐστι, δέχεται δὲ προθυμίᾳ ἀνθρώπων.[108]

But Basil is also criticized for his institution of monasticism[109] and for his doctrine that sins should be confessed to those who are familiar with spiritual matters.[110] The institution of monasticism is according to Melanchthon a specious addition to the doctrine of the *beneficia* of Christ,[111] and his views on confession are not in accord with the Scriptural statement that sins must be confessed to God.[112]

---

[106] *Enarratio Epistulae Pauli ad Romanos* (CR 15), p. 980 and *Postilla Melanchthoniana* (CR 24), p. 364.

[107] Letter to the Academics of Wittenberg, dating from 1558 (CR 9), p. 442 and (with two small variations) *Postilla Melanchthoniana* (CR 24), p. 364. We were unable to trace this quotation in Basil's works.

[108] *Postilla Melanchthoniana* (CR 24), p. 364. We were unable to trace this quotation in Basil's works.

[109] *De ecclesia et de autoritate verbi Dei* (St.A. I), p. 332 and pp. 353f. (Melanchthon expresses doubts whether the *regulae monachorum* which appear under Basil's name were all written by Basil).—This criticism of Basil is reiterated in the *Loci communes* of 1559 (St.A. II), p. 484.

[110] *Loci communes* (1521) (St.A. II), p. 154 (but Melanchthon leaves open the possibility that this work *De Institutis monachorum* was not written by Basil): quorum conscientiae angebantur aliqua de re, sanctos et peritos rerum spiritualium consulerent et ab illis absolverentur. — The reference is obviously to *Regulae brevius tractatae*, Interrogatio CCLXXXVIII (Responsio) (Migne PG 31, 1284): ἀναγκαῖον τοῖς πεπιστευμένοις τὴν οἰκονομίαν τῶν μυστηρίων τοῦ θεοῦ ἐξομολογεῖσθαι τὰ ἁμαρτήματα. Οὕτω γὰρ οἱ πάλαι μετανοοῦντες ἐπὶ τῶν ἁγίων εὑρίσκονται πεποιηκότες, see also his *Annotationes in Epistulas Pauli ad Corinthios*, dating from 1522 (St.A. IV), p. 97.

[111] *De ecclesia et de autoritate verbi Dei* (St.A. I), p. 332. The criticism of Basil's monasticism is mitigated in *Postilla Melanchthoniana* (CR 24), p. 358, where Melanchthon says that Basil's monastries were unlike those of later times and were more like schools, cf. *Conf. Aug.* (Variata) (St.A. VI), p. 67 and *Confessio Saxonica* (St.A. VI), p. 152.

[112] *Loci communes* (1521) (St.A. II), p. 154.

Further criticism is expressed of the following statement made by Basil about when man should be called a sinner, and when he should be called righteous:[113]

εἰ πλείονα τὰ ἁμαρτήματα, ἔστω ἁμαρτωλός, εἰ δὲ πλείονα τὰ δικαιώματα, ἔστω δίκαιος.

The doctrine of the Trinity

From the commandment to baptize in the name of the Father and the Son and the Holy Ghost Basil (rightly) draws the conclusion that the three persons are ὁμοούσιοι.[114]

Melanchthon repeatedly quotes Basil as saying that the Father generated the Son through selfcontuition and thought:[115]

(Basilius et alii dicunt) Filium dici λόγον, quia sit imago Patris, genita a Patre sese cogitante: Pater enim intuens se, gignit cogitationem, quae vocatur Verbum, quae cogitatio est imago Patris, in quam imaginem Pater, ut ita dicamus, transfundit suam essentiam.

It is not entirely clear where this quotation is taken from. Melanchthon may either think of *Homilia de fide* 2 (Migne PG 31, 465f.):

... ἡ εἰκὼν ἡ ἀπαράλλακτος τοῦ ἀοράτου θεοῦ, ὁ ἐκ τοῦ Πατρὸς γεννηθεὶς Υἱός ... Τῷ ὄντι γὰρ τῆς εἰκόνος ἐστὶ πάντα, ὅσα πρόσεστι τῇ πρωτοτύπῳ μορφῇ.

or (which seems more likely) of *Homilia XVI, In illud "In principio erat Verbum"*, 3 (Migne PG 31, 477):

Διὰ τί Λόγος; "Ινα δειχθῇ, ὅτι ἐκ τοῦ νοῦ προῆλθε. Διὰ τί Λόγος; "Οτι ἀπαθῶς ἐγεννήθη. Διὰ τί Λόγος; "Οτι εἰκὼν τοῦ γεννήσαντος, ὅλον ἐν ἑαυτῷ δεικνὺς τὸν γεννήσαντα.

Melanchthon seems to be familiar with both pieces of writing.[116] It should, however, be noted that in both passages from Basil there is no mention of selfcontuition by God.

---

[113] *Disputationes* (CR 12), pp. 445f., the criticism Melanchthon makes is very harsh indeed: Absurdissima est Basilii vox ... Hoc dictum abolet doctrinam de fide, et adfert desperationem. Melanchthon refers to p. 436 of the edition of Basil's works which came out in 1532, it is a reference to (Ps.-) Basil *Sermo de paen.* 2.

[114] See *Loci communes*, dating from 1559 (and already in the edition of 1535, CR 21, pp. 355f.) (St.A. II), p. 186, the reference must be to *Liber de spiritu sancto*, 24, 43, 75.

[115] *Quaestiones Academicae* (CR 10), p. 882, *Annotationes in Evangelia* (CR 14), p. 177, *Enarratio in Evang. Joannis* (CR 15), p. 10 (where Basil and Augustin are named as the sources of this tenet, and where the actual quotation from Basil points towards *Homilia* XVI: Quare dicitur λόγος? ut ostendatur quod ex mente prodierit, et sit imago genitoris, totum in se ostendens genitorem, et existens proprie, sicut et noster sermo effigies est totius cogitationis), *Explic. Symb. Nic.* (CR 23), p. 360 (with reference to Basil and Augustin) *Postilla Melanchthoniana* (CR 24), p. 74, *Post. Mel.* (CR 25), p. 18 (with reference to Basil and Gregory Nazianzen).

[116] See *Enarratio Symb. Nic.* (CR 23), p. 221.

Melanchthon refers several times to Basil as saying that the Son had to be generated by the Father, since otherwise He and the Father would be brothers.[117] Melanchthon may here have in mind the Arian objection against the orthodox doctrine that, if the Father and the Son are ὁμοούσιοι, then they are in fact brothers.[118] To this objection Basil answers that not brothers are ὁμοούσια, but that a cause and what is caused are ὁμοούσια if they are of the same nature.[119]

Basil is quoted as calling the Holy Spirit God:[120]

> ... expresse dicit (sc. Paulus) Spiritum esse Dominum; id est, Deum. Nam cum inquit: "Dominus est Spiritus", articulus tribuit nomini Spiritus locum et intellectum subiecti. Et sic Basilius eum locum citat.

Melanchthon here refers to *Homilia de spiritu sancto* (Migne PG 31, 1429):

> Ὁ δὲ Κύριος τὸ Πνεῦμά ἐστιν ... καὶ γὰρ εἰ μὴ θεότητα λέγει κατοικεῖν ἐν ἡμῖν διὰ τοῦ Πνεύματος κατοικοῦντος ... πᾶσαν ἀπολεῖ τὴν ἐλπίδα.

Basil's interpretation of *Genesis* 1:2, in which the Spirit above the waters is said to be the Holy Spirit, the third Person of the Trinity, is quoted repeatedly with approval:[121]

> Sic enim ait Bailius: Sive quod verius est et enarratum ab iis, qui ante nos fuerunt, loquitur de Spiritu sancto Dei, quia Scriptura hoc observat, ut cum ait, Spiritus Dei, intelligat Spiritum sanctum, qui est divinae Trinitatis tertia persona. Ac si hoc modo intelliges dictum Mosi, maiorem capies utilitatem. Quomodo enim ferebatur super aquas? Narrabo tibi sermonem Syri cuiusdam qui ait: Vocem hic positam significare idem, quod fovere vitali calore sicut avis incubans fovet ova.

---

[117] *Enarratio Symb. Nic.* (CR 23), pp. 221f.: Si Filius non esset natus, duae illae personae essent duo ἀδελφά, *Explic. Symb. Nic.* (CR 23), p. 366 and *Postilla Melanchthoniana* (CR 24), p. 74.

[118] See e.g. Athanasius, *Contra Arianos* 1, 14, *De Synodis* 51.

[119] See *Epistula ad canonicas* (LII) 1 and 2 (Migne PG 32, 393): Οὐ γὰρ τὰ ἀδελφὰ ἀλλήλοις ὁμοούσια λέγεται, ὅπερ τινὲς ὑπειλήφασιν· ἀλλ' ὅταν καὶ τὸ αἴτιον καὶ τὸ ἐκ τοῦ αἰτίου τὴν ὕπαρξιν ἔχον τῆς αὐτῆς ὑπάρχῃ φύσεως, ὁμοούσια λέγεται. The word ἀδελφά which is used by Basil appears in Melanchthon's reference. In *En. Symb. Nic.*, p. 222: Melanchthon (Cruciger) says that more Greek Fathers say this. One may here think, amongst others, of Athanasius who says *Contra Arianos* 1, 14: Οὐ γὰρ ἔκ τινος ἀρχῆς προϋπαρχούσης ὁ Πατὴρ καὶ ὁ Υἱὸς ἐγεννήθησαν, ἵνα καὶ ἀδελφοὶ νομισθῶσιν· ἀλλ' ὁ Πατὴρ ἀρχὴ τοῦ Υἱοῦ καὶ γεννήτωρ ἐστί, καὶ ὁ Πατὴρ πατήρ ἐστι, καὶ οὐχ υἱός τινος γέγονε· καὶ ὁ Υἱὸς δὲ υἱός ἐστι, καὶ οὐκ ἀδελφός.

[120] *Loci communes* (1559) (St.A. II), p. 206. Cf. Athanasius, *Ad Serapionem* 1, 4, who says that the article before πνεῦμα indicates that it is the Holy Spirit. (Melanchthon knew Athanasius' letters to Serapion, see *supra*, 37f.)

[121] *Loci communes* (1559) (St.A. II), pp. 207f. and (in a shorter way) in *Explic. Symb. Nic.* (CR 23), p. 379. This exegesis by Basil is already referred to in *Commentarius in Genesim*, dating from 1523 (CR 13), p. 766.

This is a correctly abbreviated quotation from *Hom. II in Hexaemeron* 6 (Migne PG 29, 44):

... διὰ τὸ τετηρῆσθαι τοῦτο ἰδιάζοντος καὶ ἐξαιρέτως τῆς τοιαύτης μνήμης ὑπὸ τῆς Γραφῆς ἀξιοῦσθαι, καὶ μηδὲν ἄλλο Πνεῦμα Θεοῦ, ἢ τὸ ἅγιον τὸ τῆς θείας καὶ μακαρίας Τριάδος συμπληρωτικὸν ὀνομάζεσθαι. Καὶ ταύτην προσδεξάμενος τὴν διάνοιαν, μείζονα τὴν ἀπ᾽ αὐτῆς ὠφέλειαν εὑρήσεις. Πῶς οὖν ἐπεφέρετο τοῦτο ἐπάνω τοῦ ὕδατος; Ἐρῶ σοι οὐκ ἐμαυτοῦ λόγον, ἀλλὰ Σύρου ἀνδρὸς σοφίας κοσμικῆς τοσοῦτον ἀφεστηκότος, ὅσον ἐγγὺς ἦν τῆς τῶν ἀληθινῶν ἐπιστήμης. Ἔλεγε τοίνυν τὴν τῶν Σύρων φωνὴν ἐμφατικωτέραν τε εἶναι, καὶ διὰ τὴν πρὸς τὴν Ἑβραΐδα γειτνίασιν μᾶλλόν πως τῇ ἐννοίᾳ τῶν Γραφῶν προσεγγίζειν. Εἶναι οὖν τὴν διάνοιαν τοῦ ῥητοῦ τοιαύτην· Τὸ, Ἐπεφέρετο, φησίν, ἐξηγοῦνται ἀντὶ τοῦ, συνέθαλπε, καὶ ἐζωογόνει τὴν τῶν ὑδάτων φύσιν, κατὰ τὴν εἰκόνα τῆς ἐπωαζούσης ὄρνιθος, καὶ ζωτικήν τινα δύναμιν ἐνιείσης τοῖς ὑποθαλπομένοις.

What Melanchthon particularly likes about Basil's doctrine of the Trinity is that he bases it on Scripture and the sound ecclesiastical tradition:[122]

Basilius inquit: Oportet nos baptizare sicut accepimus: Credere autem sicut baptizamur, glorificare autem sicut credimus Patrem, Filium et Spiritum sanctum. Fugere autem palam blasphemos eos, qui Spiritum sanctum creaturam esse dicunt.

This seems to be a reference to *Liber de spiritu sancto* 68 (Migne PG 32, 193) where Basil ironically asks the Arians:

Τὸ γὰρ ἐπὶ τοῦ βαπτίσματος συναριθμηθὲν ἀναγκαίως ᾠήθημεν δεῖν καὶ ἐπὶ τῆς πίστεως συναρμόσαι. Τὴν δὲ ὁμολογίαν τῆς πίστεως οἷον ἀρχήν τινα καὶ μητέρα τῆς δοξολογίας ἐποιησάμεθα. Ἀλλὰ τί χρὴ ποιεῖν; Νῦν γὰρ ἡμᾶς διδασκέτωσαν, μὴ βαπτίζειν ὡς παρελάβομεν· ἢ μὴ πιστεύειν ὡς ἐβαπτίσθημεν· ἢ μὴ δοξάζειν ὡς πεπιστεύκαμεν.[123]

Basil adheres to the sound ecclesiastical tradition, which appears from the quotation given from Eusebius of Palestine, and the quotations from other ecclesiastical writers, of which the one given from Eusebius is reproduced by Melanchthon.[124]

---

[122] *Explic. Symb. Nic.* (CR 23), p. 380, the same quotation is in the part of the *Enarratio Symboli Nicaeni* (CR 23) which was written by C. Cruciger, p. 235.

[123] Cruciger (see previous note) says that this statement is made in one of Basil's letters. The passage we quote is the closest parallel we could find. (The *Liber de spiritu sancto* is a defence of the divinity of the Holy Spirit and a refutation of the doctrine that the Holy Spirit is a creature.) The statement made in *Epistula* VIII 2 is less close to what Melanchthon and Cruciger provide as a quotation.

[124] *Loci communes* (1559) (St.A. II), p. 209: Sanctum Deum lucis conditorem per salvatorem nostrum Jesum cum Spiritu sancto invocantes, see *Liber de spiritu sancto* 72: Τὸν τῶν προφητῶν ἅγιον θεὸν φωταγωγὸν διὰ τοῦ Σωτῆρος ἡμῶν Ἰησοῦ Χριστοῦ σὺν ἁγίῳ Πνεύματι καλέσαντες. For the use Melanchthon makes of Basil's traditionalism see *infra*, 88f.

Basil's doctrine of the Trinity, of penitence which turns to God's grace and his doctrine of creation obviously aroused Melanchthon's admiration.[125] Although, as we have seen, he does criticize him every now and then in connection with the doctrine of grace, he belongs to what Melanchthon calls the *scriptores puriores*.[126] In his high esteem of Basil Melanchthon sharply differs from Luther who in a *Tischrede* from 1532, the year in which Erasmus' edition of Basil came out, said of him: "Basilius taug gar nichts, der ist gar ein munch, ich wollt nit ein heller umb yhn geben."[127] He is, however, in line with Erasmus, who highly praises Basil in the Preface to his edition (primarily because of Basil's eloquence) and who lists Basil with Origen, Chrysostomus, Jerome, Augustin, Athanasius, and Gregory Nazianzen among the great Fathers who are to be preferred to later scholasticism.[128]

JOHN CHRYSOSTOMUS

Although Melanchthon does not reckon him to the greatest of the Fathers[129] he does quote him repeatedly with approval.

The doctrine of Christ and grace

In connection with the person of Christ Melanchthon quotes the following statement made by Chrysostomus why the Mediator had to be God:[130]

ἄνθρωπος οὐκ ἂν ἐγένετο μεσίτης, ἔδει γὰρ καὶ τῷ θεῷ διαλέγεσθαι.

---

[125] See the first sentences on Basil in *De ecclesia et de autoritate verbi Dei* (St.A. I), p. 353: In Basilio extant utilia testimonia de Trinitate et de poenitentia contra Novatum. In concione de humilitate tradit egregiam sententiam de iustitia fidei, quae nobis aperte patrocinatur.

[126] See *De restituendis scholis*, dating from 1540 (St.A. III), p. 113, see also his *Declamatio de Basilio episcopo* (CR 11), pp. 675ff., and *Postilla Melanchthoniana* (CR 24), pp. 351ff.

[127] *Tischreden* 1, p. 106, cf. *Tischreden* 4, p. 652: ... et Basilius, der ist ein grober lerer; see also E. Schäfer, *op. cit.*, p. 174.

[128] Erasmus, *Ratio verae theologiae* (*Erasmi opera omnia*, t. V, ed. J. Clericus), p. 82 and p. 133. To Melanchthon eloquence was, in the appraisal of the Fathers, less important than to Erasmus, but Melanchthon, too, praises Basil for his lucid style which is close to Demosthenes, see *Postilla Melanchthoniana* (CR 24), p. 357: Retinet (sc. Basilius) nativam faciem linguae, non nimium ludit figuris. Est perspicuus, et quamquam est copiosus, tamen modum tenet ornamentorum. Multo propior est sermo Basilii sermoni Demosthenis quam Nazianzeni aut aliorum qui Graece scripserunt in Ecclesia; — on Demosthenes' eloquence see *Postilla Melanchthoniana* (CR 25), p. 665.

[129] See e.g. *Postilla Melanchthoniana* (CR 25), p. 320: ... errata non pauca sunt in Ambrosio et Augustino, multo plura in Chrysostomo.

[130] See *Responsio de controversiis Stancari* (St.A. VI), p. 273.

This is half of the statement made by Chrysostomus who insists that the Mediator had to be both God and man:[131]

ἄνθρωπος οὐκ ἂν ἐγένετο μεσίτης· ἔδει γὰρ καὶ τῷ θεῷ διαλέγεσθαι· Θεὸς οὐκ ἂν ἐγένετο μεσίτης· οὐ γὰρ ἂν ἐδέξαντο αὐτὸν οἷς ἐμεσίτευσεν.

In connection with the doctrine of grace and free will Melanchthon quotes time and again the words of Chrysostomus:[132]

ὁ δὲ ἕλκων (sc. θεὸς) τὸν βουλόμενον ἕλκει.[133]

Melanchthon sees his doctrine of justification confirmed by Chrysostomus as must become clear in the following quotation:[134]

Et diserte dicit, Fide non solum diligi Deum, sed vicissim credentes sentire, quod a Deo diligantur, quanquam multis modis rei sint.

Melanchthon adds to this the following interpretation and further quotation:

In hac sententia satis significat se intelligere fidem non tantum de notitia historiae, sed de fiducia, qua credimus nobis remitti peccata, et quidem

---

[131] In Epist. primam ad Timotheum, cap. II, Hom. VII (Migne PG 62, 537). Since Melanchthon in this piece of writing opposes the doctrine that Christ was the Mediator in His human nature, it is understandable that he reproduces only the first half of Chrysostomus' statement.—It seems very likely that the statement made by Chrysostomus a few sentences earlier is quoted by Melanchthon in his letter to Libius, dating from 1552, where the text in CR 7, p. 1165 only provides: ἐγ ... τῶν ὅδε φύσεων αὐτὸν ἐ ..., Chrysostomus' words are: ('Επειδὴ γὰρ δύο φύσεων μέσος γέγονεν), ἐγγὺς τῶν δύο φύσεων αὐτὸν εἶναι δεῖ. (Then in Melanchthon's letter δύο ought to be read instead of ὅδε.) In the Latin text Melanchthon quotes Chrysostomus as saying: oportuit mediatorem esse Deum et hominem, — cf. infra, 69.

[132] This sentence is quoted with very small variations, see Loci communes (1535) (CR 21), p. 376, Loci communes (1559) (St.A. II), p. 244, Liber de anima, dating from 1553 (St.A. III), p. 354, Responsiones ad impios articulos Bavaricae inquisitionis, dating from 1558 (St.A. VI), p. 323, Disputationes (CR 12), p. 672 (without giving Chrysostomus' name), Ethicae doctrinae elementa (CR 16), p. 193, p. 240 (without giving Chrysostomus' name), Enarratio Symb. Nic. (CR 23), p. 266, p. 282 (without Chrysostomus' name), Explic. Symb. Nic. (CR 23), p. 535 (without giving Chrysostomus' name), p. 544, Postilla Melanchthoniana (CR 24), p. 316 (without giving Chrysostomus' name), p. 391, Post. Mel. (CR 25), p. 60 (without giving Chrysostomus' name), p. 478 (without giving Chrysostomus' name), Examen ordinandorum (CR 23), p. 15, Explicatio Sententiarum Theognidis (CR 19), p. 131 (together with a statement made by Augustin and a line from Aeschylus, see supra, 27, note 38), Enarratio libri II. Ethicorum Aristotelis (CR 16), p. 330, cf. K. Haendler, op. cit., pp. 543f. Often this word is quoted together with (Ps.-) Basil's Μόνον θέλησον, καὶ ὁ θεὸς προαπαντᾷ, see supra, 41. (Calvin opposes these words of Chrysostomus, see Institutio religionis christianae II 3, 10.)

[133] See Chrysostomus, De ferendis reprehensionibus (Migne PG 51, 143), cf. In Joann. Hom. X (Migne PG 59, 73), In Joann. Hom. XLV (Migne PG 59, 254), Hom. XLVI, 258, Hom. LI, 283.

[134] De ecclesia et de autoritate verbi Dei (St.A. I), p. 355. This quotation is given in Greek in Commentari in Epistolam Pauli ad Romanos, dating from 1540 (CR 15), p. 520, and again in Latin in Disputationes (CR 12), p. 466.

hanc fidem discernit ab operibus, a non furando, non occidendo etc. et dicit hunc cultum superiorem esse.

This is a clear quotation from *In Epistolam and Romanos Homilia* VIII 1:

Τὸ μὲν γὰρ μὴ κλέψαι μηδὲ φονεῦσαι, καὶ τῶν τυχόντων ἐστί· τὸ δὲ πιστεῦσαι, ὅτι τὰ ἀδύνατα δύναται θεός ... ἀγάπης γνησίας τοῦτο σημεῖόν ἐστι ... καυχᾶται γὰρ πάλιν ὁ πιστός, οὐχ ὅτι τὸν θεὸν ἐφίλησε μόνον γνησίως, ἀλλ᾽ ὅτι καὶ πολλῆς παρ᾽ αὐτοῦ τιμῆς ἀπήλαυσε καὶ ἀγάπης. ῞Ωσπερ γὰρ αὐτὸς αὐτὸν ἠγάπησε μέγαλα· περὶ αὐτοῦ φαντασθείς, τοῦτο γὰρ ἀγάπης δεῖγμα· οὕτω καὶ ὁ θεὸς αὐτὸν ἐφίλησε μυρίοις ὑπεύθυνον ὄντα, οὐχὶ κολάσεως ἀπαλλάξας μόνον, ἀλλὰ καὶ δίκαιον ἐργασάμενος.

In connection with the confession of sins Chrysostomus is quoted repeatedly with approval.[135] Melanchthon quotes several times[136] these words of Chrysostomus:

οὐδὲν οὕτως τὸν θεὸν ἵλεον ποιεῖ ὡς τὸ τὰ οἰκεῖα ὁμολογεῖν ἁμαρτήματα.

This is a literal quotation from *Expositio in Psalmum* CXL 7.[137]

Melanchthon opposes the Scholastic doctrine that an enumeration of one's sins earns remission of sins.[138] This explains the importance of his reference to Chrysostomus as a proof that the ancient did not demand confession of all one's hidden sins in public:[139]

... vetustas non mandavit singulis arcana recitare, sicut clare Chrysostomus inquit in enarratione Psal. 50: Si pudet alicui dicere peccata, dicito ea quotidie in anima tua, non dico, ut confitearis conservo tuo, ut tibi exprobret, dicito Deo, qui sanat ea.

This is the spurious Homily on the fiftieth Psalm, which Melanchthon regarded as written by Chrysostomus, since it appears in the edition of a translation of Chrysostomus' works provided by Erasmus and others in 1530:[140]

---

[135] Already at the Leipzig Disputation Chrysostomus' views on penitence were the subject of discussion, see O. Seitz, *Der authentische Text der Leipziger Disputation*, pp. 207f., 211f.

[136] See *Disputationes* (CR 12), p. 553,—the quotation is given in Latin and Greek in *Postilla Melanchthoniana* (CR 24), p. 432, and only in Latin in *Post. Mel.* (CR 25), p. 187 and p. 451.

[137] Migne PG 55, 438.

[138] See e.g. *Loci communes* (1559) (St.A. II), pp. 563f. (and the explicative note by H. Engelland), and *Doctrina de poenitentia*, from 1549 (St.A. VI), pp. 437ff.

[139] *Loci communes* (1559) (St.A. II), p. 574. With some variations this quotation is also given in *Conf. Aug.* (Variata) (St.A. VI), p. 50: Peccata tua dicito, ut deleas. Si pudet dicere quod peccaveris, dicito quotidie in anima tua. Non dico, ut confitearis ea servo, ut exprobret. Dic deo, ut curet ea. — See also *Doctrina de poenitentia* (St.A. VI), p. 439, *Articuli Protestantium* (CR 4), p. 361.

[140] *In Psalmum L*, see *Opera D. Joannis Chrysostomi*, Basileae 1532, pp. 744f., for the Greek quotation see Migne PG 55, 581. The closest parallel we could find in Chrysostomus' genuine writings is in *De incomprehensibili Dei natura* V 7 (Migne PG 48, 746): Οὐδὲ γὰρ εἰς θέατρόν σε ἄγω τῶν συνδούλων τῶν σῶν, οὐδὲ ἐκκαλύψαι τοῖς ἀνθρώποις ἀναγκάζω τὰ ἁμαρτήματα ... δεῖξον τῷ μὴ ὀνειδίζοντι ἀλλὰ θεραπεύοντι.

'Αλλ' αἰσχύνη εἰπεῖν, διότι ἥμαρτες; Λέγε αὐτὰ καθ' ἡμέραν ἐν τῇ εὐχῇ σου. Καὶ τί; μὴ γὰρ λέγω, Εἰπὲ τῷ συνδούλῳ τῷ ὀνειδίζοντί σε, εἰπὲ τῷ Θεῷ τῷ θεραπεύοντι αὐτά.

In the same context the following quotation is given:[141]

> Chrysostomus enim in Epistola ad Ebreos inquit: Persuadeamus nobis peccasse nos, nec id lingua tantum pronunciet, sed etiam intima conscientia, nec tantum dicamus nos esse peccatores, sed etiam peccata specialiter computemus. Non tibi dico, ut te prodas in publicum, neque te ut apud alios accuses, sed obedire te volo Prophetae. Revela Domino viam tuam, coram Deo peccata tua confitere, apud verum iudicem cum oratione delicta tua pronuncia, non lingua, sed conscientiae tuae memoria, et tunc demum spera te misericordiam posse consequi.

This is a quotation from *In Epist. ad Hebr. cap. XII. Homilia* XXXI 3:[142]

Πείθωμεν ἑαυτοὺς ὅτι ἡμάρτομεν· μὴ τῇ γλώττῃ λέγωμεν μόνον, ἀλλὰ καὶ τῇ διανοίᾳ· μὴ ἁμαρτωλοὺς καλῶμεν ἑαυτοὺς μόνον, ἀλλὰ καὶ τὰ ἁμαρτήματα ἀναλογιζώμεθα, κατ' εἶδος ἕκαστον ἀναλέγοντες. Οὐ λέγω σοι, Ἐκπόμπευσον σαυτόν, οὐδὲ παρὰ τοῖς ἄλλοις κατηγόρησον, ἀλλὰ πείθεσθαι συμβουλεύω τῷ προφήτῃ, λέγοντι· Ἀποκάλυψον πρὸς Κύριον τὴν ὁδόν σου. Ἐπὶ τοῦ θεοῦ ταῦτα ὁμολόγησον, ἐπὶ τοῦ δικαστοῦ ὁμολόγει τὰ ἁμαρτήματα, Εὐχόμενος, εἰ καὶ μὴ τῇ γλώττῃ, ἀλλὰ τῇ μνήμῃ, καὶ οὕτως ἀξίου ἐλεηθῆναι.

Chrysostomus is further praised because he does not regard the precepts given in the Sermon on the Mount as merely *consilia*.[143]

These quotations do not, however, mean that Melanchthon was uncritical of Chrysostomus' doctrine of grace. His interpretation of Paul's doctrine of justification through faith is given the qualified approval that it is less impure than the one given by Origen, but Melanchthon says that it is also obscure and inconsistent.[144] Melanchthon explicitly opposes Chrysostomus' doctrine that concupiscence and affections are only sins when they produce a visible result:[145]

> In 7. Cap. (sc. Epistolae ad Romanos) longius currit extra septa. Ait concupiscentiam et affectus, nisi pariant externum opus, non esse peccata.

---

[141] *Conf. Aug.* (Variata) (St.A. VI), pp. 49f., *Conf. Aug.* (CR 26), p. 303.

[142] Migne PG 63, 216, the quotation follows (with minor variations) Erasmus' translation, tomus IV, p. 1858.

[143] *Adv. furiosum Parris. Theol. decr.* ... (St.A. I), p. 148 in a reference to Chrysostomus, *In Matth. Hom.* XVIII (Migne PG 57, 265ff.).

[144] *De ecclesia et de autoritate verbi Dei* (St.A. I), pp. 355f. But Melanchthon also says that Chrysostomus, just like Origen and later on Thomas Aquinas, did not distinguish clearly between Gospel and Law, see the letter to J. Anhalt (CR 8), p. 544. He criticizes Chrysostomus for opposing the condemnation of Origen, *Chronicon Carionis* II (CR 12), p. 1015.

[145] *De ecclesia et de autoritate verbi Dei*, p. 356.

This is a clear reference to *In Epist. ad Rom. Hom.* XIII 1 (Migne PG 60, 507f.):

Αὐτὰ (sc. τὰ πάθη) μὲν γὰρ οὐκ ἦν ἁμαρτία· ἡ δὲ ἀμετρία αὐτῶν μὴ χαλινουμένη τοῦτο ἐργάζεται· Οἷον, ἵν' ὡς ἐπὶ ὑποδείγματος ἐν αὐτῶν (sc. τῶν παθῶν) μεταχ-ειρίσας εἴπω, ἡ ἐπιθυμία ἁμαρτία μὲν οὐκ ἔστιν, ὅταν δὲ εἰς ἀμετρίαν ἐκπέσῃ, εἴσω τῶν τοῦ νόμου γάμων οὐκ ἐθέλουσα μένειν, ἀλλὰ καὶ ἀλλοτρίαις ἐπιδημῶσα γυναιξί, τότε λοιπὸν μοιχεία τὸ πρᾶγμα γίνεται, ἀλλ' οὐ παρὰ τὴν ἐπιθυμίαν, ἀλλὰ παρὰ τὴν ταύτης πλεονεξίαν.

Melanchthon criticizes the fact that Chrysostomus in his homilies on penitence enumerates many ways of receiving forgiveness of sins, *viz.*, alms, tears and other works, but does not mention faith.[146] His general view on Chrysostomus is that he shared many faulty views held in the church of his time, but that he also provides testimonies of sound articles of faith.[147]

In his relatively positive judgement of Chrysostomus Melanchthon sharply differs from Luther, who repeatedly calls Chrysostomus a 'Wescher' (= 'Schwätzer').[148] One of the reasons of Luther's dislike of Chrysostomus was, as Luther says himself, that Erasmus had a high esteem of him.[149] In his defence of free will Erasmus often refers to Chrysostomus as an authority.[150] Melanchthon obviously had the feeling that Chrysostomus provided more support for the doctrine of grace than Luther, frightened off by Erasmus' use of Chrysostomus, believed.[151]

---

[146] *Op. cit.*, p. 355: In tractatu de poenitentia cum colligit multos modos consequendae remissionis peccatorum, scilicet eleemosynas, lacrymas, et alia opera, tamen non facit mentionem fidei, de qua oportuit dici, — the reference is to *De poenitentia hom.* II 2ff. (Migne PG 49, 285ff.). There seems to be a brief reference to this passage in *Apol. Conf. Aug.* B (CR 27), pp. 567f.: (Item Chrysostomus inquit.) In corde contrito, in ore confessio, in opere tota humilitas.

[147] *Op. cit.*, p. 355: Chrysostomi aetas multos iam vitiosos mores receperat, quos ipse recensens non reprehendit, *op. cit.*, p. 356: Sed tamen, si quis attente et cum iudicio leget commentarios illos, multa inveniet testimonia multorum articulorum.

[148] See *Tischreden* I, p. 85 (in connection with his commentary on the letter to the Hebrews, from which Melanchthon quotes with approval, see *supra*, 48), p. 106: Chrisostomus gillt bei mir auch nichts, ist zur ein wescher; cf. E. Schäfer, *op. cit.*, pp. 174f.

[149] *Tischreden* 2, p. 515: Porro cum garrulus sit Chrisostomus, placet Erasmo.

[150] See e.g. *Hyperaspistae Diatribes Liber I* (*Erasmi opera omnia*, t. X, ed. J. Clericus), p. 1511, where he quotes Chrysostomus as explaining *John* 6:44 in the following way: Verum hoc nostrum non tollit arbitrium, sed divino egere auxilio ostendit, nec invitum, sed omni conatu contendentem venire. — Erasmus reckons Chrysostomus amongst the great Fathers who are to be preferred to the Scholastics, *Ratio verae theologiae* (*Erasmi opera omnia*, t. V, ed. J. Clericus), pp. 82f., 121, 133.

[151] On the question of in how far Melanchthon's views on free will, which after the first edition of the *Loci communes* differed from Luther's, influenced his judgement on the Greek Fathers' doctrine of grace see *infra*, 132ff.

CLEMENT OF ALEXANDRIA

The doctrine of grace

Melanchthon several times[152] quotes a definition of justice given in Clement's writings:

δικαιοσύνη ἐστὶ κοινωνία θεοῦ μετὰ ἰσότητος.[153]

Melanchthon has mixed feelings about this definition. First he is very critical of it and says that the definition omits the Mediator, faith and forgiveness of sins.[154] Then he says that, rightly understood, it comprises the two tables of the Law, *viz.*, the right knowledge of God and the right relation with one's neighbour.[155]

Very often[156] Melanchthon reproduces a verse of Sophocles, quoted by

---

[152] See his letter to Cranmer (CR 8), p. 9, the Testimony dating from January 1st 1556 (CR 8), p. 658, the Testimony dating from August 1st 1557 (CR 9), p. 190, the *Enarratio Epist. Pauli ad Romanos* (CR 15), p. 857 (without Clement's name being given), *Examen ordinandorum* (CR 23), p. 17, *Definitiones multarum appellationum quarum in Ecclesia usus est*, dating from 1552/53 (St.A. II), p. 792. Melanchthon perhaps has this statement in mind when he says in a letter to Stathmion that to a philosopher δικαιοσύνη is ἰσότης (CR 7), p. 622.

[153] This is a quotation from Epiphanes given by Clement in *Stromata* 3, 2, 6, 1. On Melanchthon's interpretation of this definition see also P. Fraenkel, *Testimonia Patrum*, pp. 294f.

[154] (CR 8), p. 10: Non fit mentio Mediatoris in definitione iustitiae, et omittitur id, quod praecedere necesse erat, videlicet remissio peccatorum, et reconciliatio propter Mediatorem, filium Dei ... Ita tota definitio loquitur de iustitia operum interiorum et exteriorum, non de ea, quam Paulus nominat iustitiam fidei.

[155] (CR 9), pp. 190f.: Iustitia est societas, qua sese Deus nobis communicat, et est aequalitatis conservatio. Duas partes iustitiae complectitur: alteram, quae proprie in prima tabula Decalogi traditur, quae est agnitio vera Dei ... Altera pars comprehendit secundam tabulam, quae praecipit aequalitatem inter homines, iuxta dictum: diligas proximum sicut te ipsum. This interpretation was briefly given a year before, see CR 8, p. 658, and in the commentary on the Letter to the Romans of the same year, CR 15, p. 857.

[156] See the letter to Roggius, dating from 1532 (CR 2), pp. 614f., to Collinus, dating from 1553 (CR 8), p. 117, to Camerarius, dating from 1553 (CR 8), p. 132, to Heckerus, dating from 1555 (CR 8), p. 620, to Matthias, dating from 1556 (CR 8), pp. 731f., to Collinus, dating from 1557 (CR 9), p. 129, to Clausius, dating from 1557 (CR 9), p. 147, to Libius, dating from 1557 (CR 9), p. 186, to Stigelius, dating from 1558 (CR 9), p. 434, to Delius, dating from 1558 (CR 9), p. 436, to Stigelius, again dating from 1558 (CR 9), p. 666, to Heresbachius, dating from 1559 (CR 9), p. 719, again to Stigelius, dating from 1559 (CR 9), p. 803, *Declamatio de Gregorio Nazianzeno* (CR 12), p. 279. — This often recurring quotation is indicative of the often careless way in which Melanchthon uses his sources: Clement himself gives this as a quotation from Sophocles, see *Stromata* 6, 2, 10, 5. Melanchthon first follows Clement, then in the letter to Camerarius, dating from 1553 (CR 8), p. 132, he says that according to Clement this is a verse from Euripides (this may be caused by the fact that in Clement this quotation from Sophocles is followed by one from Euripides), but doubts whether the verse can be found in Euripides, then in the letter to Heckerus, dating from 1555, he again says that the quotation is from Sophocles (CR 8), p. 620, in the letter to Matthias, a year later (CR 8), p. 731 he says that the verse cannot be found in Sophocles, then he gives the quotation repeatedly without an author's name,

Clement of Alexandria, without adding any qualification that this word might imply the goodness of human nature:

ἄπαν τὸ χρηστὸν τὴν ἴσην ἔχει φύσιν.

Once Melanchthon explains this as meaning:[157]

Boni retinent similes naturas et voluntates, nec fortuna mutantur.

Melanchthon reproduces this statement (with one exception) only in his letters. He may not have felt it necessary to add the qualification that this only applies to those who live from God's grace, since he uses this saying in human relations which to a certain degree are ruled by common human wisdom.[158]

In defending his doctrine that Adam fell through his own guilt Melanchthon once refers to Clement:[159]

Observate dictum Clementis: Dicam omnia potius quam Deum esse causam peccati: 'Ερῶ πάντα μᾶλλον ἢ τὸ προνοοῦν εἶναι αἴτιον κακοῦ.

This is a quotation from *Stromata* 4, 12, 81 where Basilides is quoted as saying:

πάντ' ἐρῶ μᾶλλον ἢ κακὸν τὸ προνοοῦν ἐρῶ.

Clement is not an important Patristic source of Melanchthon,[160] he is certainly less important to Melanchthon than he was to Erasmus.[161]

CYPRIAN

The doctrine of Christ and grace

When Melanchthon in his writing *De ecclesia et de autoritate verbi Dei* lists the subjects on which Cyprian provides useful testimonies he begins with

---

then again says that the verse cannot be found in Sophocles (CR 9, p. 436 and p. 719) and after that he again says that Sophocles is the author of the verse, see the letter to Stigelius (CR 9), p. 803.

[157] See the letter to Matthias, dating from 1556 (CR 8), p. 731.

[158] Cf. the letter to Stigelius, dating from 1558 (CR 9), p. 434 where he says after quoting the verse: Scio etiam, te velle, nos in Ecclesia tueri coniunctionem iuxta dictum: 'Ο θεὸς ἀγάπη ἐστί, καὶ ὁ μένων ἐν ἀγάπῃ, ἐν θεῷ μένει, καὶ ὁ θεὸς ἐν αὐτῷ. Hae leges inter nos ratae sint, nec repeti earum commemorationem in Epistolis semper opus est.

[159] *Postilla Melanchthoniana* (CR 25), p. 381.

[160] Apart from the quotations referred to see *Postilla Melanchthoniana* (CR 25), p. 273 and the letter to H. Troll, dating from 1557 (CR 9), p. 194, where the quotation from the *Evangelium Aegyptiorum* in *Stromata* 3, 9, 63-64 is reproduced and the quotation in the *Definitiones*, dating from 1552/53 (St.A. II), p. 811 from *Stromata* 2, 20, 116, 3-4 (the reference to p. 161 is to the edition in Bibliotheca Medica, Forence 1550).

[161] Erasmus lists Clement with Chrysostomus, Cyprian, Jerome, Ambrose, and Augustin amongst the important Fathers, *Ratio verae theologiae* (*Erasmi opera omnia*, t. V, ed. J. Clericus), p. 83.

the doctrine of the Trinity.[162] The only quotation from Cyprian we could find in connection with the divinity of Christ is in later pieces of writing, where Melanchthon reproduces Cyprian's prayer to Christ before his execution (and the fact that the prayer is directed to Christ implies according to Melanchthon Christ's divinity):[163]

> Ego in tuo nomine peto, ut tu a Patre petas, ut detur mihi.[164]

As such this sentence does not appear in Cyprian's prayer, but all the elements contained in this quotation appear in Cyprian's prayer:

> The deprecor filium Dei vivi ... tu nobis testamentum fecisti et pollicitus es dicens: petite et accipietis ... quodcunque a patre meo petieritis in nomine meo, ego in tuo nomine peto ut accipiam ... per nomen tuum te deprecor ut optimam des victoriam in inimicum meum.[165]

In the *Loci communes* of 1521 he claims that Cyprian often says that the saints remain sinners, which he interprets as support of his doctrine that justification only begins in this life. But he gives no quotations to corroborate this view.[166] It could be that he here has in mind a passage from *De oratione dominica* which he quotes in other pieces of writing[167] and which he knew at the time of the first edition of the *Loci communes* through Augustin:[168]

> (Et Cyprianus in enarratione orationis dominicae), Ne quis sibi quasi innocens placeat, et se extollendo plus petat, instruitur et docetur peccare quotidie, dum quotidie pro peccatis iubetur orare.

Later on Melanchthon gives a quotation from Cyprian which endorses his doctrine of the *beneficia* of Christ:[169]

---

[162] *Op. cit.*, (St.A. I), p. 350: Continet (sc. Cyprianus) utilia testimonia: De Trinitate ...

[163] *Loci communes*, dating from 1559 (St.A. II), p. 197: Adoratio tribuit divinitatem, *Responsiones ad art. inqu.* (St.A. VI), p. 338: Ideoque invocatio est honos, qui tantum Deo tribuitur.

[164] See *Resp. ad art. Bav. inqu.* (St.A. VI), p. 337 (where the reference is to Erasmus' edition from 1540), and *Quaestiones Academicae* (CR 10), p. 860, where the prayer is quoted with some variations: Fili Dei Domine Jesu Christe, Te peto, ut petas pro me, ut mihi detur, cf. *Postilla Melanchthoniana* (CR 24), p. 839.

[165] See Cyprian, *Orationes* (CSEL 3, 3), pp. 150ff.

[166] *Loci communes* (1521) (St.A. II), p. 130.

[167] *Apol. Conf. Aug.* B (CR 27), p. 505.

[168] See *De oratione dominica* 22. This section is quoted by Augustin, *Contra duas epistulas Pelagianorum* 4, 10, 27, to which Melanchthon refers in *Adversus curiosum Parris. Theol. decr.* ... (St.A. I), p. 147.

[169] See *Commentarii in priorem epist. Pauli ad Cor.*, dating from 1551 (CR 15), p. 1112. In *De Erasmo et Luthero elogion* etc., dating from 1522 (CR 20), p. 705, he expresses the following qualified praise: et in causa gratiae certae Cyprianum non aspernandum puto; sed et ipse non raro scripturas torquet.

Et Cyprianus complectitur utrumque finem, adfirmat accipienda esse beneficia Christi, et vicissim agendas esse gratias: Pietas inter data et condonata tanti beneficii largitori gratias agit.

The closest parallel we could find to this is from *Epistola* LXIII 18:[170]

Quare si in lumine Christi ambulare volumus, a praeceptis et monitis eius non recedamus, agentes gratias quod, dum instruit in futurum quid facere debeamus, de praeterito ignoscit quod simpliciter erravimus.

Important in connection with the doctrine of grace is, of course, that Cyprian provides testimonies for infant baptism.[171] He quotes him as follows:[172]

So schreibet Cyprianus zu Fido einen guten unterricht, das die Kirch nicht sol die Kinder von der tauff und gnaden ausschliessen, sondern sey schuldig jnen die tauff mitzuteilen. Denn so vil an ir ist, ist sie schuldig, allen menschen, jung und alt, jr ampt mitzuteilen. Und saget dabey deutlich, das die kinder derhalben der tauff bedurffen, das sie durch Gottes gnad and werck jnn der tauff erlangen vergebung der Erbsund.

This is a free quotation from *Epistola* LXIV 5:[173]

Propter quod neminem putamus a gratia consequenda impediendum esse ... sed omnem omnino admittendum esse ad gratiam Christi ... prohiberi non debet infans qui recens natus nihil peccavit, nisi quod secundum Adam carnaliter natus contagium mortis antiquae prima nativitate contraxit, quid ad remissam peccatorum accipiendam hoc ipso facilius accedit quod illi remittuntur non propria sed aliena peccata.

But Melanchthon is also critical of Cyprian in the context of the doctrine of grace, especially in connection with penitence and ecclesiastical censure. Cyprian is wrong in saying that forgiveness of sins is invalid unless one has completed what ecclesiastical censure asks.[174] He opposes Cyprian's doctrine that baptism forgives sins committed before it, but that after baptism one has to seek remission of sins through alms.[175] He

---

[170] Migne PL 4, 400.

[171] See *De ecclesia et de autoritate verbi Dei* (St.A. I), pp. 350f.

[172] See *Verlegung etlicher unchristlicher Artikel, welche die Widerteuffer fürgeben* (St.A. I), p. 319.

[173] (CSEL 3, 2), p. 720. Melanchthon refers to the same passage in *Loci communes* (1559) (St.A. II), p. 514.

[174] *De ecclesia et de autoritate verbi Dei* (St.A. I), p. 351: ... Ut de poenis canonicis admodum duriter scribit, ait non valere absolutionem, nisi illae poenae fuerint persolutae, cf. p. 332. Melanchthon may here have in mind *De lapsis* 13ff., especially 18: Ceterum si quis praepropera festinatione temerarius remissionem peccatorum dare se cunctis putat posse aut audet Domini praecepta rescindere, non tantum nihil prodest sed et obest lapsis.

[175] *Op. cit.*, p. 351, the reference is to *De opere et eleemosynis* (CSEL 3, 1), p. 374, and to *De lapsis* 35 (CSEL 3, 1), pp. 262ff.

disagrees with his views on celebacy.[176] But Melanchthon mitigates his criticism by saying that these are faults which Cyprian would have corrected himself if they had been pointed out to him.[177]

When Melanchthon describes Cyprian as a witness of the doctrine of the Trinity and of infant baptism, this means that he regards him as one of the important Fathers (since infant baptism was important to Melanchthon's doctrine of grace). Luther seems to have held a less favourable view of Cyprian. He calls him a saint martyr, but a weak theologian.[178] Just like Melanchthon he is critical of his very rigid attitude towards ecclesiastical discipline.[179] But he also praises Cyprian for his ardent treatment of faith.[180]—As appears from the Preface to the edition of the works of Cyprian, Erasmus had a high esteem of him: He praises Cyprian's eloquence, his evangelical piety. He criticizes his view that those baptized by heretics had to be rebaptized, but immediately excuses this mistake by saying that it was caused by hatred of the heretics and love of the unity of the Church.[181]

CYRIL OF ALEXANDRIA

The doctrine of Christ

In his defence of the doctrine that Christ as a Mediator was both God and man Melanchthon gives two quotations from Cyril which he says are in the twelfth book of the *Thesaurus*:[182]

---

[176] *Op. cit.*, p. 351, the reference must be to *De clericorum singularitate*, this is a spurious piece of writing, Melanchthon may not have doubted the authenticity, since it appears in Erasmus' edition, pp. 384ff. (although Erasmus himself expresses doubts about its authenticity, see the first page of the Preface to the edition. Luther, too, doubted it, see *Tischreden* 4, p. 190).

[177] *Op. cit.*, p. 351: Haec sunt plena absurditatis, quae admonitus haud dubie correxisset, cf. p. 332: Fortasse sentiebat commodius quam locutus est.

[178] *Tischreden* 1, p. 330: Cyprianus est sanctus martyr, sed theologus imbecillus. On Luther and Cyprian see also E. Schäfer, *op. cit.*, pp. 177f.

[179] See *Resolutiones disputationum de indulgentiarum virtute* (W.A. 1), p. 547: ... Cyprianus vel rigidissimus ecclesiasticarum censurarum et disciplinarum observator.

[180] *Tischreden* (aus verschiedenen Jahren), 5, p. 649: Ph. Melanchthon Basilium commendavit, qui clare posuit fidem iustificantem supra locum: Qui gloriatur, in Domino glorietur. Econtra Doctor Martinus Lutherus Cyprianum summis extulit laudibus, qui constantissime et summo ardore fidem tractasset, deinde Irenaeum ... On Melanchthon's use of Basil in this context see *supra*, 40.

[181] See the letter of dedication to Cardinal Laurentius Puccius, pp. 1-4 of the edition of 1519.—Erasmus lists Cyprian with Chrysostomus, Jerome, Ambrose, Augustin, and Clement amongst the great theologians of the early church, see *Ratio verae theologiae* (*Erasmi opera omnia*, t. V, ed. J. Clericus), p. 83.

[182] *Responsio de controversiis Stancari* (St.A. VI), p. 274.

(Cyrilli longa est commemoratio in Thesauri libro 12.) Mediator Dei et hominum Jesus Christus est non solum quia reconciliavit homines Deo, sed etiam, quia naturaliter et substantialiter et Deus et homo est in una hypostasi. Item, Est autem Christus Mediator Dei et hominum, quia in eo uno Deus et homo coniunguntur.

This is a literal quotation from the Latin translation of Cyril's works in *Operum D. Cyrilli Al. tomi quattuor*, Basel 1546, tom. II, p. 156 (the Latin translation differs somewhat from the Greek text in Migne PG 75, 504).[183]

Melanchthon refers repeatedly to Cyril (together with Athanasius and Ps.-Justin) as saying that the union of the divine and the human nature in Christ can be compared with the union of the soul and the body in man.[184]

Also in the context of the two natures of Christ he quotes Cyril as saying against the Arian argument, that if the Son will be subjected to the Father (*I Cor.* 15:28), He cannot be the Father's equal:

(Cyrillus breviter respondet:) subiectio seu obedientia non tollit aequalitatem essentiae et potentiae, sed ostendit ordinem personarum.[185]

This is not the quotation of a brief statement made by Cyril, but a brief summary of a lengthy argument given by him.[186]

---

[183] After the first sentence quoted above the translation continues: Hoc enim modo naturam nostram sibi Deus reconciliavit. Nam aliter quomodo unum mediatorem Christum Paulus dixisset. The Greek text runs as follows (Migne PG 75, 504): Εἰ μεσίτης ἐστὶ θεοῦ καὶ ἀνθρώπων Ἰησοῦς ὁ Χριστός, οὐ φύσει καὶ οὐσιωδῶς θεῷ τε καὶ ἀνθρώποις συναπτόμενος, διαλλάττων δὲ μόνον, καὶ εἰς φιλίαν εἰσάγων τὰ τῆς πρὸς ἄλληλα κοινωνίας ἀποστήσαντα, τούτεστιν ἄνθρωπον καὶ θεόν, πῶς ἕνα φησὶν ὁ Παῦλος αὐτόν. So the Greek text argues: if He was not essentially God and man, how could He have been the one Mediator? The Latin text argues: He was essentially God and man, how otherwise could He have been the Mediator? (The difference is only in formulation, not in thought.)—The second sentence quoted by Melanchthon runs in Greek: μεσίτης δὲ θεοῦ καὶ ἀνθρώπων ἐστὶν ὁ Χριστὸς πρόδηλον ὅτι θεοῦ μὲν ὡς θεός, ἀνθρώπων δὲ ὡς ἄνθρωπος ἅπτεται φυσικῶς.

[184] (Ps.-) Justin is in this context sometimes explicitly quoted (see *infra*, 73f.), Athanasius and Cyril are only referred to, see *Responsio de controversiis Stancari* (St.A. VI), p. 266, *Refutatio erroris Serveti* (St.A. VI), p. 375, *Disputationes* (CR 12), p. 593, p. 616, p. 649, *Explic. Symb. Nic.* (CR 23), p. 510, *Postilla Melanchthoniana* (CR 24), p. 560. See e.g. Cyril, *Epistula* XLV (Migne PG 77, 233).

[185] See *Explic. Symb. Nic.* (CR 23), p. 513, cf. *Postilla Melanchthoniana* (CR 24), p. 553, cf. *Resp. de contr. Stanc.* (St.A. VI), p. 267.

[186] See *Dialogus de Trinitate* V, 582ff., in the edition used by Melanchthon this is in *Tomus* II, pp. 342ff., cf. *Thesaurus*, Assertio XXXIX.—In *Explic. Symb. Nic.* (CR 23), p. 373 he quotes him in connection with Christ's work in the incarnation as saying: nec missio et obedientia tollunt aequalitatem potentiae (the punctuation in the CR is misleading). Either Melanchthon here applies to the incarnation what Cyril says in *De Trin.* V, 582ff. about *I Cor.* 15:28, or he has in mind *Adv. Nest.* 3, 1 (Migne PG 76, 115ff.), from *Resp. de contr. Stanc.* (St.A. VI), p. 265 and p. 271 it appears that he knows about this passage, since he quotes Nestorius' objection: Si Christus secundum naturam

Cyril of Alexandria was obviously to Melanchthon one of the useful witnesses to the divinity of Christ, a witness of whom he made use every now and then.

JOHN OF DAMASCUS

In the first edition of the *Loci communes* John of Damascus is one of the first ecclesiastical writers whom Melanchthon attacks, because he regards him as being too much influenced by philosophy.[187] In the letter of dedication to the edition of the *Loci communes* dating from 1535 he merely refers to him as an example of someone who wrote a *methodus*.[188] In the beginning of the final edition of the *Loci communes* there is no reference to John of Damascus. Melanchthon seems to have become less critical of him.

The doctrine of Christ

We found two quotations from John of Damascus in connection with the doctrine of Christ:

quod semel adsumsit, nunquam deseruit nec deseret.[189]

This could be a reference to *De fide orthodoxa* 3, 17 (Migne PG 94, 1069) where John says, quoting and explaining Gregory Nazianzen:

ὡς φησιν ὁ θεολόγος Γρηγόριος «ὧν τὸ μὲν ἐθέωσε, τὸ δὲ ἐθεώθη, καὶ θαρρῶ λέγειν, ὁμόθεος. Καὶ ἄνθρωπον γενέσθαι τὸ χρίσαν, καὶ Θεὸν τὸ χριόμενον.» Ταῦτα γὰρ οὐ κατὰ μεταβολὴν φύσεως, ἀλλὰ κατὰ τὴν οἰκονομικὴν ἕνωσιν, τὴν καθ' ὑπόστασιν λέγω, καθ' ἣν ἀδιασπάστως τῷ Θεῷ Λόγῳ ἥνωται.

The other quotation is:

Humana natura subsistit in divina.[190]

This is an abbreviated quotation from *De fide orthodoxa* 3, 9 (Migne PG 94, 1017):

Οὐ γὰρ ἰδιοσυστάτως ὑπέστη ἡ τοῦ Θεοῦ Λόγου σάρξ, οὐδὲ ἑτέρα ὑπόστασις γέγονε παρὰ τὴν τοῦ Θεοῦ Λόγου ὑπόστασιν, ἀλλ' ἐν αὐτῇ ὑποστᾶσα, ἐνυπόστατος μᾶλλον, καὶ οὐ καθ' ἑαυτὴν ἰδιοσύστατος ὑπόστασις γέγονε.

---

divinam esset Sacerdos, sibi ipsi offerret. — In his reply Cyril says *inter alia*: ῞Οτε τοίνυν ὁ κατὰ φύσιν ἰδίαν ἐλεύθερος, ὡς θεός, ὁ ἐν μορφῇ καὶ ἰσότητι τοῦ γεγεννηκότος, κεχρημάτικε δοῦλος τῶν ὑπὸ ζύγα δουλείας τὸ μέτρον οὐ διωθούμενος οἰκονομικῶς, ἀνθ' ὅτου δέδιας αὐτὸν καὶ ἀρχιερέα καλεῖν διὰ τὸ ἀνθρώπινον.

[187] *Loci communes* (1521) (St.A. II), p. 5: Nimium enim philosophatur Damascenus.

[188] See (CR 2), p. 921 and (CR 21), p. 333.

[189] *Enarratio Symb. Nic.* (CR 23), p. 341, *Examen ordinandorum* (CR 23), p. 5, here the quotation is given with small variations: Naturam humanam, quam semel assumpsit *logos* numquam deserit. See apart from *De fide orth.* 3, 17 also 3, 27.

[190] *Postilla Melanchthoniana* (CR 24), p. 560.

Epiphanius

Although Epiphanius is not quoted very often by Melanchthon (with the exception of one sentence) he does list him among the important early Christian writers.[191] The reason is that Epiphanius was a strong defender of orthodoxy against the various heresies.[192] Of particular value to Melanchthon is Epiphanius' opposition to Origen's allegorical exegesis of the Bible, which Melanchthon rejected as well. In this context the following quotation from *Adversus Haereses* II, tom. I, 61, 6 (Migne PG 41, 1048) is given once in this way:[193]

πάντα τὰ θεῖα ῥήματα οὐκ ἀλληγορίας δεῖται, ἀλλ' ὡς ἔχει, θεωρίας δὲ δεῖται καὶ αἰσθήσεως, εἰς τὸ εἰδέναι ἑκάστης ὑποθέσεως τὴν δύναμιν.

Of this the following translation is given:

> Divinus sermo non indiget allegorica interpretatione, sed in propria sententia intelligatur. Indiget autem speculatione et sensu, ut materiae discernantur, et recte accipiantur.

This means that according to Melanchthon's understanding of this sentence allegorical exegesis is excluded in all instances. But more often Melanchthon quotes the text in a slightly different way, and then says that not all Biblical texts ought to be explained in an allegorical way:[194]

τὰ θεῖα ῥήματα οὐ πάντα ἀλληγορίας δεῖται, ἀλλὰ ὡς ἔχει, κτλ.

---

[191] See *infra*, note 199.

[192] *De ecclesia et de autoritate verbi Dei* (St.A. I), p. 355: Continet enim Epiphanius refutationes veterum haeresium, praecipue de Trinitate et paucis aliis materiis, quem quidem historicum praecipuum legendum esse censeo, cf. also the letter to Camerarius, dating from 1535 (CR 2), p. 877: Volumina (sc. Epiphanii) sunt non tam propter disputationes quam propter historiam Ecclesiasticam digna lectu, the letter to Spalatinus, dating from 1537 (CR 3), p. 329, the letter to Longus, dating from 1543 (CR 5), p. 45.

[193] The quotation is given in this way in *Declamatio de dicto: Sermo Christi habitet* etc., dating from 1550 (CR 11), p. 899. For Melanchthon's use and interpretation of this sentence see S. Wiedenhofer, *op. cit.*, pp. 336ff. For Melanchthon's approval of Epiphanius' rejection of Origen's allegorical method see also P. Fraenkel, *Testimonia patrum*, p. 344, note 24.

[194] *Responsio ad criminationes Staphyli* (St.A. VI), p. 466, *Disputationes* (CR 12), p. 659, *Hist. coll. Worm.*, dating from 1558 (CR 9), p. 460, Praefatio to *Tabulae locorum communium theologicorum*, dating from 1560 (CR 9), p. 1024, in a letter to Barinius, dating from 1556 (CR 8), p. 863 (and in the *Dictum* reproduced in CR 8, p. 60, where θεοῦ is given instead of θεῖα and, more important, αἰσθήσεως instead of ἐκθήσεως) the quotation appears with some variations: οὐ πάντα θεοῦ ῥήματα ἀλληγορίας δεῖται, ἀλλ' ὡς ἔχει. θεωρίας δὲ δεῖται καὶ ἐκθήσεως εἰς τὸ εἰδέναι ἑκάστης ὑποθέσεως τὴν δύναμιν. Of this Melanchthon gives the following translation: Non omnia verba Dei transformanda sunt in allegorias, sed ut nativa significatio sermonis postulat. Speculatione autem et sensu opus est, ut intelligatur cuiusque argumenti propositum. (In the Latin translation of Epiphanius, which came out in Basel in 1542 the sentence is translated as follows, p. 243: Imo omnia divina verba non allegoria opus habent, sed prout se habent accipienda sunt. Speculatione autem indigent

The following literal quotation from *Adv. Haer.* II, I, 64, 5 (Migne PG 41, 1077f.) is given in the same context:[195]

(Sic enim scribit de eo (sc. Origene) Epiphanius:) καὶ ὅσα μὲν ἐν προσομιλίαις, καὶ διὰ τῶν προοιμίων εἰς ἤθη τε καὶ εἰς φύσεις ζῴων τε καὶ τῶν ἄλλων εἴρηται, μέσος φερόμενος, πολλάκις χαριέντα διηγήσατο, ὅσα δὲ εἰς δόγματα ἐδογμάτισε, καὶ περὶ πίστεως καὶ μείζονος θεωρίας, τῶν πάντων ἀτοπώτατα τῶν πρὸ αὐτοῦ, καὶ μετ' αὐτὸν εὑρίσκεται.

The doctrine of the Trinity

In the *Explicatio Symboli Nicaeni* Melanchthon quotes Epiphanius as follows:[196]

Apud Epiphanium saepe repetitae sunt satis perspicuae asseverationes, contra Sabellianos, ἐνυπόστατον ὁ πατήρ, ἐνυπόστατον ὁ υἱός, ἐνυπόστατον τὸ ἅγιον πνεῦμα. Item contra πνευματομάχους, Spiritus vere est ex Deo, et non alienus a Patre et Filio, sed ὁμοούσιος Patri et Filio.

This statement is indeed made by Epiphanius against the Sabellians[197] and against the *Pneumatomachi*.[198]

Melanchthon lists Epiphanius with Athanasius, Basil, Ambrose, and Augustin among the most important ecclesiastical writers,[199] or with Irenaeus, Athanasius, Basil, Gregory Nazianzen, and Theodoretus.[200] This high esteem of Epiphanius was shared by Luther.[201]

---

ac sensu, ad cognoscendam uniuscuiusque propositi argumenti vim ac facultatem. — A brief reference to this statement is given in *Postilla Melanchthoniana* (CR 25), p. 205. (The *speculatio* is usually explained by Melanchthon as *ordo in docendo*.) As Bretschneider (CR 8), p. 59 points out Melanchthon for a while used to write these words into books which he gave to friends, so he regarded these words as very true and useful. (See further *De norma iudicii in Ecclesia* (CR 9), p. 1083, *Quaestiones Academicae* (CR 10), p. 895, *Decl. de cura recte loquendi* (CR 12), p. 219. On Epiphanius' rejection of Origen see *Chronicon Carionis* II (CR 12), p. 1015.)

[195] *Annotationes in Epist. Pauli ad Rom.* (CR 15), p. 466.

[196] (CR 23), p. 380, cf. *Enarratio Symb. Nic.* (CR 23), p. 235.

[197] See *Adv. Haereses* II, Tom. I, Haeres. LXII (Migne PG 41, 1053, 1060), this quotation is also given in the part of the *Enarratio Symb. Nic.* which was written by C. Cruciger, p. 220.

[198] See *Adv. Haereses* III, Tom. I, Haeres. LXXIV (Migne PG 42, 496): ... ὡς καὶ αὐτὸ ὄντως ἐκ θεοῦ ἕν, καὶ οὐκ ἀλλότριον Πατρὸς καὶ Υἱοῦ, ἀλλ' ὁμοούσιον Πατρὶ καὶ Υἱῷ ... This sentence is also quoted in *Disputationes* (CR 12), p. 591.

[199] See his letter, dating from 1541 about the Colloquium at Worms (CR 4), p. 38, *Responsio ad scriptum quorundam delectorum a Clero Secundario Coloniae Agrippinae*, dating from 1543 (St.A. VI), p. 402.

[200] See his letter to Patriarch Joseph of Constantinopel, dating from 1559 (CR 9), p. 922.

[201] See *Tischreden* 5 (aus verschiedenen Jahren), p. 650: Epiphanius longe ante Hieronymum scripsit historias ecclesiasticas longe utilissimas, si eas a contentionis argumentis separare possemus, dignae esset ut excuderentur; cf. E. Schäfer, *op. cit.*, p. 175.

GREGORY NAZIANZEN

Gregory Nazianzen is one of the witnesses of orthodoxy, so he is primarily quoted in later writings. But Melanchthon betrays knowledge of him as early as 1519.[202]

The doctrine of grace

There is one statement made by Gregory about the relation between man's free will and God's grace which Melanchthon obviously likes very much and which he often quotes:[203]

πᾶν τὸ κατορθούμενον παρὰ θεοῦ ἐστι, δέδοται δὲ τοῖς καλουμένοις καὶ οὕτω νεύουσι.

This is a free quotation from *Oratio* 37, 13:[204]

("Όταν ἀκούσῃς, Οἷς δέδοται, πρόσθες,) δέδοται μὲν τοῖς καλουμένοις καὶ οὕτω νεύουσι ... Ἐπειδὴ γάρ εἰσί τινες οἱ τοσοῦτον μεγαλοφρονοῦντες ἐπὶ τοῖς κατορθώμασιν, ὥστε τὸ πᾶν ἑαυτοῖς διδόναι ... διδάσκει τούτους ὁ λόγος, ὅτι καὶ τὸ βούλεσθαι καλῶς, δεῖται τῆς παρὰ θεοῦ βοηθείας.

Also quoted with approval in connection with good works which must glorify God's grace is the statement:[205]

ἀρχὴν ἁπάντων καὶ τέλος ποίει θεόν.

This is a quotation from *Carm. liber* I, Sectio II:

ἀρχὴν ἁπάντων καὶ τέλος ποιοῦ θεόν.[206]

Against the Anabaptists who want to constitute a sinless church, Gregory's statement against the Donatists is quoted with approval:[207]

Eadem est figura sigilli, sive aureo sive ferreo annulo insculpta sit, ita idem esse ministerium inquit, sive boni sive mali teneant.

---

[202] *Epistola de Lipsica disputatione* (St.A. I), p. 6, cf. *infra*, 84.

[203] See *Responsiones ad impios Articulos Bav. Inquis.* (St.A. VI), dating from 1558, p. 323, *Declamatio de Gregorio Nazianzeno*, also dating from 1558 (CR 12), p. 283, *Disputatio*, dating from 1559 (CR 12), p. 651, Letter to J. Mollerus, dating from 1558 (CR 9), p. 670, *Quaestio Academica*, dating from 1557 (?) (CR 10), p. 872, *Postilla Melanchthoniana* (CR 25), p. 478 (in this latter case the quotation is given in Latin). So Melanchthon became acquainted with this statement rather late in his life; cf. K. Haendler, *op. cit.*, pp. 543f., H. Engelland, *Melanchthon. Glaube und Handeln*, pp. 394ff.

[204] Migne PG 36, 297.

[205] *Philosophiae moralis epitomes liber* I (St.A. III), p. 165, *Postilla Melanchthoniana* (CR 24), p. 202.

[206] Migne PG 37, 908, cf. 1577.

[207] *Loci communes* (1559) (St.A. II), p. 489 and *Declamatio de Gregorio Nazianzeno* (CR 12), p. 283.

This is a reference to *Oratio* 40, 26:

Ἔστω χρυσός, ἔστω σίδηρος, δακτύλιοι δὲ ἀμφότεροι, καὶ τὴν αὐτὴν ἐγκεχαράχ-θωσαν εἰκόνα βασιλικήν, εἶτα κηρὸν ἐντυπούτωσαν· τί διοίσει ἡ σφραγίς αὕτη τῆς σφραγίδος ἐκείνης; Οὐδέν ... Οὕτω ἔστω σοὶ πᾶς βαπτιστής, κἂν τῇ πολιτείᾳ προέχῃ, ἀλλ' ἥ γε τοῦ βαπτίσματος δύναμις ἴση.[208]

In a similar context he quotes Gregory with approval when he states against the Novatians that the saints remain sinners:[209]

Nazianzenus irridet illos καθαρούς: dicit illos nescire, quid sit peccatum, et quod in sanctis quoque sit peccatum.

This is a reference to *Oratio* 39, 18-19, where Gregory points to David and Peter as saints who remained sinners.[210]

There is one statement which Melanchthon ascribes to Gregory and quotes quite often and which sounds rather 'optimistic' from the point of view of Melanchthon's doctrine of sin:[211]

Sic inquit Nazianzenus: οὐδὲν οὕτως εὐφραίνειν ἡμᾶς εἴωθεν, ὡς συνειδὸς καθαρὸν καὶ ἐλπίδες ἀγαθαί.

The reason why he has no objection to a statement like this one is presumably the same one as why he freely quotes an equally 'optimistic' statement by Sophocles which he found in Clement of Alexandria.[212] This quotation is one of the examples of the sometimes careless way in which Melanchthon uses his sources: He ascribes this sentence to Gregory Nazianzen, but it was in fact made by Chrysostomus.[213]

Melanchthon also expresses criticism of Gregory in connection with the doctrine of grace and sin. He quotes Gregory (and Origen) as saying that revenge is permitted, but that it is a more perfect virtue not to take revenge. This distinction between precepts and counsels is rejected by Melanchthon:[214]

Origenes et Nazianzenus fingunt concessum esse vindicare, sed perfec-tiorem virtutem esse non vindicare.

This is a reference to *Oratio* 5, *Contra Julianum* II.[215]

---

[208] Migne PG 36, 396.

[209] *Postilla Melanchthoniana* (CR 25), p. 718.

[210] Migne PG 36, 356f.

[211] Letter to Pannonius, dating from 1547 (CR 6), p. 426, to Langus, also dating from 1547 (CR 6), p. 538, to Wellerus, dating from 1548 (CR 6), p. 892 (with the addition: Hanc sententiam saepe recito, et multis velo notam esse), to the Students, dating from 1548 (CR 7), p. 106, *Postilla Melanchthoniana* (CR 24), p. 799.

[212] See *supra*, 50f.

[213] See Chrystostomus, *Contra eos qui subintroductas habent virgines* (Migne PG 47, 511).

[214] *Loci communes* (1559) (St.A. II), p. 714, Melanchthon adds: Has ineptias supra refutavi, ubi de praeceptis et consiliis dictum est. See on this matter further *infra*, 106.

[215] Migne PG 35, 712.

The doctrine of the Trinity

The doctrine of the Trinity was to Melanchthon the most valuable part of Gregory Nazianzen. In 1539 he refers to this doctrine as the most important article of faith in Gregory,[216] and in 1543 he repeats a similar statement.[217] (The approving statements in connection with the doctrine of grace appear in later writings as well, as we have seen).

Melanchthon once refers to the question debated in Patristic theology whether the Son was generated by the will of God or by the nature of God. This was discussed, he says, at the Synod of Rimini and in the writings of Gregory Nazianzen:[218]

> Agitata est etiam tunc (sc. in Synodo Ariminensi) quaestio de his modis loquendi: Pater natura genuit filium, non genuit voluntate, id est, contingenter, sicut contingenter creaturas condidit. De his modis loquendi extant commonefactiones in Nazianzeno, et in Longobardo, libro 1. dist. 6.

Melanchthon here must have in mind the *Oratio theologica* III 6 (Migne PG 36, 80f.), where this question is discussed, but the reference is somewhat free and fits more with Petrus Lombardus[219] than with what is said at the Synod of Rimini and by Gregory Nazianzen. At this synod[220] and in Gregory, *Oratio Theol.* III 6 the question is whether the Son is generated by free will or by necessity. The answer given by the Synod and by Gregory is that He was *generated* by free will, but that He was not *created* by God's free will (as creation is). So the question there was whether the Son was generated by free will or by necessity. Melanchthon quotes them as dealing with the question whether the Son was generated by nature or by free will. In this form the question appears in Petrus Lombardus and amongst the Fathers in Athanasius.[221]

There are a few statements in connection with the doctrine of the Trinity which Melanchthon likes to quote:

> λόγον ait dici, quia sit ἐξαγγελτικός proferens vocem Evangelii ex arcano sinu patris.[222]

---

[216] *De ecclesia et de autoritate verbi Dei* (St.A. I), p. 354: Nazianzenus tractavit articulum de Trinitate, alia dogmata leviter attingit.

[217] Letter to Hessus (CR 5), p. 57: Perspexi totum (sc. codicem Nazianzeni), et quamquam monumentum est dignum Bibliothecis, propter controversiam de Trinitate, tamen praeter eam causam, non multa continet διδασκαλικά.

[218] *Chronicon Carionis* II (CR 12), p. 986.

[219] See *infra*, 100.

[220] See Migne PG 26, 740.

[221] See Athanasius, *Contra Arianos* 3, 59ff. Athanasius says that the dilemma: Did God create the Son out of free will or did He have a Son by necessity? is a false one, and that the truth is that the Father generated the Son out of His nature, be it not against His own will, — see on this matter E. P. Meijering, *Orthodoxy and Platonism in Athanasius. Synthesis or Antithesis?*, Leiden 1974², pp. 69ff., and *God Being History. Studies in Patristic Philosophy*, Amsterdam-Oxford 1975, pp. 103ff.

This is a reference to *Oratio* 30, 20 (Migne PG 36, 129):

Λόγος δέ, ὅτι οὕτως ἔχει πρὸς τὸν Πατέρα, ὡς πρὸς νοῦν λόγος· οὐ μόνον διὰ τὸ ἀπαθὲς τῆς γεννήσεως, ἀλλὰ καὶ τὸ συναφὲς καὶ τὸ ἐξαγγελτικόν.

Several times[223] Melanchthon gives the following quotation:

'Εκ φωτὸς Πατρὸς καταλαμβάνομεν φῶς τὸν Υἱὸν φωτὶ ἁγίῳ Πνεύματι.

This is an almost literal quotation from *Oratio Theologica* V 3:[224]

Καὶ νῦν ἡμεῖς καὶ τεθεάμεθα, καὶ κηρύσσομεν, ἐκ φωτὸς τοῦ Πατρός, φῶς καταλαμβάνοντες τὸν Υἱόν, ἐν φωτὶ τῷ Πνεύματι, σύντομον καὶ ἀπέριττον τῆς Τριάδος θεολογίαν.

The saying that the Son is generated by the thought and selfcontuition of the Father Melanchthon refers, apart from to Augustin and Basil,[225] also to Gregory Nazianzen.[226] Melanchthon may here again have in mind *Oratio* 30, 20 (*Oratio Theol.* IV 20) where Gregory says about the Son as the Image:[227]

Εἰκὼν δὲ ὡς ὁμοούσιον, καὶ ὅτι τοῦτο ἐκεῖθεν, ἀλλ' οὐκ ἐκ τούτου Πατήρ· αὕτη γὰρ εἰκόνος φύσις, μίμημα εἶναι τοῦ ἀρχετύπου.

This would be a very free reference, but equally free is another reference to this chapter in the *Explicatio Symboli Nicaeni*:[228]

Apud Nazianzenum in fine secundae orationis de filio Dei extat brevis declaratio appellationum. Filius unigenitus dicitur, ut discernantur a Christo filii adoptionis. Unicus est autem Filius unigenitus, qui est de essentia Patris, Deus de Deo, Lumen de Lumine. Sed homines renati nominantur filii adoptionis, qui propter unigenitum diliguntur.

Since the fourth (theological) oration is indeed the second one on the Son and since towards the end of it, in chapter 20, Gregory does give a

---

[222] *Declamatio de Gregorio Nazianzeno* (CR 12), p. 283, see further (with minor variations) *Refutatio erroris Serveti*, dating from 1558 (St.A. VI), p. 373, *Quaestio academica*, dating from 1555 (CR 10), p. 849 (cf. p. 882), *Disputatio*, dating from 1554 (CR 12), p. 610 and p. 622 where a longer quotation is twice given in Greek (with some minor variations), *Explic. Symb. Nic.* (CR 23), p. 501, *Postilla Melanchthoniana* (CR 25), p. 18.

[223] See the letter to Strigelius, dating from 1552 (CR 7), p. 1057, letter to Aurifaber and Chytaeus, dating from the same year (CR 7), p. 1068, letter to Strigelius, dating from 1553 (CR 8), p. 191, letter to John Calvin, dating from 1554 (CR 8), p. 362 (here with the qualification that few sentences about the right knowledge of God are found in Gregory).

[224] Migne PG 36, 136.

[225] See *supra*, 29, 42.

[226] *Postilla Melanchthoniana* (CR 25), p. 18: Basilius dicit λόγον nominari, quia nascitur cogitatione Patris. Nazianzenus dicit idem.

[227] Migne PG 36, 129, on the Son as the product of the thought of God see the quotation given *supra*, 61f.

[228] (CR 23), p. 515.

list of Christ's titles this must be meant as a reference to this chapter. But the quotation is very free and comprises additional interpretation. Gregory says:

Δοκεῖ γάρ μοι λέγεσθαι, Υἱὸς μὲν ὅτι ταὐτόν ἐστι τῷ Πατρὶ κατ' οὐσίαν· καὶ οὐκ ἐκεῖνο μόνον, ἀλλὰ κἀκεῖθεν. Μονογενὴς δέ, οὐχ ὅτι μόνος ἐκ μόνου καὶ μόνον, ἀλλ' ὅτι καὶ μονοτρόπως, οὐχ ὡς τὰ σώματα.

Gregory here wants to stress the unique way of generation, which differs from the way in which human beings are generated. The motive which Melanchthon here supposes, viz., that Gregory wants to make clear the difference between the only begotten Son of God and men who can become sons of God through adoption, is absent in Gregory's own words. Melanchthon will have been led to this interpretation by the fact that what he says about the adopted sons and the only begotten Son was also a commonplace in early Christian writers.[229]

The doctrine of creation

In his commentary on Genesis dating from 1523 Melanchthon quotes with approval Gregory as saying:[230]

Nazianzenus bene explicans quod a Basilio dictum est, ait, primo die lucem esse conditam, diffusam passim in totam universitatem mundi, quae postea ceu undique collecta atque coacta sit in solem.

This seems to be a free reference to *Oratio* 44, 4 (Migne PG 36, 609):

Καὶ τοῦτο οὐκ ὀργανικὸν ἀπ' ἀρχῆς ἀναδείξας, οὐδὲ ἡλικόν, ὡς ὁ ἐμὸς λόγος, ἀλλ' ἀσώματον, καὶ ἀνήλιον· ἔπειτα δὲ καὶ ἡλίῳ δοθέν, καταφωτίζειν πᾶσαν τὴν οἰκουμένην.

Melanchthon gives cautious praise to Gregory Nazianzen. He quotes him with approval in connection with the doctrine of free will and of the Trinity, and he once lists him amongst the *scriptores puriores*.[231] Here he takes up a position between Luther and Erasmus. Luther simply says of him: "Nazianzenus est nihil."[232] Erasmus lists him amongst the great exegetes of the Bible.[233] In the edition of the works of Gregory which came out in Basel in 1550 and was re-edited together with the works of

---

[229] See e.g. Irenaeus, *Adv. Haer.* 3, 6, 1, Hilary, *De Trinitate* 6, 23, cf. P. Smulders, *La doctrine trinitaire de S. Hilaire de Poitiers*, Rome 1944, pp. 151ff.

[230] (CR 13), p. 769.

[231] *De restituendis scholis* (St.A. III), p. 113.

[232] *Tischreden* 5, p. 154, he calls him a Wesscher (= Schwätzer) in *Tischreden* 5, p. 415; cf. E. Schäfer, *op. cit.*, p. 174.

[233] *Ratio verae theologiae* (*Erasmi opera omnia*, t. V, ed. J. Clericus), p. 133.

Basil a year later by the same editor, there are a few introductory remarks on Gregory quoted from Erasmus. He praises Gregory's piety and eloquence, but adds that Gregory likes to come forward with difficult *argutiae* and philosophizes about almost inexplicable things. This deterred Erasmus from translating his works into Latin.[234]

GREGORY OF NEOCAESAREA

The doctrine of the Trinity

In his *Explicatio Symboli Nicaeni* Melanchthon repeatedly[235] quotes in connection with the doctrine of the Trinity the Confession of Faith of Gregory of Neocaesarea which appears in Rufinus' Latin translation of Eusebius' *Historia ecclesiastica* VII 25:

> Unus Deus Pater, viventis Verbi, sapientiae subsistentis et imaginis suae integer integrae genitor, Pater Filii unigeniti, unus Dominus, solus ex solo, imago Patris, verbum efficax, Filius sempiternus ex sempiterno, Unus Spiritus sanctus ex Deo substantiam habens qui per Filium apparuit sanctificans, per quem Deus super omnia et in omnibus cognoscitur.

Melanchthon obviously identified himself with Gregory of Neocaesarea: As Gregory opposed Paul of Samosata, so he himself opposes the new Paul of Samosata, *viz.*, Servet.[236]

---

[234] D. Erasmi Roterodami de Gregorio Nazianzeno iudicium: Gregorio Nazianzeno pietas propemodum ex aequo certat cum facundia, sed amat significantes argutias: quas eo difficilius est latine reddere quod pleraeque sunt in verbis sitae ... Adde quod de rebus divinis, quae vix ullis verbis humanis explicari possunt, libenter ac frequenter philosophatur ... Me certe a vertendo Gregorio semper deterruit dictionis argutia, et rerum sublimitas, et allusiones subobscurae. — This quotation is taken from Erasmus' introductory letter to the Latin translation by B. Pirckheymer of Gregory's *Orationes* which came out in Paris in 1532.

[235] (CR 23), p. 363, p. 380, p. 527 (on p. 363 he quotes unus ex uno instead of solus ex solo, — the quotation also appears in the part of the *Enarratio Symb. Nic.* which was written by C. Cruciger (CR 23), p. 220). This is an abbreviated quotation with some variations from Rufinus' text which runs as follows: Unus Deus pater verbi viventis, sapientiae subsistentis et virtutis suae, et figurae, perfectus perfecti genitor, pater filii unigeniti. Unus Dominus, solus ex solo, figura et imago deitatis, verbum perpetrans, sapientia comprehendens omnia, et virtus qua tota creatura fieri potuit. Filius verus veri, et invisibilis ex invisibili, et incorruptibilis ex incorruptibili, et immortalis ex immortali, et sempiternus ex sempiterno. Unus spiritus sanctus, ex Deo substantiam habens, et qui per filium apparuit, imago filii perfecti, perfecta viventium causa, sanctitas sanctificationis praestatrix, per quem Deus super omnia et in omnibus cognoscitur. — See also *Refutatio erroris Serveti et Anabaptistarum* (St.A. VI), p. 369 and *Responsio ad criminationes Staphyli*, dating from 1558 (St.A. VI), p. 465, letter to the Senate of Venice, dating from 1539 (CR 3), p. 749, letter to R. Palatinus, dating from 1539 (CR 3), p. 879.

[236] See the letter to the Princes of Henneberg, dating from 1553 (CR 8), p. 2, *Declamatio de Basilio Episcopo* (CR 11), pp. 678f. On Gregory as an old witness to the doctrine of the

HILARY OF POITIERS

The doctrine of the Trinity

Although Hilary was one of the great defenders of Nicene orthodoxy in the early Church, Melanchthon only quotes him a few times in connection with the doctrine of the divinity of Christ and of the Trinity.

There is a general reference to Hilary when Melanchthon stresses the personal pre-existence of Christ as the Word of God:[237]

> Et Ambrosius et Hilarius dicunt, Filium cum patribus locutum esse.

Melanchthon here obviously has in mind books 5 and 6 of the *De Trinitate*.

There is an explicit quotation from Hilary in the *Annotationes et conciones in Evang. Joannis*:[238]

> Sic Hilarius discernit personas, infinitas in aeterno, libro secundo, species in imagine, usus in munere.

This is a literal quotation from *De Trinitate* 2, 1:

> Nec deesse quicquam consummationi tantae reperietur, intra quam sit in Patre et Filio et Spiritu sancto infinitas in aeterno, species in imagine, usus in munere.

This is a difficult sentence, commented upon by many ever since Augustin.[239] Melanchthon merely quotes it without offering an explanation.

Melanchthon mildly criticizes Hilary's interpretion of *John* 17:3: Ut cognoscant te solum verum Deum, et quem misisti Jesum Christum:[240]

> Hilarius contra Arianos sic interpretatur hanc sententiam, ut cognoscant te et Jesum Christum solum esse verum Deum. Mihi videtur simpliciter locutus esse in hanc sententiam: Ut cognoscant, te solum esse verum Deum, te scilicet, qui Pater es, Filius et Spiritus sanctus.

This is a reference to *De Trinitate* 3, 14 and 9, 32ff., see especially 9, 36:[241]

Trinity see e.g. the letter to Cranmer, dating from 1549 (CR 7), p. 348, letter to Prince Albert, dating from 1549 (CR 7), p. 391.

[237] *Annotationes in Evangelia* (CR 14), p. 177.

[238] (CR 14), p. 1050.

[239] See Augustin, *De Trinitate* 6, 10, 11, see further e.g. Bonaventura, *Breviloquium* 1, 6, 1, 3, Thomas Aquinas, *Summa Theologica* III, qu. 75, art. 1, Petrus Lombardus, *Sent.* I dist. xxxi, 2.

[240] *Annotationes et conciones in Evang. Joannis* (CR 14), p. 1205.

[241] Cf. E. P. Meijering (in close co-operation with J. C. M. van Winden), *Hilary of Poitiers on the Trinity. De Trinitate 1, 1-19, 2, 3*, Leiden 1982, pp. 154f.

> Sed ecclesiae fides solum verum Deum patrem confessa, confitetur et
> Christum. Neque verum Christum Deum confitendo, non et solum verum
> Deum Patrem confitendo: neque rursum solum verum Deum Patrem con-
> fessa, non confitetur et Christum. Per id enim Christum confessa Deum
> verum est, quod solum verum Deum confessa sit Patrem.

It should be noted that Melanchthon's interpretation of this verse
hardly differs from the one given by Hilary. Melanchthon's *simpliciter*
may indicate that he objects more the way in which Hilary reaches his
conclusion (in lengthy discussions with the Arians instead of immediately
grasping the true meaning of the verse) than to Hilary's actual exegesis.

In the context of the doctrine of grace Melanchthon refers with
approval to the fact that Hilary regards the precepts given in the Sermon
on the Mount as *leges necessariae* (and not as *consilia*):[242]

> Hilarius, Exigunt, inquit, Evangelia ulciscendae iniuriae dissimulationem.

This is an abbreviated quotation from Hilary, *Comm. in Matthaeum* 4,
25:

> Atque ita non solum ab iniquitatibus nos abesse evangelia praecipiunt,
> verum etiam ulciscendae iniuriae exigunt dissimulationem.

Although Melanchthon does list Hilary among the *scriptores puriores*[243]
he does not make extensive use of his writings. This is surprising in so far
as both Luther and Erasmus (who edited the *De Trinitate* in 1523) had a
high esteem of him. Luther praises him (and Augustin) because he wrote
excellent things against the heretics about the Trinity and about justification.[244] Erasmus lists him among the important exegetes of the Bible.[245]
He praises his method of exegesis which tries to find out what the Biblical
writers want to say and does not impose preconceived ideas on the
Biblical texts.[246] Of particular importance seems that in the introduction
to his edition of Hilary's *De Trinitate* Erasmus says that Hilary was

---

[242] *Adv. furiosum Parris. Theol. decr.* ... (St.A.), p. 148.

[243] *De restituendis scholis* (St.A. III), p. 113, cf. his letter to the Doctores Iurisconsulti of
Wittenberg, dating from 1521 (CR 1), p. 430: ... Hilarius, vir nulli Episcoporum
occidentalis Ecclesiae secundus.

[244] *Tischreden* 5, p. 154 and p. 414. As a struggler against heresy not even Augustin can
be compared with Hilary, *Tischreden* 2, p. 344.

[245] *Ratio verae theologiae* (*Erasmi opera omnia*, t. V, ed. J. Clericus), p. 133.

[246] *Ratio verae theologiae*, p. 127, the reference is to Hilary, *De Trinitate* 1, 18, see on this
passage E. P. Meijering, *Hilary of Poitiers on the Trinity*, pp. 58ff. In his commentary on
Psalms 1-4 (*Erasmi opera omnia*, t. V, ed. J. Clericus), pp. 117ff. Erasmus frequently refers
to Hilary's *Enarrationes in Psalmos*.

opposed to curiosity, which ought to have been very much to Melanchthon's liking.[247]

As early as 1521 Melanchthon says of Irenaeus that he was in his time the only theologian in the Western Church who was still filled with the Apostolic spirit.[248] The number of passages from Irenaeus which are quoted by Melanchthon are not very large, but some of them appear very often.

The doctrine of Christ and the Trinity

In a letter to Brentius, in 1533, Melanchthon says that Servet interprets Tertullian and Irenaeus wrongly when he tries to draw support from them for his doctrine that the Logos is no entity of His own. Melanchthon claims to have studied Tertullian and Irenaeus diligently on this matter.[249] In the case of Tertullian Melanchthon immediately thought Servet to be mistaken, in the case of Irenaeus he first expressed some doubts, as appears from the letter to Camerarius, written three months before the letter to Brentius.[250] The quotation he gives in the refutation of Servet time and again with minor variations and in various abbreviations is:[251]

---

[247] See Erasmus' edition of Hilary in 1523, pp. aa 4. Erasmus does criticize the harshness of Hilary's polemics against the Arians, pp. bb ff.

[248] *Didymi Faventini adv. Th. Placentinum* (St.A. I), p. 117: Irenaeus, qui vir unus illis temporibus mihi reliquus fuisse videtur in occidentis Ecclesia, qui vere Apostolico spiritu fuerit. Cf. P. Fraenkel, *Testimonia patrum*, p. 84, note 168, p. 179, note 54.

[249] (CR 2), p. 660: Περὶ τοῦ λόγου, εἰ ἔστιν ὑπόστασις, iniuriam facit (sc. Servetus) Tertulliano, et, ut mihi videtur, etiam Irenaeo, diligenter enim horum inquisivi sententias, cf. his letter to the Senate of Venice, dating from 1539 (CR 3), p. 749, cf. P. Fraenkel, *Testimonia patrum*, p. 47.

[250] (CR 2), p. 640: Tertulliano prorsus facit iniuriam ... Irenaeus subobscurus est. — Obviously Melanchthon studied Irenaeus on this matter in the spring of 1533. — According to H. Tollin, *Ph. Melanchthon und Servet. Eine Quellenstudie*, Berlin 1876, pp. 81ff. it is not Servet, but Melanchthon who interprets Irenaeus and Tertullian wrongly, since, as every Patristic scholar now knows, Irenaeus and Tertullian do not provide a Nicene doctrine of the Father and the Son. This statement by Tollin is too rash, — the question is not whether Irenaeus and Tertullian provide Nicene orthodoxy, but whether they teach that the Son is an entity of His own, and Melanchthon is right in saying that they do teach this.

[251] *Loci communes* (1559) (St.A. II), p. 193, *Refutatio erroris Serveti* (St.A. VI), p. 370, *Testimonium Gotho datum* (CR 6), p. 830, letter to Kuntelius, dating from 1548 (CR 7), p. 75, letter to Camerarius, dating from 1548 (CR 7), p. 105, Preface to *De novissimis verbis David*, dating from 1550 (CR 7), p. 582, *Quaestio Academica*, dating from 1557 (CR 10), p. 866, *Declamatio de nativitate Christi*, dating from 1552 (CR 11), p. 1036, *Chronicon Carionis* II

> Ostenso manifeste, quod in principio λόγος existens apud Deum, per quem omnia facta sunt, qui et semper aderat humano generi, hunc novissimis temporibus secundum praefinitum tempus a Patre, unitum suo plasmati, passibilem hominem factum misit.

This is an almost literal quotation from *Adversus Haereses* 3, 19, 1 (ed. Harvey). Another statement made by Irenaeus about "the two natures of Christ" of which Melanchthon was obviously very fond and which he quotes very often is:[252]

> Et Irenaeus erudite et pie inquit pagina 185 Christum crucifixum et mortuum esse requiescente verbo, ut crucifigi et mori posset.

This is a reference to *Adv. Haer.* 3, 20, 3:

> Sicut enim homo erat ut tentaretur: sic et Verbum ut glorificaretur: requiescente quidem Verbo, ut posset tentari, et inhonorari, et crucifigi, et mori, absorpto autem homine in eo quod vincit, et sustinet ... et resurgit, et assumitur.[253]

It should be noted that Melanchthon uses this quotation partly for his doctrine of the forgiveness of sins, whilst in Irenaeus it plays a role in the doctrine of the gift of immortality.[254]

(CR 12), p. 924, *Annotationes in Evangelia*, dating from 1544 (CR 14), p. 177, *Enarratio in Evang. Joannis*, dating from 1546 (CR 15), p. 57, *Explic. Symb. Nic.* (CR 23), p. 363, p. 503, *Postilla Melanchthoniana* (CR 24), p. 117 and (CR 25), p. 554. Melanchthon sometimes says that this quotation can be found in the second chapter of the third book of the *Adversus Haereses*, sometimes that it can be found in the twentieth chapter. The quotation is from the twentieth chapter of the edition of Irenaeus by Erasmus in 1526 (= *Adv. Haer.* 3, 19, 1, ed. Harvey).

[252] We give this quotation after *Loci communes* (1559) (St.A. II), p. 198. (The reference to p. 185 is to Erasmus' edition.) Melanchthon adds an interpretation of his own to this statement of Irenaeus: id est, natura divina non est quidem lacerata aut mortua, sed fuit obediens Patri, quievit, cessit irae aeterni Patris adversus peccatum generis humani, non est usa sua potentia non exeruit suas vires. (This interpretation is also given several times in the passages which have been listed in this note). — For further instances of quotation of this passage from Irenaeus see *Loci communes* (1559) (St.A. II), p. 203, *Responsio de controversiis Stancari*, dating from 1553 (St.A. VI), p. 264 (here the explanation is added: Non ait, naturam divinam mortuam esse, sed quievisse, ut natura assumpta mori posset), *Refutatio erroris Serveti*, dating from 1558 (St.A. VI), p. 374 (here there is a brief reference to the Greek text which is preserved in this section, but which does not appear in Erasmus' edition: ἡσυχάζοντος τοῦ λόγου), letter to Buchholzer, dating from 1552 (CR 7), p. 1093, letter to Collinus, dating from 1554 (CR 8), p. 234, *Chronicon Carionis* II (CR 12), p. 1029 (here in a reference to the Greek text which is given by Theodoretus, *Dialogus III, Impatibilis*, Migne PG 83, 284), *Enarratio in Evang. Joannis*, dating from 1536 (CR 15), p. 81, p. 240, p. 280, p. 373, p. 420, *Explic. Symb. Nic.* (CR 23), p. 371, p. 375, p. 508.
[253] The text in the edition by Erasmus does not differ from the text in Harvey's edition.
[254] See note 252, cf. *infra*, 69.

In connection with the two natures of Christ he once gives the following quotation from Irenaeus:[255]

> Oportebat Mediatorem Dei et hominum per suam ad utrosque cognationem in amicitiam et concordiam utrosque reducere, et facere, ut Deus reciperet hominem, et homo restitueretur Deo. Qua enim ratione Filii adoptionis esse possemus, nisi per Filium, et nisi Verbum caro factum esset, et nostrae naturae sociatum esset?

This is a quotation from *Adv. Haer.* 3, 19, 6 with some alterations:[256]

> Oportuerat enim mediatorem dei et hominum per suam ad utrosque domesticitatem in amicitiam et concordiam utrosque reducere, et facere ut deus assumeret hominem, et homo se dederet deo. Qua enim ratione filiorum adoptionis eius participes esse possemus, nisi per filium eam quae est ad ipsum recepissemus ab eo communionem, nisi verbum eius communicasset nobis, caro factum.

The most important alterations are that Melanchthon gives "homo restitueretur Deo" instead of "et homo se dederet Deo" and that he leaves out "eam quae est ad ipsum recepissemus ab eo communionem"—in both cases the motive may have been to stress God's grace and suppress a possible synergistic interpretation.—There is one possible reference to Irenaeus in connection with the doctrine of the incarnation and the history of salvation:

Melanchthon is confronted with the question what new was brought by Christ if everything of what is said in the New Testament was predicted in the Old Testament. Melanchthon's answer is: He brought Himself and the beginning of a new and eternal Kingdom.[257] There is no explicit reference to Irenaeus here, but in Irenaeus we do find a similar answer to the same question.[258]

---

[255] *Responsio de controversiis Stancari* (St.A. VI), p. 273. It seems very likely that Melanchthon has this passage in mind in his letter to Libius, dating from 1552 (CR 7), p. 1165 where he says that Irenaeus and Chrysostomus say that the Mediator had to be God and man, whilst he himself prefers to say that it was becoming for the Mediator to be God and man: Non utor hac phrasi: *necesse fuit, oportuit* mediatorem esse Deum et hominem, sed utor hac phrasi: *necesse* ... Sed tuo more loquuntur Irenaeus et Chrysostomus, — cf. *supra*, 46.

[256] We give the text from Erasmus' edition, pp. 183f.

[257] *Postilla Melanchthoniana* (CR 25), p. 914: Omnia quae in Novo Testamento dicuntur, prius dicebantur. Quid ergo novi attulit Christus? Respondeo. Attulit se ipsum et inchoationem regni novi et aeterni.

[258] In *Adv. Haer.* 4, 55, Irenaeus shows that the whole life of Christ has been predicted by the prophets. Then he goes on in 4, 56, 1: Si autem subit vos huiusmodi sensus, ut dicatis: Quid igitur novi Dominus attulit veniens? cognoscite, quoniam omnem novitatem attulit semetipsum afferens, qui fuerat annuntiatus. Hoc enim ipsum praedicabatur, quoniam novitas veniet innovatura et vivificatura hominem.

Because of his doctrine of the person of Christ Melanchthon had a high esteem of Irenaeus. Repeatedly he declares that he wants to be in line with Irenaeus.[259] The reason is that Irenaeus' doctrine of the Trinity is based on Scripture.[260] Luther praises Irenaeus for his (doctrine of) faith.[261] Erasmus praises him for his knowledge of the Bible, for the way in which he explains the Catholic faith, but criticizes him for his chiliasm and for certain aspects of his doctrine of the resurrection.[262] In the Preface to his edition of Irenaeus Erasmus says that in his writings the old evangelical vigour is to be found,[263] a view which had been expressed by Melanchthon before Erasmus.[264]

JEROME

Of Jerome Melanchthon says in general that he wrote little about the dogmas.[265] This fact means that he was not so important to Melanchthon as he had been so far to the ecclesiastical tradition (and still was to e.g. Erasmus).

The doctrine of Christ and grace

Jerome is quoted as saying:[266]

> Secundum illud passus est (sc. Christus) quod pati poterat, id est non secundum illam substantiam quae assumsit, sed secundum illam, quae assumta est.

---

[259] *Responsiones ad impios articulos Bav. inquis.*, dating from 1558 (St.A. VI), p. 291: Quare adfirmamus nos nec discedere nec discessisse ... a Patribus, Irenaeo, Ambrosio, Augustino etc., cf. *Responsio ad criminationes Staphyli et Avii* (St.A. VI), p. 464, *Declamatio in Funere Lutheri* (CR 11), p. 728, *Declamatio de maxilla Simsonis*, dating from 1546 (CR 11), p. 745.

[260] *De ecclesia et de autoritate verbi Dei* (St.A. I), p. 337.

[261] See the quotation given *supra*, note 180. On Luther and Irenaeus see also E. Schäfer, *op. cit.*, pp. 176f.

[262] *Enarratio in Psalmum XXXVIII* (*Erasmi opera omnia*, t. V, ed. J. Clericus), p. 432: Irenaeus omnibus disciplinis affatim instructus, et in sacris litteris sic versatus, ut dicas illum nihil aliud scisse, qui sic tractavit rem fidei Catholicae, ut sentias illum amasse quod docuit, tamen prolapsus est in dogma Chiliastarum, nec de resurrectione per omnia docuit quod nunc docet Ecclesia Catholica.

[263] See Erasmus' edition of 1528, p. a 2: Spirant enim illius scripta priscum illum Evangelii vigorem ...

[264] See *supra*, 67, note 248.

[265] *De ecclesia et de autoritate verbi Dei* (St.A. I), p. 357: De dogmatibus pauca scripsit.

[266] *Refutatio erroris Serveti*, dating from 1558 (St.A. VI), p. 374, *Explic. Symb. Nic.* (CR 23), p. 373, the same quotation is given with this addition: mortuus est Dei Filius iuxta Scripturas secundum id quod mori poterat, and p. 509: Nos autem ita dicimus a Dei Filio susceptum esse passibile nostrum, ut Deus impassibilis permaneret.

Melanchthon adds that this sentence can be found in Jerome's confession to Damasus. The quotation is almost literal.[267]

In connection with the doctrine of grace Melanchthon comments on two statements which may be from the Epistle to Demetrias which was ascribed to Jerome and played an important part in the discussions between Catholics and Protestants in the sixteenth century:[268]

> Anathema sit, si quis dixerit Deum impossibilia praecepisse.

And:

> Anathema sit, si quis dicit Legem posse fieri sine gratia.[269]

The first sentence could be a free quotation from *Ep. ad Dem.* 16 (Migne PL 30, 32):

> O caecam insaniam ... Simulque (proh nefas!) ascribimus iniquitatem iusto ... dum eum primo impossibile aliquid praecepisse conquerimur.

The second sentence could be a very free reference to the statement ascribed to the same letter quoted *supra*, 32:

> Nec ob aliud datur praeceptum, nisi ut quaeratur praecipientis auxilium.

Melanchthon does not dispute the authenticity of these words, but tries to explain away the first sentence by saying that this one applies to external actions and was directed against the Manicheans and interprets the second one in a Lutheran way by saying that the grace spoken of is the "gratuita imputatio propter Christum". If our assumption is right that these are free quotations from the letter to Demetrias, then Melanchthon obviously did not further check these quotations, since he ascribes the letter to Ambrose, see *supra*, 32.

For the rest Melanchthon is fairly critical of Jerome's doctrine of sin and grace. There is some praise for his opposition against Pelagianism:[270]

> In dialogo contra Pelagium recte disputat, renovationem non fieri tantum viribus liberi arbitrii, sed opus esse auxilio Spiritus sancti.

This is a reference to *Dialogus contra Pelagianos* 1, 4 (Migne PL 23, 522):

> Non sic donata est liberi arbitrii gratia, ut Dei per singula tollatur adminiculum.

---

[267] The text is to be found in Migne PL 45, 1717.

[268] See H. A. Oberman, *Werden und Wertung der Reformation*, pp. 87f.

[269] See *Loci communes* (1559) (St.A. II), p. 250ff., *Enarratio Symb. Nic.* (CR 23), p. 289, *Explic. Symb. Nic.* (CR 23), pp. 438f., 545ff. But Melanchthon refers to the second sentence also as "to a decree in those times", see *Chronicon Carionis* (CR 12), p. 1017: Extabat illis temporibus decretum illud: Impossibile est legem fieri sine gratia ...

[270] *De ecclesia et de autoritate verbi Dei* (St.A. I), p. 358.

Melanchthon goes on to say:

> Recte etiam negat sanctos esse sine peccato et ponit memorabile dictum: Tunc iusti sumus, quando nos peccatores esse fatemur, et iustitia nostra non ex proprio merito, sed ex Dei misericordia contingit.

This is a reference to *Dial. c. Pel.* 2, 7 (Migne PL 23, 568):

> sic perfectio hominis non ex natura, sed ex gratia veniens, imperfectos eos qui perfecti videntur esse, demonstrat ... manifeste ostendit, non in hominis merito, sed in Dei gratia esse iustitiam qui sine legis operibus credentium suscipit fidem.

and to *Dial. c. Pel.* 1, 19 (Migne PL 23, 535):

> Nullus ergo sanctorum quandiu in isto corpusculo est, cunctas potest habere virtutes? Nullus ...

But Melanchthon criticizes in the same context Jerome's interpretation of sins as actual sins like lust and anger and not as constant interior doubt, carelessness, concupiscence. He says somewhere that Jerome's refution of the Pelagians was too weak.[271] Jerome's views on marriage and celibacy are rejected by Melanchthon.[272] He attacks Jerome's views on ascetism, especially on the drinking of wine and the eating of meat.[273]

The doctrine of creation

Jerome is quoted as the source of information when Melanchthon in his commentary on Genesis refers to the fact that many Fathers explained the beginning in which heaven and earth were created as being the Son. Just like Jerome Melanchthon rejects this interpretation.[274]

---

[271] *Declamatio de vita Hieronymi* (CR 11), p. 741: Pelagianos refutat languidius, cf. *De Erasmo et Luthero elogion* etc., dating from 1522 (CR 20), p. 704: Hieronymus ne in dialogis quidem, aut Pauli commentariis adsequutus est Pauli sententiam.

[272] See *De ecclesia et de autoritate verbi Dei* (St.A. I), p. 357, *Annotationes in priorem Epist. Pauli ad Cor.* (St.A. IV), p. 44. See Jerome, *Adversus Jovianum* I-II (Migne PL 23, 222ff.). In a letter he makes a more qualified remark: he does not deny that chastity is a virtue, but strongly denies that this virtue makes people Christians. He does not want to be regarded as a Christian Epicurean (as Jerome puts it), see CR 1, p. 195: Nolim Jovinianos aut Christianos Epicureos, ut cum Hieronymo loquar, exclames. This is a reference to *Adv. Jovianum* I 1 (Migne PL 23, 221), where Jovian is called the 'Epicurus Christianorum'.

[273] *De ecclesia et de autoritate verbi Dei* (St.A. I), p. 358: Ridicula vox est, quam ponit: Si vis perfectus esse, bonum est vinum non bibere, et carnem non manducare, ubi male detorsit dictum Pauli, qui cum inquit: "Bonum est carnem non edere" addit, si fratri noceat exemplum. This is a reference to *Epist.* XXII 8 (Migne PL 22, 399). But in the *Scholia in Epist. Pauli ad Col.*, dating from 1527, he quotes Jerome's exegesis of *Col.* 2:23 with approval in which Jerome says: ... Paulum ... iubere tribui corpori, quantum satis sit (St.A. IV), p. 260.

[274] *Commentarius in Genesin*, dating from 1523 (CR 13), p. 763: De principio multa fabulati sunt, et pro eo quod est in principio, quidam in Filio legerunt, ut et Hieronymus

Furthermore Jerome is quoted as one of the sources for the explanation of *Genesis* 1:2 which says that the 'ferri' of the Spirit above the water should be interpreted as 'fovere', which shows that it is the Holy Spirit and not any kind of wind.[275]

Melanchthon's attitude towards Jerome was lukewarm, this attitude is summed up in the words with which he concludes his observations on Jerome in his piece of writing *De ecclesia et de autoritate verbi Dei*: "It is obvious that in the writings of Jerome there are many not insignificant errors."[276] In this he is closer to Luther than to Erasmus who—at least for a while—placed Jerome above Augustin.[277]

Ps.-Justin

A manuscript of the piece of writing *Expositio rectae confessionis* (which as we now know was written by Theodoretus of Cyrus under the name of Justin Martyr) was discovered by Melanchthon in 1549. It was useful to him in one aspect:

The doctrine of Christ

The following quotation is given fairly often when Melanchthon wants to explain the relation between the divine nature and the human nature in Christ:

> Aliqui unionem, velut animae ad corpus cogitantes, sic declaraverunt. Id exemplum concinnum quidem est, quanquam non prorsus congruit, sed tamen secundum aliquid congruit.[278]

It is also quoted in Greek:

> τινὲς μὲν ἕνωσιν ὡς ψυχῆς πρὸς σῶμα νοήσαντες, οὕτως ἐκδεδώκασιν, καὶ ἁρμόδιόν γε τὸ παράδειγμα εἰ καὶ μὴ κατὰ πάντα, κατὰ τὶ γοῦν.[279]

---

indicat: nos simplicissime literam sequemur, ut debemus, siquidem ea sola facit ad aedificandam fidem. Principium significat exordium temporis et rerum. See Jerome, *Liber Hebraicarum quaestionum in Genesin* (Migne PL 23, 985ff.): Plerique extimant ... in Hebraeo haberi: "In Filio fecit Deus caelum et terram", quod falsum esse ipsius rei veritas comprobat, see further *infra*, 123ff.

[275] (CR 13), p. 766, see Jerome, *Liber Heb. quaest. in Gen.*, 987f.

[276] (St.A. I), p. 358: Constat igitur multos esse in scriptis Hieronymi non exiguos lapsus.

[277] See *supra*, 30. On Luther and Jerome see also E. Schäfer, *op. cit.*, pp. 181ff.

[278] See *Responsio de controversiis Stancari* (St.A. VI), p. 266.

[279] *Refutatio erroris Serveti* (St.A. VI), pp. 375f. The quotation is also given in Greek in *Disputationes* (CR 12), p. 593, p. 616, p. 649, *Chronicon Carionis* II (CR 12), p. 961, p. 1019, *Examen ordinand.* (CR 23), p. 6, *Explic. Symb. Nic.* (CR 23), p. 510, a brief reference to this statement is given in *Postilla Melanchthoniana* (CR 24), p. 560.

This is a literal quotation from *Expos. rectae conf.* 11.[280]

Melanchthon refers to the fact that as early as this piece of writing the doctrine of the Trinity is expressed in the words οὐσία and ὑποστάσεις.[281] These words do indeed occur in the third chapter of the *Expositio*. Melanchthon shows himself enthusiastic about the discovery of this piece of writing and expresses the hope that it will be edited (perhaps by himself), since it is an old testimony to the doctrine of the Trinity. It seems as if Melanchthon had slight doubts about the authenticity, since he says that the writing is useful *if* it is old.[282]

ORIGEN

As early as 1520 Melanchthon says that not too much attention should be given to Origen and to those who followed his exegesis.[283] The *Loci communes* of 1521 open with an attack on Origen, primarily because of his allegorical exegesis.[284] When the issues with which Melanchthon was concerned widened, he became milder in his judgement of Origen. In his writing *De ecclesia et de autoritate verbi Dei* he lists the following positive aspects of Origen's theology: He is a useful witness on the basis of the Bible and of ecclesiastical writers to the doctrine of the Trinity, the two natures of Christ, infant baptism, original sin, the eucharist, and some other articles of faith.[285] But he opposes him on his doctrine of a plurality of worlds, the finitude of the punishment of the devil and on his doctrine of justification.[286]

---

[280] Migne PG 6, 1225.

[281] See his letter to Camerarius, dating from 1549 (CR 7), p. 489: Inveni hic Justini Martyros libros, in quibus tres pagellae sunt, hoc titulo, ἔκθεσις πίστεως περὶ τῆς ὀρθῆς ὁμολογίας, ἤτοι περὶ τῆς ἁγίας καὶ ὁμοουσίου Τριάδος. diserte loquitur περὶ οὐσίας καὶ ὑποστάσεων et de duabus naturis in Christo nato ex Virgine, and his letter to Baumgartner, dating from 1551 (CR 7), p. 854.

[282] See his letter to Camerarius: Si est vetus scriptum, profecto illustre testimonium est doctrinae Ecclesiasticae. Valde cuperem eas pagellas edi, et familiares fieri piis, and his letter to Baumgartner: Decrevi etiam edere libellum Justini Martyris recens allatum ... ac si antiquum scriptum est, profecto et illustre testimonium.

[283] Letter to Hessus (CR 1), p. 159: Nolo nimium tribuas Origeni, aut qui hunc secuti sunt in enarratione sacrorum, cf. *De Erasmo et Luthero elogion* etc., dating from 1522 (CR 20), pp. 704f.

[284] (St.A. II), pp. 4f.: Ex Origene si tollas inconcinnas allegorias et philosophicarum sententiarum silvam, quantulum erit reliquum? Et tamen hunc auctorem magno consensu sequuntur Graeci et ex Latinis, qui videntur esse columnae, Ambrosius et Hieronymus. On Melanchthon's attack on allegorical exegesis see also *supra*, 33 and 57, cf. also K. Haendler, *op. cit.*, pp. 192ff.

[285] (St.A. I), p. 345: Origenes citans Apostolorum et veterum Ecclesiarum exempla et sententias, est testis utilis posteritati de aliquot articulis: De Trinitate, de duabus naturis in Christo, de baptismo infantum, de peccato originali, de usu coenae Domini et de aliis quibusdam.

[286] (St.A. I), p. 346: Fingit ante hunc mundum fuisse plures mundos, fingit diabolorum et damnatorum poenas cessaturas esse. On his opposition against Origen's doctrine of justification see *infra*, 76ff.

The doctrine of Christ and grace

Origen is one of those ecclesiastical writers who quote the apostles in support of their doctrine of the Trinity.[287] Melanchthon may here be thinking of what Origen says in the Preface to the *De Principiis* (Praef. 4):

> Species vero eorum quae per praedicationem apostolicam manifeste tradun-tur, istae sunt. Primo quod unus est Deus, qui omnia creavit ... Tum deinde quia Christus Jesus, ipse qui venit, ante omnem creaturam natus ex patre est ... Tum deinde honore ac dignitate patri ac filio sociatum tradiderunt spiritum sanctum.

Origen gives testimony to the personal pre-existence of the Logos:[288]

> Nemo putet, inquit, nos ἀνυπόστατον quiddam dicere, cum Dei sapientiam nominamus. Et postea: Si ergo semel et recte receptum est unigenitum Filium Dei sapientiam eius esse substantialiter subsistentem.

These are almost literal quotations from *De principiis* 1, 2, 2.

In his doctrine of "the two natures of Christ" he compares the relation between the two natures of Christ with iron heated by fire:[289]

> Origenes, etsi similitudinem huius coniunctionis propriam afferri posse negat tamen comparat eam ferro ignito. Sicut ignis penetrat ferrum et undi-que ei miscetur, sic λόγος assumens humanam naturam lucet in ea tota, et natura humana velut accensa lumine λόγῳ unita est.

This is a correct summary of what Origen says in *De Principiis* II 6, 6. In connection with the doctrine of sin and grace Origen is useful because he testifies to infant baptism:[290]

> Baptismum infantium constat a veteribus scriptoribus Ecclesiae probari. Nam Origenes et Augustinus scribunt ab apostolis receptum esse.

Elsewhere he states this more exactly:[291]

> Origenes 6. cap. ad Rom. sic scribit: Itaque Ecclesia ab apostolis tradi-tionem accepit etiam parvulis dare Baptismum.

---

[287] *De eccl. et de autoritate verbi Dei* (St.A. I), p. 337.

[288] *Loci communes* (1559) (St.A. II), p. 193.

[289] *Loci communes* (1559) (St.A. II), pp. 193f., in a somewhat altered way the quotation also appears in *Enarr. Symb. Nic.* (CR 23), p. 342: ... utamur hac Origenica umbra, ut fumus in flamma fit ignis, ita utcumque cogitemus arctissimam esse copulationem divinae et humanae naturae.

[290] *Adversus anabaptistas iudicium*, dating from 1528 (St.A. I), p. 281.

[291] *Loci communes* (1559) (St.A. II), p. 514, the same reference already in *De ecclesia et de autoritate verbi Dei* (St.A. I), pp. 327f., and in *Confessio Saxonica*, dating from 1551 (St.A. VI), p. 127.

With a not unusual carelessness Melanchthon says that this quotation can be found in the commentary on the sixth chapter of the Epistle to the Romans, it is in fact in the commentary on the fifth chapter:

> Pro hoc et Ecclesia ab apostolis traditionem suscepit, etiam parvulis baptismum dare.[292]

In his commentary on the Epistle to the Romans from 1532 Melanchthon repeatedly criticizes Origen's views on justification:
In explaining *Rom.* 3:28 Melanchthon says:

> Illud est ridiculum, quod quidam hic interpretantur 'legem operum' legem Mosi, 'legem fidei' legem naturae'.[293]

This is a reference to Origen, *Comm. in Epist. ad Rom.* 3, 9:[294]

> Considera etiam ipse, qui legis, utrum ad legem Moysi et legem naturalem sermo hic debeat inclinari an ad legem litterae et legem spiritus.

In explaining *Rom.* 4:2, 3 Melanchthon criticizes an interpretation which says:[295]

> ... Paulum in hoc testimonio ... simpliciter tribuere fidei iustificationem tamquam bono operi per synecdochen, quod requiratur ad iustificationem cum aliis bonis operibus.

This is a reference to Origen, *Comm. in Epist. ad Rom.* 4, 1:[296]

> Iam sane considerabis, sicut de fide dictum est quia reputata est ei ad iustitiam, ita et de aliis virtutibus dici possit quia, verbi gratia, misericordia unicuique reputari potest ad iustitiam ...

In explaining *Rom.* 5:1 he criticizes Origen in the following way:[297]

> Origenes corrupit lectionem et transformavit evangelii doctrinam in legem hoc modo: Iustificati fide pacem habeamus. Et hic "pacem" interpretatus est de officiis dilectionis erga homines.

This is a fairly free reference to Origen, *Comm. in Epist. ad Rom.* 4, 8.[298]
In explaining *Rom.* 7:1-6 Melanchthon states:[299]

---

[292] Migne PG 14, 1047.

[293] (St.A. V), pp. 118f.

[294] Migne PG 14, 955.

[295] (St.A. V), p. 128, as R. Schäfer observes this criticism reoccurs in *De ecclesia et de autoritate verbi Dei*, p. 346 and in his commentary, dating from 1540 (CR 15), pp. 520f., it appears further in the letter to Cranmer, dating from Jan. 1st 1553 (CR 8), p. 9, *Explic. Symb. Nic.* (CR 23), p. 457.

[296] Migne PG 14, 963.

[297] (St.A. V), p. 156.

[298] Migne PG 14, 989 where Origen says in explaining this text: unum dicamus omnes, eadem sapiamus, nec intra nosmetipsos, nec extrinsecus ad invicem habeatur ulla dissensio (see R. Schäfer's note to the text of Melanchthon (St.A. V), p. 156).

[299] (St.A. V), p. 216, cf. *De ecclesia et de autoritate verbi Dei* (St.A. I), p. 347.

Origenes detorquet haec tantum ad ceremonias.

This is a reference to Origen, *Comm. in Epist. ad Rom.* 6, 7:[300]

> Non enim idcirco Christus nos abstraxit a lege peccati, ut vetustati litterae serviamus, id est ut circumcisionem recipiamus, et Sabbata vel caetera quae vetustas legis litterae continet.

In his writing *De ecclesia et de autoritate verbi Dei* some points of criticism which he expressed in the commentary on the Epistle to the Romans from 1532 are repeated and a few more are added:

Every now and then Origen makes correct statements which he later on again corrupts. Melanchthon approves of Origen when he says:[301]

> Initium iustificationis a Deo est fides, quae credit in iustificantem, et haec fides, cum iustificata fuerit, tanquam radix imbre suscepto haeret in animae solo, ut cum per legem Dei excoli coeperit, surgunt in eo rami, qui fructus operum ferant. Non ergo ex operibus radix iustitiae, sed ex radice fructus operum crescit, illa scilicet radice iustitiae, qua Deus acceptam fert iustitiam sine operibus.

This is an almost literal quotation from *Comm. in Epist. ad Rom.* 4, 1.[302] He also approves of Origen when he says:[303]

> Ubi est gloriatio tua? Videtur iam proprior esse Paulinae sententiae, admittit exclusivam, homines sola fide iustificari, et allegat latronem in cruce et mulierem apud Lucam: "Fides tu salvam te fecit."

This is a correct reference to *Comm. in Epist. ad Rom.* 3, 9:[304]

> Per fidem enim iustificatus est hic latro sine operibus legis ... Sed et mulier illa de qua in Evangelio secundum Lucam refertur ... ex nullo legis opere, sed pro sola fide ait ad eam: "Remittuntur tibi peccata tua" et iterum: "Fides tua te salvam fecit." ...

But Origen spoils this interpretation by adding:[305]

> hominem initio consequi remissionem peccatorum sola fide. Postea iustum esse caeteris virtutibus, sicut ipse postea inquit: Fides reputatur ad iustitiam ei qui convertitur, sed postea iustitia reputatur ad iustitiam.

Melanchthon may here have in mind what Origen says in *Comm. in Epist. ad Rom.* 4, 6:[306]

---

[300] Migne PG 14, 1076.
[301] (St.A. I), p. 346.
[302] Migne PG 14, 965.
[303] (St.A. I), p. 346.
[304] Migne PG 14, 953.
[305] (St.A. I), p. 346.
[306] Migne PG 14, 981f. It is not clear what he means with this praise of Origen when he says (St.A. I), p. 347: In capite septimo clare dicit, Sanctos repraesentare alienam per-

> Et puto quod prima salutis initia, et ipsa fundamenta fides est: profectus
> vero et augmenta aedificii spes est: perfectio autem et culmen totius operis
> charitas ... Et forte per haec singula sicut de fide dictum est, quia fides
> reputatur ad iustitiam, ita et de charitate dici potest, quia reputata est
> charitas ei ad iustitiam, aut pietas, aut misericordia.

Melanchthon opposes Origen when he interprets *Rom.* 3:21 as
meaning:[307]

> sine lege naturali sunt traditae novae leges Evangelicae, ut illa: Nesciat dex-
> tra, quid faciat sinistra. Haec, inquit, lex erat ante ignota.

This is a clear reference to Origen, *Comm. in Epist. ad Rom.* 3, 7:[308]

> Numquid naturaliter potest sentire de illa iustitia quae dicit ... "ut nesciat
> sinistra tua quid faciat dextra tua". Haec et huiusmodi iusta dictare non
> potest lex naturae, et ideo dicit Apostolus: "Nunc autem sine lege",
> naturae scilicet, "iustitia Dei manifestata est."

Melanchthon criticizes Origen's exegesis of *Romans* 8:3:[309]

> Quod erat impossibile legi, quia infirmabatur per carnem, Transfert
> carnem ad legem, Caro legis erat infirma, id est, ceremoniae erant im-
> possibiles, inutiles etc.

This is a clear reference to *Comm. in Epist. ad Rom.* 6, 12:[310]

> Ipse (sc. intellectus) enim et impossibilis erat, et infirmus, si secundum
> carnem, id est secundum litteram sentiretur. Quid enim tam impossibile
> quam Sabbati observatio secundum litteram legis.

Melanchthon's rejection of Origen's interpretation of the doctrine of
justification through faith leads him to very harsh criticism of Origen:
His writings and those of Pelagius corrupted the purity of the Gospel.[311]
As a Reformer Melanchthon opposed Origen right from the beginning
because of his speculations and moralism. He mitigated under the
influence of the controversy with the anti-trinitarians his criticism of

---

sonam, cum sibi tribuunt peccatum. This is a reference to Origen, *Comm. in Epist. ad Rom.*
VI 9 (Migne PG 14, 1089f.), but Origen says this in connection with his doctrine that sin
can be overcome through conversion and he takes this fact as an example that saints can
look back on their previous life, — and this is a doctrine to which Melanchthon is completely opposed.

[307] (St.A. I), p. 347, cf. *Enarratio in Epist. Pauli ad Rom.*, dating from 1556 (CR 15), pp.
860f.

[308] Migne PG 14, 943.

[309] (St.A. I), p. 347.

[310] Migne PG 14, 1094.

[311] *Confessio Saxonica* (St.A. VI), p. 95, *Articuli Protestantium Caesari traditi* (CR 4), p. 350:
Pelagius drew his ideas from Origen, Preface to the second volume of Luther's works (CR
6), pp. 166f., *Annotationes in Evangelia* (CR 14), p. 296, *Declamatio de vita Augustini* (CR 11),
p. 453.

Origen's speculations, but he remained completely opposed to Origen's moralism. Amongst the early Christian writers Origen was regarded by Melanchthon as one of the greatest enemies of the Gospel. Melanchthon is here in line with Luther,[312] but differs sharply from Erasmus.[313] To Erasmus Origen was (one of) the greatest interpreters of the Bible.[314]

TERTULLIAN

The doctrine of Christ and grace

Tertullian's doctrine about the person of Christ is according to Melanchthon important, because it goes back to the Apostles.[315] Melanchthon here has in mind that Tertullian says of the *regula fidei* which he quotes in *Adversus Praxean* 2 that it goes back right to the beginning of the preaching of the gospel: Hanc regulam ab initio evangelii decucurrisse.[316]

Against Servet Melanchthon points out repeatedly that Tertullian taught the personal pre-existence of the Logos:[317]

Nam Tertullianus adversus Praxeam expresse movet hanc quaestionem, an λόγος sit natura subsistens seu (ut nunc dicimus) persona, et respondet affir-

---

[312] See e.g. *Tischreden* 1, p. 106: Origenem hab ich schon in bann getan, p. 136: In toto Origene non est verbum unum de Christo; see further E. Schäfer, *op. cit.*, pp. 171f.

[313] Cf. J. D. Tracy, *Erasmus, The Growth of a Mind*, pp. 101f.

[314] *Enchiridion* (*Erasmi opera omnia*, t. V, ed. J. Clericus), p. 8, *Ratio verae theologiae* (*Erasmi opera omnia*, t. V), p. 133: Imo partem laboris adimat nobis veterum labor, adiuvemur illorum commentariis, dummodo primum ex his deligamus optimos velut Origenem, qui sic primus, ut nemo cum illo conferri possit. When criticism of Origen is voiced by Erasmus, it is often in order to show that even the greatest can fail. It is interesting that Erasmus once says that where Origen failed this was due to Platonic philosophy, see *Enarratio in Psalmum* XXXVIII (*Erasmi opera omnia*, t. V, ed. J. Clericus), p. 432: Magnus ecclesiae doctor fuit Origenes, de cuius fontibus ferme Graecorum ingenia sunt irrigata: ad haec martyris filius, ipse martyrii candidatus: sed quam multa in huius viri scriptis leguntur plusquam haeretica. Ruinae occasio fuit philosophia Platonica. — See also the way in which Erasmus explains historically Origen's allegorical exegesis of all Old Testament texts, *De Ratione concionandi* (*Erasmi opera omnia*, t. V, ed. J. Clericus), p. 1029. W. Maurer, *Historischer Kommentar zur CA*, 1, pp. 62f., supposes that when Origen is not included in the list of heretics given in the text of the CA which was sent to Nuremberg on June 15th 1530 this was done in order not to offend Erasmus and his friends, see also p. 66.

[315] *De ecclesia et de autoritate verbi Dei* (St.A. I), p. 337: Ut de Trinitate citant eos (sc. apostolos) Origenes, Tertullianus ... qui cum testentur doctrinam de Trinitate ab Apostolis acceptam esse, valde confirmant pios, p. 349: Continet (sc. Tertullianus) utilia testimonia de Trinitate, recitans non suam sententiam, sed veterem acceptam ab Apostolis.

[316] *Adv. Prax.* 2, 2, this statement must be seen in connection with Tertullian's tenet (of which Melanchthon approves), that in matters of faith the old is true, see on this *infra*, 92f.

[317] *Loci communes* (1559) (St.A. II), p. 192, cf. *Refutatio erroris Serveti* (St.A. VI), pp. 369f., Letter to the Senate of Venice (CR 3), p. 749, *Enarratio in evangelium Joannis* (CR 15), p. 57, *Postilla Melanchthoniana* (CR 24), p. 867.

mans esse personam seu ὑπόστασιν, et hanc sententiam longa oratione exponit, in qua haec sunt verba: Quaecumque ergo substantia sermonis fuit,
illam dico personam et illi nomen Fillium agnosco et secundum a Patre
defendo.

This is an almost literal quotation from *Adv. Prax.* 7, 9.

But Melanchthon also expresses criticism of Tertullian's doctrine of
Christ:[318]

Tertullianus male loquitur, cum inquit ad Ethnicos: Vos colitis Deum per
Orphea, Iudaei per Mosen, nos per Christum. Et addit: Sicut vos dicitis,
Fatum esse sapientiam Dei: Sic nos dicimus, λόγον esse consilium Dei.

The first quotation is a free one from *Apologeticum* 21, 29:

(Deum colimus per Christum ...) Ut Iudaeis respondeam, et ipsi Deum per
Moysen colere didicerunt, ut Graecis occurram, Orpheus Prieriae,
Musaeus Athenis ... initiationibus homines obligaverunt.

The second quotation is a free one from *Apologeticum* 21, 10f.:

Apud vestros quoque sapientes λόγον, id est sermonem atque rationem,
constat artificem videri universitatis ... eundem et fatum vocari et deum et
animum Iovis et necessitatem omnium rerum ... Et nos autem sermonem
atque rationem ... per quae omnia molitum Deum ediximus, propriam
substantiam spiritum adscribimus.

One of the reasons why Melanchthon criticizes these statements made
by Tertullian is that in saying this he confuses, just like Paul of Samosata,
the Logos with the Idea of the Platonists.[319] Perhaps Melanchthon was
unaware of the serious implications of this criticism. According to him
Servet is the Paul of Samosata of his own days, and according to
Melanchthon Servet wrongly wants to draw support from Tertullian for
his rejection of Christ's pre-existence. If, however, Tertullian, just like
Paul of Samosata, identifies Christ with the Platonic Idea, then Servet
does have a point in seeking support in the writings of Tertullian.

In connection with the doctrine of grace Melanchthon quotes a few
times:[320]

---

[318] *Postilla Melanchthoniana* (CR 24), p. 463, cf. p. 774 where Tertullian is quoted as
saying: Quare vos ethnici obiurgatis nos quod Deum invocemus per Christum, cum
tamen toleretis Iudaeos per Mosen, et non vituperetis Thraces invocantes per Orphea,
Graecos per Musaeum.

[319] *Postilla Melanchthoniana* (CR 24), p. 463: Ita Samosatenus Platonicorum Ideam
voluit conciliare cum λόγῳ. On p. 774 his criticism is that then Christ is no more than a
Legislator and Teacher.

[320] *Postilla Melanchthoniana* (CR 24), p. 503, letter to Libius, dating from 1560 (CR 9),
p. 1045 (here the first line is correctly quoted: Si apud Deum deposueris iniuriam, ipse
ultor est, in the same way the quotation is given in the Preface to the *Corpus doctrinae christianae*, dating from 1560 (CR 9), p. 1055.

Si deposueris apud Deum tristitiam, ipse consolator est: si damnum restitutor est: si dolorem medicus est: si mortem resuscitator est.

With the exception of the first line, which in Tertullian is: si iniuriam deposueris penes eum, ultor est, this is an almost literal quotation from *De patientia* 15, 1.

In his defence of the doctrine that sin is a corruption of human nature and lack of faith and fear God, he refers with approval to the following words of Tertullian which lift up the conscience:[321]

Bonum est paenitere an non? quid revolvis? Deus praecipit! At ille non praecipit tantum, sed etiam hortatur, invitat praemio salutis, iurans etiam: Vivo dicens, cupit credi sibi. O beatos, quorum causa Deus iurat. O miserrimos, si nec iuranti Domino credimus.

This is an almost literal quotation from *De paenitentia* 4, 7.—The second half of this passage is quoted in order to show that Tertullian supports the Lutheran doctrine of faith:[322]

(Nam Tertullianus egregie de fide liquitur ... Sic enim ait Tertullianus:) Invitat praemio salutis etc.

Although Melanchthon finds a number of useful quotations in him, Tertullian is amongst the early Christian writers of secondary importance to Melanchthon.

THEODORETUS

The doctrine of Christ

In the *Refutatio erroris Serveti* Melanchthon quotes Theodoretus as saying:[323]

κατὰ τὴν πρόσληψιν σαρκὸς ἐσταύρωται.

This is an abbreviated quotation from Theodoretus, *Dialogus* II (Inconfusus):[324]

'Αλλ' ἐπειδὴ οὗτος θεός τε καὶ ἄνθρωπος, κατὰ μὲν τὴν θεότητα θεός, κατὰ δὲ τὴν πρόσληψιν τῆν σαρκὸς ἄνθρωπος 'Ιησοῦς Χριστὸς ὁ Κύριος τῆς δόξης ἐσταυρῶσθαι λέγεται.

---

[321] *Disputationes* (CR 12), p. 505.
[322] *Apol. Conf. Aug.* B (CR 27), p. 553.
[323] (St.A. VI), p. 374, the reference is to p. 42 of Theodoretus, this applies to *Theodoreti Episcopi Cyri Dialogi tres contra quasdam Haereses*, Romae 1546.
[324] Migne PG 83, 185.

In defending the doctrine of the *communicatio idiomatum* he gives the following quotations:[325]

κοινὰ τοῦ προσώπου γέγονε τὰ τῶν φύσεων ἴδια.

and:

οὐ σύγχυσιν εἰργάσατο τῶν φύσεων ἡ κοινότης τῶν ὀνομάτων.

These are literal quotations from *Dialogus* III (Impatibilis).[326]

Theodoretus was obviously not very important to Melanchthon. It seems that he became acquainted with him rather late, after the edition of some of his works in 1546. Melanchthon may have liked him, because Theodoretus was a clear traditionalist, just like Melanchthon himself, and because he presented his readers with quotations from ecclesiastical authorities in earlier times.

VIGILIUS

The doctrine of Christ

In connection with the doctrine that Christ died in his human nature the following quotation is given:[327]

> Ipse igitur unus idemque Dei Filius, Dominus Jesus Christum mortuus est secundum formam servi, et non est mortuus secundum formam Dei.

This is a literal quotation from *Contra Eutychem* IV 5.[328]
On Christ who is the Mediator as God and man the following quotations are given:[329]

> 1) Talis hostia requirebatur, quae ita media esset inter Deum et homines, ut et morti succumberet per illud, quod hominis habebat, et mortem vinceret, eo quod divinitatem in se tenebat.

This is an almost literal quotation from *Contra Eutychem* V 15.[330]

> 2) Nisi talis Mediator existeret, qui de coelestibus veniens couniretur terrenis. Unde etiam medius erit, si utrumque non habuerit, quia nisi talem

---

[325] *Refutatio erroris Serveti* (St.A. VI), p. 375. The reference is to p. 67 and p. 68 in the edition quoted in the previous note. The first one of these two quotations is also given in *Chronicon Carionis* (CR 12), p. 1029.

[326] Migne PG 83, 277.

[327] *Resp. de controversiis Stancari* (St.A. VI), p. 263.

[328] Migne PG 62, 121. There is a reference to this statement in *Explic. Symb. Nic.* (CR 23), p. 373.

[329] *Resp. de contr. Stanc.* (St.A. VI), pp. 273f.

[330] Migne PG 62, 145. The second passage is also quoted by Petrus Lombardus, *Sent.* III, dist. xix, cap. 7, 2.

dederis inter Deum et homines, ut ex utroque utrumque sit, id est, ut et
Deus sit propter divinitatis, et idem homo propter humanitatis naturam,
humana divinis quemadmodum reconcilientur, non ostendis.

This is an almost literal quotation from the same passage, with this
alteration that the first sentence quoted by Melanchthon is given by
Vigilius not before but after the second one.

Conclusions

The conclusion of our survey is that Melanchthon refers to Patristic
sources fairly often, but that he repeatedly comes forward with the same
quotations. We feel entitled to draw this conclusion despite the fact that
we do not claim to have provided an exhaustive list of the Patristic quotations in Melanchthon. We believe we have given not only the most important quotations, but also the majority of quotations in connection with
the doctrine of the Trinity, christology and creation, and free will. There
are a substantial number of quotations in connection with ethics and the
eucharist which have not been dealt with, and we leave the possibility
open that we have overlooked a number of quotations in the fields we are
concerned with, but we do not believe that those quotations would alter
the picture significantly. It seems very likely that he had collected quotations under various headings and tended to produce them as soon as that
particular subject was raised. He presents himself as a teacher who wants
to provide his readers and listeners with *perspicua brevitas*: a few clear
quotations from the Fathers are enough to lend authority to what
Melanchthon says.—He collected his quotations with a certain
carelessness. Often they are not literal, sometimes they are given in such
a way that they become closer to Melanchthon's own views, sometimes in
such a way that the difference between Melanchthon and the source
quoted becomes greater than it in fact is.

One cannot say that an increasing knowledge of the Fathers influenced
Melanchthon's theology, e.g. in accordance with the appearance of
Erasmus' editions of the various Fathers. Around the time of the first edition of the *Loci communes* Melanchthon betrays knowledge not only of the
Latin but also of the Greek Fathers. When in the course of his life
theological developments influenced Melanchthon's thought on various
issues these developments also made him look for more and other quotations from the Fathers which suited him. First the quotations centred
around the doctrine of grace and human will, later on also around the
doctrine of the Trinity and the person of Christ, and once he had
modified his views on grace and human will Greek Fathers are also

quoted in support of his views on this subject.[331] Sometimes the quotations are well known, in the sense that they had often been produced by earlier Christian writers,[332] sometimes they were also given by others in the theological discussions of Melanchthon's days.[333]

It is well known that Melanchthon's theological position was somewhere in between Luther and Erasmus (though closer to Luther). This also appears from his evaluation of the Fathers. Greek Fathers like Basil, Gregory Nazianzen, and Chrysostomus are judged much more positively by Melanchthon than by Luther, and in this respect the influence of Erasmus may be detected. But like Luther Melanchthon makes the doctrine of grace the overriding criterion in his judgement, and this leads him to harsh criticism of e.g. Origen who was greatly admired by Erasmus. To Erasmus the 'subjective' side of the Fathers is very important, primarily their eloquence and piety, to Melanchthon they are witnesses of the pure evangelical doctrine.[334] This also means that their authority is subjected to the authority of the Bible.[335]

As we have seen,[336] some contradiction can be detected in Melanchthon: he claims to reproduce the consent of the early Christian Fathers and he admits that the Fathers often contradict each other. In the context

---

[331] The steady growth in the number of quotations has rightly been called "expansion rather than fundamental change" by P. Fraenkel, *Testimonia Patrum*, p. 44.

[332] Cf. *supra*, 29, 65, 79.

[333] Cf. *infra*, 133ff.

[334] Instances of praise of the 'subjective' side of the Fathers are fairly limited in Melanchthon. The following examples may be given: In the *Epistula de Lipsica disputatione*, from 1519 (St.A. I), p. 6 he refers to Gregory Nazianzen who says that discussions should be held in a quiet and peaceful way (and Melanchthon in this respect compares Gregory with Erasmus), this is a possible reference to Gregory's letter CXXX (to Procopius), see Migne PG 37, 225, a letter to which Melanchthon refers explicitly in his *Declamatio de Gregorio Nazianzeno* (CR 12), pp. 282f. See also his words of praise for Gregory in his *Declamatio* on him p. 283: ... vita ... exemplum est viri modesti, non discedentis ab officio propter iniurias, amantis veritatem et pacem (these words are significantly followed by a much larger enumeration of his *testimonia* of orthodoxy). Of Ambrose he says in his *Declamatio* about him (CR 11), p. 598: ... coelestibus donis pie usus est ... Quare adolescentes et pietatem et studia Ambrosii imitamini. But the following warning is also given in this context: Nec tantum exempla actionum nos invitant ad virtutis studium, ad constantiam, ad pudicitiam. Haec a multis sumi possunt: sed singulorum controversiae erudiunt posteritatem, et vox piorum quorum iudicia comprobata sunt testimoniis divinis, valde confirmat imbecilliores. Similarly he says of Basil in his *Declamatio* about him (CR 11), p. 682: Recitavi res gestas, in quibus et genus doctrinae conspicitur, et lucent Basilii virtutes multae ... Fides quae est omnium virtutum mater in genere doctrinae et constantia confessionis cernitur, and of Jerome in his *Declamatio* about him (CR 11), p. 741: Studium vero et constantiam voluntatis in bonis consiliis et tolerantiam virorum imitemur ... Talis cum fuerit Hieronymus ... (In the *Declamationes* the humanistic side of Melanchthon is manifest.) See on this matter also P. Fraenkel, *Testimonia patrum*, p. 240.

[335] See *supra*, 7ff.

[336] See *supra*, 10.

of the latter view he makes the fine observation that everybody can draw from the Fathers what seems to suit him, just like bees collect honey and spiders venom out of the same flowers.[337] Melanchthon himself certainly had the idea that he collected honey out of the writings of the various Fathers. It is interesting to see that when he attacks the Eclectics in philosophy he uses the same image of the bees and the honey and rejects this kind of eclecticism, but concedes that this method is valid as long as one chooses under the guidance of God's light just as the bees under the guidance of nature avoid venom.[338] The implication of this is that he regards it as legitimate to collect under the guidance of God's truth quotations from the Fathers which testify to the truth. But doing this differs from presenting any *consensus* of the Fathers. Melanchthon used the Fathers as an eclectic who chooses what suits his purpose and who ignores or rejects what does not. Melanchthon's use of the Fathers shows that he does not reproduce any kind of Patristic *consensus*. As Melanchthon was aware himself that *consensus* did not exist and the claim that he reproduces it was made for apologetic purposes:[339] With this claim he wanted to counter the Catholic accusation that the Reformers came forward with heretical novelties.

Melanchthon often gives the same quotations, and he gives them with considerable freedom and not seldom even carelessness, and this is understandable: Melanchthon did not try to analyse the thoughts of the Fathers, but used the Fathers in support of his own doctrine. This fact does not, however, entirely excuse his carelessness, since Melanchthon himself once accuses one of his opponents of not quoting Luther exactly and with precise reference, and of doing so out of fear of being refuted.[340]

---

[337] *De ecclesia et de autoritate verbi Dei* (St.A. I), p. 376: Et excerpit pro suo adfectu quisque, quod videtur commodum, ut ex eisdem floribus apes mella legunt, araneae venena.

[338] *Erotemata Dialectices* (CR 13), p. 656: Sed clamant aliqui, ut apes ex magna varietate florum succos colligunt, ita doctrinam ex variis sectis excerpendam esse. Hi refutandi sunt hoc ipso exemplo, ut enim apes natura duce vitant venena, ita nos praelucente Deo, vitemus falsas opiniones. Melanchthon here uses a commonplace in ancient writers, see e.g. Lucrece, *De rerum natura* 3, 11-12: floriferis ut apes in saltibus omnia libant,/ omnia nos itidem depascimur aurea dicta, cf. C. Bailey, *T. Lucreti De rerum natura libri VI*, volume II, Oxford 1963⁴, p. 989 and J. H. Waszink, *Biene und Honig als Symbol des Dichters und der Dichtung in der griechisch-römischen Antike*, Rheinisch-Westfälische Akademie der Wissenschaften, Vorträge G 196, 1974, pp. 22f. Melanchthon probably found this comparison in Basil, *Sermo de legendis libris gentilium* 3 (Migne PG 31, 570): Κατὰ πᾶσαν δὴ οὖν τῶν μελιττῶν τὴν εἰκόνα τῶν λόγων ὑμῖν μεθεκτέον. Ἐκεῖναί τε γὰρ οὔτε ἅπασι τοῖς ἄνθεσι παραπλησίως ἐπέρχονται, οὔτε μὴν οἷς ἂν ἐπιπτῶσιν ὅλα φέρειν ἐπιχειροῦσιν, ἀλλ᾿ ὅσον αὐτῶν ἐπιτήδειον πρὸς ἐργασίαν λαβοῦσαι, τὸ λοιπὸν χαίρειν ἀφῆκαν. Melanchthon knew this piece of writing by Basil as appears from *Explicatio Sententiarum Theognidis* (CR 19), p. 57: Scitis extare libellum Basilii quomodo sint legendi ethnici scriptores.

[339] Cf. F. W. Kantzenbach, *Evangelium und Dogma. Die Bewältigung des theologischen Problems der Dogmengeschichte im Protestantismus*, Stuttgart 1959, p. 37, and K. Haendler, *op. cit.*, pp. 83ff., 223ff.

[340] *Did. Faventini adv. Th. Placentinum* (St.A. I), p. 133: Nam quod quaedam e Lutheri

The fairly limited number of quotations does not in itself point towards a clearly limited knowledge of the Fathers, since—consciously or un-consciously—he could have reproduced in his writings what he had read in the Fathers without giving names.

ADDENDA

Before we try to analyse how the authority of the Fathers functioned in the theology of Melanchthon two complex questions have to be dealt with. It is Melanchthon's view that Scripture is the only authority for the Christian believers, the Pope has no authority, Medieval theology is to a large degree a corruption of the truth and the Fathers are to a certain degree witnesses of the truth. Melanchthon tries to draw support from the Fathers for his view that Scripture is the exclusive authority, and that the ecclesiastical tradition must be judged after Scripture. This is the first question we want to deal with: How does he draw his support from the Fathers in this respect? The second question is how Melanchthon quoted and judged Medieval theologians in connection with the doctrine of Christ and grace, the Trinity and the creation.

A. PATRISTIC TESTIMONIES FOR MELANCHTHON'S VIEWS ON THE AUTHORITY OF THE POPE, THE ECCLESIASTICAL TRADITION AND SCRIPTURE

Ambrose

According to Melanchthon Luther explained "Tu es Petrus et super hanc petram" etc. in the same way as amongst others Ambrose.[341] This explanation says that Jesus was speaking to all apostles, the whole church,[342] and that the rock is Peter's and the whole church's faith.[343] Melanchthon here obviously has in mind Ambrose, *Expos. in Lucam* VI 93 (Migne PL 15, 1780):

> Et ideo licet caeteri apostoli sciant, Petrus tamen respondit prae ceteris: Tu es Christus ...

and *Expos. in Lucam* VI 98 (Migne PL 15, 1781):

> Petra tua fides est, fundamentum Ecclesae fides est.

---

scriptis citas et obscure et improbe citas, ut qui nec locum adscripseris, unde petisti, nec integram retuleris sententiam, ne, si candide citares, nihil ad rem facere videretur quod producis. — This criticism can not seldom be made of Melanchthon himself.

[341] *Defensio contra Joh. Eckium* (St.A. I), p. 19, see also *De potestate Papae*, dating from 1537 (CR 3), p. 277.

[342] See *Resolutio Lutheriana super propositione XIII de potestate Papae* (W.A. 2), p. 188.

[343] (W.A. 2), p. 190.

AUGUSTIN

Augustin confirms Luther's explanation of "Tu es Petrus" etc.[344] Melanchthon here has obviously in mind *Sermo* LXXVI 1, 1 (Migne PL 38, 479):[345]

> Unus pro multis dedit (sc. Petrus) responsam, unitas in multis ... Hoc autem ei nomen, ut Petrus appellaretur, a Domino impositum est: et hoc in ea figura ut significaret ecclesiam. Quia enim Christus petra, Petrus populus christianus.

Augustin places Scripture above later Christian authors:[346]

> (Divus Augustinus contra Donatistas ait), Scripturam Canonicam veteris ac novi omnibus posterioribus litteris ita praeponi, ut de ea dubitari ac disceptari non possit, utrum verum vel utrum rectum sit, quidquid in ea scriptum esse constiterit. (Et paulo post:) Concilia, quae per singulas regiones vel provincias fiunt, plenariorum conciliorum autoritati, quae fiunt ex universo orbi christiano, sine ullis ambagibus cedere ipsaque plenaria saepe priora posterioribus emendari. (Vides quid scripturae, quid conciliis tribuat Augustinus, haec enim labi posse fatetur, de illa vero dubitare nefas censet.)

These are almost literal quotations from *De baptismo contra Donatistas* II 3, 4 (Migne PL 43, 128). The following quotation must prove the same:[347]

> Et Augustinus contra Petiliani Epistolam inquit, Nec catholicis Episcopis consentiendum est, sicubi forte falluntur, aut contra canonicas Dei scripturas aliquid sentiunt.

This does not appear in the *Libri contra Litteras Petiliani*, it seems to be a reference to *De baptismo contra Donatistas* II 3, 4, as well.

In the same context Melanchthon refers to the fact that according to Augustin not men but Christ speaks with authority in the Church:[348]

> Quaestio est, Ubi sit Ecclesia? quid ergo facturi sumus? In verbis nostris eam quaesituri sumus, an in verbis capitis sui, Domini nostri Jesu Christi?

---

[344] See *supra*, notes 341 and 342, cf. P. Fraenkel, Quelques observations sur le "Tu es Petrus" chez Calvin, au Colloque de Worms en 1540 et dans l'*Institution* de 1543, *Bibliothèque d'Humanisme et de Renaissance, Travaux et Documents*, Genève 1965, p. 610, p. 617.

[345] According to Melanchthon Augustin says this 'in homilia'.

[346] *Declamatiuncula in divi Pauli doctrinam* (St.A. I), p. 50, cf. P. Fraenkel, *Testimonia Patrum*, p. 17, n. 30.

[347] *Conf. Aug.* (CR 26), p. 324, cf. p. 407, *Conf. Aug.* (Variata) (St.A. VI), p. 74.

[348] *De ecclesia et de autoritate verbi Dei* (St.A. I), p. 336.

> Puto quod in illius verbis quaerere debemus, quia veritas est et optime novit
> corpus suum.

This is a quotation from *De unitate ecclesiae* (Migne PL 43, 392).

There is one statement made by Augustin in this context which causes Melanchthon clear difficulties:

> Evangelio non crederem, nisi me Ecclesiae Catholicae commoveret autoritas.[349]

Melanchthon repeatedly struggles with this statement.[350] He says that Augustin does not mean that the church has more authority than Scripture or that the church can abolish articles of faith which belong to Biblical tradition, but that the church teaches and testifies to the Gospel. We could not believe the Gospel if the church did not teach us and testified that this doctrine finds its origin in the apostles.[351]—It seems as if Melanchthon is to a certain degree right in this interpretation, for Augustin does say in that context: "ipsi evangelio Catholicis praedicantibus credidi", but he also says: "quibus praecipientibus Evangelio credidi", and: "utramque Scripturam similiter mihi catholica commendat auctoritas".

BASIL

Basil bases his doctrine of the Trinity on Scripture, hereby clearly indicating his belief in the authority of the Bible.[352] Against the novelties of heresy the church needs according to Melanchthon certain fences of protection, these are the testimonies received from the apostles and certain later authors (whose orthodoxy cannot be doubted). In this context Melanchthon refers amongst others to Basil, who received his faith from his grandmother and nurse who instructed him in the doctrine she had received from Gregory of Neocaesarea, who refuted Paul of Samosata

---

[349] *Contra epistulam Man.* 5, 6. See on this subject extensively P. Fraenkel, *Testimonia Patrum*, pp. 228ff., cf. also F. W. Kantzenbach, *Das Ringen um die Einheit der Kirche im Jahrhundert der Reformation*, p. 104, J. N. Bakhuizen van den Brink, Traditio in de Reformatie en het Katholicisme in de zestiende eeuw, pp. 37f., and S. Wiedenhofer, *op. cit.*, p. 292.

[350] See e.g. *De ecclesia et de autoritate verbi Dei* (St.A. I), p. 326, p. 339, *Disputatio* (dating from 1531) (CR 12), pp. 482ff., *Quaestiones Academicae* (CR 10), pp. 726f.

[351] (St.A. I), p. 339: Non sentit Augustinus, maiorem esse ecclesiae autoritatem quam verbi divini, aut ecclesiam posse abolere articulos in verbo Dei traditos, sed sentit Ecclesiam esse doctricem et testem. Non crederemus Evangelio, nisi ecclesia doceret nos, et testaretur, hanc doctrinam ab Apostolis traditam esse.

[352] See the quotations given *supra*, 44.

and who wrote a confession of faith in the Trinity (and whose orthodoxy was therefore beyond doubt): [353]

> Basilius allegat nutricem suam cuius pietatem ait tunc in primis fuisse laudatam, et addit eam accepisse doctrinam a Gregorio Neocaesarensi, qui illo tempore eruditione et miraculis claruit, et refutavit Samosatenum, ac reliquit brevem confessionem fidei quae continet illustre testimonium de Trinitate.

This is a reference to *Epistola* CCIV 6 (Migne PG 32, 752f.):

> Πίστεως δὲ τῆς ἡμετέρας τίς ἂν καὶ γένοιτο ἐναργεστέρα ἀπόδειξις ἢ ὅτι τραφέντες ἡμεῖς ὑπὸ τίτθῃ μακαρίᾳ γυναικί, παρ' ὑμῶν ὡρμημένῃ; Μακρίναν λέγω τὴν περιβόητον, παρ' ἧς ἐδιδάχθημεν τὰ τοῦ μακαριωτάτου Γρηγορίου ῥήματα, ὅσα πρὸς αὐτὴν ἀκολουθίᾳ μνήμης διασωθέντα αὐτή τε ἐφύλασσε, καὶ ἡμᾶς ἔτι νηπίους ὄντας ἔπλαττε καὶ ἐμόρφου τοῖς τῆς εὐσεβείας δόγμασιν. [354]

Melanchthon makes Basil establish the general rule that in the church doctrines have to be put forward which are clearly taught by Scripture and do not conflict with the Fathers: [355]

> Et inquit (sc. Basilius) in Ecclesia dogmata esse proponenda, quae Scripturae Apostolicae certo tradunt,m et quae non pugnant cum patribus.

CHRYSOSTOMUS

Chrysostomus is quoted in order to prove that the "super hanc petram" etc. does not refer to the person of Peter, but to his confession of faith: [356]

---

[353] *De ecclesia et de autoritate verbi Dei* (St.A. I), p. 327, cf. S. Wiedenhofer, *op. cit.*, pp. 275f. For Basil's dependence on Gregory see also *Alloquia et breves conciones* (CR 10), p. 1005 and *De dignitate studii theol.* (CR 11), pp. 326f., especially 327: Tantum autem ei (sc. Gregorio) tribuit Basilius, ut dicat sibi adhuc personare aures voce Gregorii, eiusque testimonium opponi Sabellicis perturbantibus ecclesias Neocaesariensium. This is a fairly free reference to Basil, *Epist.* CCX (directed to the 'primores' of Neocaesarea) 3 (Migne PG 32, 771): Πίστεως διαστροφὴ παρ' ὑμῖν μελετᾶται, ἐχθρὰ μὲν τοῖς ἀποστολικοῖς δόγμασιν, ἐχθρὰ δὲ τῇ παραδόσει τοῦ μεγάλου ὡς ἀληθῶς Γρηγορίου ... οὗ τὰ διδάγματα ἔναυλα ὑμῖν ἐστιν ἔτι καὶ νῦν δηλόνοτι. Τὸ γὰρ τοῦ Σαβελλίου κακόν, πάλαι μὲν κινηθέν, κατασβεσθὲν δὲ τῇ παραδόσει τοῦ μεγάλου ἐπιχειροῦσι νῦν ἀνανεοῦσθαι οὗτοι ... Cf. *Phil. moral. epitomes* II (St.A. III), p. 241 and *De iure reformandi* (CR 3), p. 257, *Enarratio in Evang. Joannis* (CR 15), pp. 56f., with his not unusual carelessness Melanchthon says elsewhere that Basil said that the words of Athanasius (instead of Gregory) and others still sounded in his ears, *Quaestiones Academicae* (CR 12), p. 726; cf. further *Postilla Melanchthoniana* (CR 24), p. 357.

[354] Cf. *Epistula* CCXXIII 3, for Basil's traditionalism see also *Liber de spiritu sancto* 71ff. where he quotes from earlier Christian writers in support of his doctrine of the Trinity, especially the divinity of the Holy Spirit. But Melanchthon also accuses Basil of having introduced new institutions, especially the monastery, see *supra*, 41.

[355] *Quaestiones Academicae* (CR 10), p. 726. Melanchthon obviously believes that this is a correct summary of the quotations he gives from Basil in connection with Basil's view on the Scriptural basis of the doctrine of the Trinity, see *supra*, 44.

[356] See *De potestate Papae* (CR 3), p. 277.

(Sic ait Chrysostomus:) Super hanc petram ait (sc. Dominus), non super Petrum. Non enim super hominem, sed super fidem Petri aedificavit Ecclesiam suam. Quae autem erat fides? Tu es Christus, filius Dei vivi.

This is an almost literal quotation from the (spurious) *Sermo I in Pentecosten.*[357]

CYPRIAN

The special authority of the Pope is refuted with a summary of Cyprian's letter to Florentius Pupianus, *Epist.* LXIX:

Oportere unum esse, cui audiat populus non quidem totius orbis, sed singularum diocesium.

These words do not appear in this letter of Cyprian, but Melanchthon trusts that the diligent reader will come to the same judgement on this matter as he.[358]

HILARY OF POITIERS

Hilary, too, is quoted in order to prove that the *petra* on which the church is built is not the person of Peter but his confession of faith:[359]

Petro revelavit Pater, ut diceret: Tu es filius Dei vivi. Super hanc igitur confessionis petram ecclesiae aedificatio est. Haec fides ecclesiae fundamentum est.

This is an abbreviated quotation from Hilary, *De Trinitate* 6, 36.

As we have seen,[360] Hilary was a typical Biblicist who did not want to go beyond Scriptural revelation. Melanchthon could have drawn quite a few quotations from Hilary in support of his Biblicism, but he does not do so, which could be an indication that he did not know the writings of Hilary too well.

IRENAEUS

Irenaeus is referred to in connection with the doctrine of the fences of defence which the church needs against new heresies:[361]

Irenaeus contra Florinum allegat autoritatem superiorum ac nominatim Polycarpi qui fuerat auditor Johannis Apostoli. Inquit enim execraturum

---

[357] Migne PG 52, 806. Melanchthon did not doubt the authenticity of this sermon.
[358] *Defensio contra Joh. Eckium* (St.A. I), p. 20.
[359] *De potestate Papae* (CR 3), p. 277.
[360] See *supra*, 12.
[361] See *supra*, 88.

fuisse dogmata Florini, si ea audiisset, et vitaturum locum, in quo illa dicta essent, tanquam pollutum.[362]

This is a brief summary of what Eusebius narrates in *Hist. eccl.* V 20, 3-8. Similarly Melanchthon quotes Irenaeus as saying that he received his doctrine about the two natures of the Son of God from Polycarpus, who received it from the apostle John.[363] This is a free reference to Irenaeus, *Adv. Haer.* 3, 3, 4 where Irenaeus says that Polycarpus was instructed by the Apostles and that he himself as a young man saw Polycarpus. Irenaeus says this in the context of the apostolic tradition. The context of this tradition is *inter alia* that Jesus is the Christ (see e.g. *Adv. Haer.* 3, 16ff.), but Irenaeus does not say that he received his doctrine of the two nature of Christ via Polycarpus from John.[364]

JEROME

The following quotation from Jerome is given against the exclusive authority of the Pope:[365]

at dicis, super Petrum fundatur ecclesia, licet id ipsum in alio loco super omnes apostolos fiat et cuncti claves regni coelorum accipiant, et ex aequo super eos ecclesiae fortitudo solidetur, tamen propterea inter duodecim unus eligitur, ut Scismatis tollatur occasio.

This is with one not unimportant omission (Jerome says at the end of this passage ... ut *capite constituto* schismatis tollatur occasio) a literal quotation from *Adv. Jovianum* I 26 (Migne PL 23, 258). The omission is important, since it was a point of discussion between Catholics and Protestants whether the church needs a head or not.[366]

The following quotation from *Epist.* CXLVI 1 (Ad Evangelum) (Migne PL 22, 1194) must support the same view:[367]

---

[362] *De ecclesia et de autoritate verbi Dei* (St.A. I), p. 327.

[363] *Articuli Protestantium Caesari traditi* (CR 4), p. 351: Irenaeus narrat, se accepisse doctrinam de duabus naturis in filio Dei a Polycarpo, Polycarpum a Johanne, cf. *De restituendis scholis*, dating from 1549 (St.A. III), p. 110. Erasmus, too, draws attention to the connection John-Polycarp-Irenaeus, see P. Fraenkel, *Testimonia patrum*, p. 83, note 166.

[364] On the tradition John-Polycarpus-Irenaeus see also *Alloquia et breves conciones* (CR 10), p. 1005: Ita refutat Irenaeus Marcionitas, citans Polycarpum quem audierat, qui fideliter custodierat doctrinam a Joanne apostolo traditam, (this is a free reference to *Adv. Haer.* 3, 3, 4: Et ipse autem Polycarpus Marcioni aliquando occurrenti sibi, et dicenti, Cognoscis nos?, respondit: Cognosco te primogenitum Satanae) and *De dignitate studii theol.* (CR 11), p. 326, *Explic. Symb. Nic.* (CR 23), p. 363.

[365] *Defensio contra Joh. Eckium* (St.A. I), p. 20.

[366] Melanchthon tells in his *Epistula de Lipsica disputatione* (St.A. I), p. 8, that Eck said that the Pope is the head of the church whilst according to Luther Christ is the head of the church, see also O. Seitz, *Der authentische Text der Leipziger Disputation*, p. 63.

[367] *De potestate Papae* (CR 3), p. 275. This statement by Jerome was also discussed at Leipzig, see O. Seitz, *op. cit.*, p. 65.

Si autoritas quaeritur, orbis est maior urbe, ubicumque Episcopus fuerit, sive Romae, sive Eugubii, sive Constantinopoli, sive Rhegii, sive Alexandriae, eiusdem meriti est, et eiusdem sacerdotii: potentia divitiarum et humilitas paupertatis sublimiorem vel inferiorem facit.

ORIGEN

Origen gives the right exegesis of "Tu es Petrus et super hanc petram" etc., and this exegesis is followed by Luther.[368]

Melanchthon here obviously has in mind *Comm. in Matth.* XII 10 (Migne PG 13, 997):

... ἐὰν ὡς ὁ Πέτρος λέγωμεν ... καὶ αὐτοὶ γινόμεθα ὅπερ καὶ ὁ Πέτρος, ὁμοίως αὐτῷ μακαριζόμενοι ... Πέτρα γὰρ πᾶς ὁ Χριστοῦ μαθητής, ... καὶ ἐπὶ πᾶσαν τὴν τοιαύτην πέτραν οἰκοδομεῖται ὁ ἐκκλησιαστικὸς πᾶς λόγος.

Somewhat strangely he criticizes Origen for saying that Peter excelled above the other apostles, because it was said to him in the plural: "What thou shall bind on earth shall be bound in heaven." This is an interpretation which is in fact explicitly rejected by Origen, see *Comm. in Matth.* XII 11 (Migne PG 13, 1001):

Καὶ γὰρ ἐνταῦθα μὲν ὡς πρὸς Πέτρον εἰρῆσθαι δοκεῖ τά· «Ὅσα ἂν δήσῃς ἐπὶ τῆς γῆς, ἔσται δεδεμένα ἐν τοῖς οὐρανοῖς» καὶ τὰ ἑξῆς· ἐν δὲ τῷ κατὰ Ἰωάννην δοὺς Πνεῦμα ἅγιον ὁ Σωτὴρ τοῖς μαθηταῖς διὰ τοῦ ἐμφυσήματος, φησί «Λάβετε Πνεῦμα ἅγιον» καὶ τὰ ἑξῆς.

Origen's views on Scripture as the primary authority appear according to Melanchthon from the fact that he draws support for infant baptism from the Apostles,[369] and that the bases his doctrine of the Trinity on Scripture.[370]

TERTULLIAN

Tertullian is quoted in support of the doctrine that the church needs certain fences of defence:[371]

Tertullianus contra Praxeam inquit, hanc regulam tenendam esse adversus omnes haereses, Rectum esse quodcumque primum est, adulterium vero

---

[368] *Defensio contra Joh. Eckium* (St.A. I), p. 20, cf. *De potestate Papae* (CR 3), p. 277.

[369] *De ecclesia et de autoritate verbi Dei* (St.A. I), pp. 327f.: Origenes allegat apostolos de baptismo infantum. Ait enim in cap. 6 ad Romanos, Ecclesias accepisse traditionem ab apostolis, ut baptizentur infantes, see further, *supra*, 75f.

[370] See *supra*, 74.

[371] *De ecclesia et de autoritate verbi Dei* (St.A. I), p. 327, see further the letter to the Senate of Venice, dating from 1539 (CR 3), p. 746, letter to Johannes Fredericus, dating from 1552 (CR 7), pp. 1079f., letter to archbishop Sigismundus (CR 9), p. 535, *Postilla Melanchthoniana* (CR 25), p. 83, *Comm. in Epist. Pauli ad Cor.*, dating from 1551 (CR 15), p. 1168, cf. P. Fraenkel, *Testimonia Patrum*, pp. 187ff., K. Haendler, *op. cit.*, pp. 200ff.

quodcumque posterius. Et quidem vocat primum quod Apostoli certo tradiderunt, sic enim ipse sese interpretatur.

This is a clear reference to *Adv. Prax.* 2, 2:

Hanc regulam ab initio evangelii decucurrisse ... quo peraeque adversus haereses iam hinc praeiudicatum sit id esse verum quodcumque primum, id esse adulterum quodcumque posterius.

Tertullian is further praised for basing his doctrine of the Trinity on Scripture.[372]—The fact that Tertullian wants to base his theological expositions on the *regula fidei* and advizes not to discuss Biblical texts with the heretics[373] was either unknown to Melanchthon or conveniently ignored by him.

According to Melanchthon the theology of the Fathers is fairly close to Scriptural revelation, not as close as Melanchthon himself claims to be, but certainly much closer than the Scholastics. This also becomes apparent, according to Melanchthon, in their attitude towards the Bible. They want to use Scripture as the exclusive norm of their theology, but do not follow this intention consistently, since they also come forward with new traditions which are incompatible with the revelation given in Scripture.

B. MELANCHTHON AND MEDIEVAL THEOLOGIANS

It is more difficult to describe Melanchthon's relation to Medieval theologians than to the Fathers, since he often refers to 'the Scholastics' without giving names (and then he often thinks of Thomas Aquinas, Duns Scotus, Occam, and their followers in his own days.) We shall follow the same method as in describing his relation to the Fathers: We shall try to trace the quotations he gives from Medieval theologians in connection with the doctrine of Christ and grace, the Trinity, and we shall reproduce Melanchthon's judgement on the theologians he quotes. But even less than was the case with the Fathers are these quotations indicative of Melanchthon's knowledge of Medieval theology, since he often attacks scholastic doctrines without giving names. But we hope that our collection can give an answer to the question of how far Melanchthon's attitude towards Medieval theologians differed from his attitude

---

[372] *De ecclesia et de autoritate verbi Dei* (St.A. I), p. 337, p. 349: Continet utilia testimonia de Trinitate, recitans non suam sententiam, sed veterem acceptam ab Apostolis.
[373] See *supra*, 13.

towards the Fathers. (As with the Fathers we shall review the Medieval theologians in alphabetical order.)

ANSELM

The doctrine of Christ and grace

As late as 1553 Melanchthon says that he has read Anselm's *Cur deus homo*, and he expresses a general, though qualified approval.[374] The late Melanchthon several times gives reasons for the incarnation. In this context he once explicitly refers to Anselm, who is said to be following the Fathers in this respect: The Mediator had to be God so that the price paid for our sins was equivalent.[375] This is a reference to *Cur deus homo* II 6-7. But there are more reasons given which Melanchthon may have found in Anselm's *Cur deus homo*: In the incarnation satisfaction had to be given to God's justice.[376] If the decree of the incarnation had not been taken men would have perished.[377] This, too, is found in Anselm (and Athanasius).[378]

Melanchthon repeatedly quotes Anselm's definition of original sin with approval.[379]

(Anselmus ... ait) peccatum originis esse carentiam iustitiae origine.

This is, as Melanchthon observes himself, the generally known definition of original sin given by Anselm, a definition which is an abbreviation of the following words:[380]

---

[374] Letter to G. P. Anhalt (CR 8), p. 30: Legi Anselmi scriptum, *Cur dus homo*: quod etsi tenuius et obscurius est, tamen non sit ignotum studiosis.

[375] *Postilla Melanchthoniana* (CR 24), p. 579: Quare Mediator est Deus? Scilicet ut sit pretium aequivalens. Hoc est exaggeratum ab antiquitate: Cogitarunt omnia peccata in mundo esse minora illo pretio, quod Filius praestitit pro nobis. Anshelmus pulchre commoratus est in illo affectu: In hoc commoremini et vos, et haec est tertia causa. Cf. *Explic. Symb. Nic.* (CR 23), p. 370, *Postilla Melanchthoniana* (CR 24), p. 79, p. 569, p. 621.

[376] *En. Symb. Nic.* (CR 23), pp. 338f., *Explic. Symb. Nic.* (CR 23), p. 370, *Postilla Melanchthoniana* (CR 24), p. 78, p. 621, *Disputationes* (CR 12), p. 593, *Enarratio epist. prioris ad Tim.* (CR 15), pp. 1321f., cf. Anselm, *Cur deus homo* I 19f.; Athanasius, *De Inc.* 9, says something similar, but it seems unlikely that this statement by Athanasius caught Melanchthon's attention, since he gives a quotation from *De Inc.* 9 and then gives an interpretation to that quotation in which he ignores what Athanasius gives as his own interpretation: God had to be consistent in His threat (justice) and in His goodness, see *supra*, 35.

[377] *Explic. Symb. Nic.* (CR 23), p. 370, *Postilla Melanchthoniana* (CR 24), p. 78, p. 578.

[378] Anselm, *Cur deus homo* II 1-4, cf. Athanasius, *De incarnatione verbi*, 5ff.

[379] *Commentarii in Epist. Pauli ad Rom.*, dating from 1532 (St.A. V), p. 172, cf. *Loci communes* (1559) (St.A. II), p. 257: Mihi non displicet retineri Anselmi descriptionem: Peccatum originis est carentia iustitiae originalis debitae inesse, *Commentarii in Epist. Pauli ad Rom.*, dating from 1544 (CR 15), p. 623, *Enarratio Epist. Pauli ad Rom.*, dating from 1556 (CR 15), p. 917, cf. *Enarratio Symb. Nic.* (CR 23), p. 260 (this is in the part written by C. Cruciger), *Explic. Symb. Nic.* (CR 23), p. 583.

[380] *De conceptu virginali et originali peccato* 3.

Si Deus non damnat nisi propter iniustitiam, damnat autem aliquem propter originale peccatum: ergo non est aliud originale peccatum quam iniustitia. Quod si ita est, et iniustitia non est aliud quam absentia debitae iustitiae: non enim videtur esse iniustitia, nisi in natura, quae cum debet habere, iustitiam non habet, utique originale peccatum clauditur sub eadem definitione iniustitiae.

What Melanchthon likes about this view is that it implies a loss of all the moral vitues which man had before the fall.[381]

It seems that Melanchthon had the idea that he could find in Anselm some support for his doctrine of Christ and grace.

BERNARDUS OF CLAIRVAUX

The doctrine of grace

In the *Loci communes* of 1521 Melanchthon refers to Bernardus' piece of writing *De libero arbitrio* and says that Bernardus is inconsistent in his views[382] and that his own views on this matter are preferable to those of Bernardus or any other Scholastics.[383] In the course of time Melanchthon took a more favourable view of Bernardus on account of several statements made by Bernardus which seemed to be in line with Melanchthon's views on grace and justification: Melanchthon repeatedly gives the following quotation in connection with the doctrine of the forgiveness of sins:[384]

Necesse est primo omnium credere quod remissionem peccatorum habere non possis nisi per indulgentiam Dei, sed adde, ut credas et hoc quod per ipsum peccata tibi donantur. Hoc est testimonium, quod perhibet Spiritus sanctus in corde tuo dicens: Dimissa sunt tibi peccata tua. Sic enim arbitratur Apostolus gratis iustificari hominem per fidem.

---

[381] See note 379.

[382] (St.A. II), p. 8: Scripsere de libero arbitrio Augustinus et Bernardus ... Bernardus non est similis sui. At the Leipzig Disputation Eck sought support for his doctrine that man must consent with God's grace in the writings of Bernardus, see Melanchthon's *Epistula de Lipsica Disputatione*, dating from 1519 (St.A. I), p. 7 and O. Seitz, *Der authentische Text der Leipziger Disputation*, pp. 16ff.

[383] (St.A. II), p. 17: Vides, lector, quanto certius de libero arbitrio scripserimus quam vel Bernardus vel ulli scholastici. On Melanchthon's views on Bernardus' doctrine of free will and grace see further H. O. Günther, *op. cit.*, pp. 30f.

[384] *Loci communes*, dating from 1559 (St.A. II), p. 368. Melanchthon adds the following comment on these sentences: In hoc dicto perspicue et proprie recitatur sententia ecclesiarum nostrarum, et extant similia testimonia apud hunc auctorem. This quotation is (sometimes partly) repeated in *Confessio Saxonica* (St.A. VI), p. 102, letter to Pfauser, dating from 1556 (CR 8), p. 711, *Disputationes*, dating from 1546 (CR 12), p. 545, *Commentarii in Epist. Pauli ad Romanos*, dating from 1544 (CR 15), p. 520, *Enarratio Epist. Pauli ad Romanos*, dating from 1556 (CR 15), p. 935, *Apol. Conf. Aug.* B (CR 27), p. 549, p. 633.

This is a quotation from the *Sermo in festo Annuntiationis beatae virginis*, 1 and 3 (Migne PL 183, pp. 383A, 384A).

From chapter 1 of this piece of writing is also the literal quotation:[385]

> (Bernardus gravissime dicit) Deinde quod nihil prorsus habere queas operis boni, nisi et hoc dederit ipse. Postremo quod aeternam vitam nullis potes operibus promereri, nisi gratis detur et illa.

In connection with the (in-)sufficiency of human merits the following almost literal quotation is given:[386]

> Sufficit ad meritum scire quod non sufficit meritum.

Bernardus' words are:[387]

> Sufficit ad meritum scire quod non sufficiant merita.

Bernardus is even made to express the doctrine of justification through faith *disertis verbis*:[388]

> (Recte loquitur Bernardus in sermone tricesimo secundo in Cantico, si sine calumnia intelligatur:)"Quisquis pro peccatis compunctus esurit et sitit iustitiam et credit in te, qui iustificas impium, is per solam iustificatus pacem habebit apud Deum." (Haec verba recte intellecta suffragantur nostrae sententiae.)

This is a very free reference to the thirty second sermon on the *Cantica Canticorum* in which Bernardus describes the difference between him who expects Christ as the Bridegroom and him who expects Christ as a Saviour. The words which are closest to thin quotation are:[389]

> Qui ... compunctus magis actuum recordatione suorum, loquens in amaritudine animae suae dicit Deo: Noli me condemnare ... hic talis non sponsum requirit, sed medicum, ac per hoc non oscula quidem vel amplexus, sed tantum remedia vulneribus accipiet suis ...

Melanchthon can only mean that if this sermon is rightly understood, then the core of it is expressed in the words which he puts into Bernardus' mouth.

These quotations make Melanchthon make the general claim that Bernardus supports his doctrine of justification.[390] He puts him on the same level as ancient Christian writers like Basil, Ambrose, Epiphanius,

---

[385] *Apol. Conf. Aug.* B (CR 27), p. 633.
[386] *Loci communes*, dating from 1559 (St.A. II), p. 436, *Annotationes in Evangelia*, dating from 1544 (CR 14), p. 217.
[387] See *Sermo LXVIII 6 in Cantica Canticorum* (Migne PL 183, 1111).
[388] *Responsiones ad impios articulos Bavaricae inquisitionis* (St.A. VI), p. 327.
[389] *Sermo XXXII 3 in Cantica Canticorum* (Migne PL 183, 946).
[390] Letter to G. Pontanus, dating from 1543 (CR 5), p. 234.

Polycarpus, Irenaeus, Gregory of Neocaesarea, and even Augustin.[391] He belongs to the small number of Medieval theologians who were witnesses of the evangelical truth.[392] This positive view on Bernardus was also held by Luther.[393] But Melanchthon in later years also criticizes Bernardus, e.g. when he says that works like fasting make justification perfect.[394] But on the whole it is obvious that in the course of time Melanchthon became much more sympathetic to Bernardus than he was in the beginning.

BONAVENTURA

The doctrine of grace

Melanchthon somewhere says in general terms that Bonaventura said right things about justification.[395] No specifice quotation is given in this context. He could here have in mind the same statement as to which he refers elsewhere:[396]

> ... Bernardus, Bonaventura in vera tentatione discunt acquiescere fiducia filii Dei, non suorum operum.

This is possibly a reference to *Dominica II Post Pascha Sermo* I (Opera omnia IX, p. 295):

> Et propter hoc, carissime, cum insurgit diaboli fraudulentia, ingredere in petram id est Christum, impendendo meditationes, cogitationes et affectiones, quia numquam potest diabolus melius vinci quam in memoria passionis Christi. Unde Bernardus: Nullus unquam daemonum stare poterit, videns gladium, in quo devictus fuit.

There are a few quotations in connection with the doctrine of original sin:[397]

---

[391] *Loci communes*, dating from 1559 (St.A. II), p. 483, *Declamatio in funere Lutheri* (CR 11), p. 728, *Disputationes* (CR 12), p. 676, *Commentarii in Epist. Pauli ad Rom.*, dating from 1544 (CR 15), p. 495, *En. in Epist. Pauli ad Rom.*, dating from 1556 (CR 15), p. 803.

[392] See apart from some of the references given in the previous note also *Confessio Saxonica* (St.A. VI), p. 95, *Praefatio* to the edition of Augustin's *De spiritu et littera*, dating from 1545 (CR 5), p. 805, *In Danielem Prophetam Comm.* (CR 13), p. 956, *Annotationes et conciones in Evang. Matthaei* (CR 14), p. 991, *Comm. in Epist. Pauli ad Cor.*, dating from 1551 (CR 15), p. 1068, *Postilla Melanchthoniana* (CR 25), p. 862 (although here less praise is given to him than to others: Aliquid luci etiam in Bernardo fuit).

[393] See e.g. *Tischreden* 1, p. 330: Inter ecclesiasticos doctores Augustinus primas tenet, Ambrosius secundas, Bernhardus tertias; see also E. Schäfer, *op. cit.*, pp. 191f.

[394] Letter to Luther, dating from 1530 (CR 2), p. 230, see Bernardus, *Sermo* CV (Migne PL 183, 732).

[395] Letter to G. Pontanus (CR 5), p. 234: Sunt et Bonaventurae quaedam satis bonae sententiae (sc. de iustificatione).

[396] *Comm. in Epist. Pauli ad Cor.* (CR 15), p. 1068.

[397] *Disputationes* (CR 12), p. 438, cf. *Loci communes*, dating from 1559 (St.A. II), p. 258.

(Bonaventura et quidam alii agnoscunt vicium in mente et voluntate esse, pugnans cum lege Dei). Laudat enim dictum Hugonis, qui ait: Peccatum originis est ignorantia in mente, et concupiscentia in carne.

This is a quotation from *Sent.* II, dist. xxx, art. 2, qu. 2 (Opera omnia II, p. 724):

Item, Hugo in libro de Sacramentis in septima parte: "Originale peccatum est vitium, quod nascendo trahimus per ignorantiam in mente et con-cupiscentiam in carne." Ergo videtur, quod originale peccatum sit ignoran-tia.

Melanchthon quotes with approval Bonaventura's definition of original sin:[398]

Et Bonaventura, Cum quaeritur quid sit originale peccatum, recte respondetur, quod sit concupiscentia immoderata.

This is an abbreviated quotation from *Sent.* II, dist. xxx, art. 2, qu. 1 (Opera omnia II, p. 722):

Concedendum est igitur ... quod originale peccatum est concupiscentia, et haec non quaecumque, sed concupiscentia, prout claudit in se debitae iustitiae carentiam. Haec autem est concupiscentia immoderata et intensa, adeo ut sit carnis ad spiritum praedominantia.

In the same context also the following quotation is given with approval:[399]

Homo est spoliatus in gratuitis: et vulneratus in naturalibus. (Sunt verba Bonaventurae.)

This is an almost literal quotation from *Sent.* II, dist. xxviii, art. 1, qu. 1 (Opera omnia II, p. 676).

Melanchthon obviously had the feeling that because of his doctrine of original sin Bonaventura could be used as a witness to the Lutheran doc-trine of justification through faith alone. A similar view on Bonaventura was also held by Luther.[400]

HUGO OF ST VICTOR

The doctrine of grace

Melanchthon repeatedly reproduces Hugo's definition of original sin, and does so in different ways. One way is:[401]

---

[398] *Apol. Conf. Aug.* B (CR 27), p. 425.

[399] *Postilla Melanchthoniana* (CR 25), p. 382.

[400] See e.g. *Tischreden* 1, p. 330: Bonaventura inter scholasticos doctores optimus est, see further E. Schäfer, *op. cit.*, pp. 445f.

[401] *Disputationes* (CR 12), p. 438, *Apol. Conf. Aug.* B (CR 27), p. 426.

(dictum Hugonis, qui ait:) Peccatum originis est ignorantia in mente, et concupiscentia in carne.

Since he explicitly says that this statement is quoted by Bonaventura he must have in mind *De Sacramentis* I, pars vii, cap. 28 (which is quoted by Bonaventura):[402]

Si ergo quaeritur quid sit originale peccatum in nobis intelligitur corruptio sive vitium quod nascendo trahimus per ignorantiam in mente, per concupiscentiam in carne.

The other way is:[403]

Hugo praeclare dicit, peccatum originis esse ignorantiam in mente et inobedientiam in voluntate.

Here Melanchthon quotes and interprets his source with his not unusual carelessness. Melanchthon obviously thought that both definitions imply the same and express what Hugo wants to say. But Hugo applies the disobedience only to Adam and Eve[404] and explicitly denies that in Adam's and Eve's descendants original sin is voluntary disobedience.[405] In itself Melanchthon agrees that original sin is not voluntary disobedience.[406]

Because of his definition of original sin Melanchthon regards Hugo of St. Victor (together with e.g. Bernardus and Tauler) as belonging to those Medieval theologians who were witnesses to the Evangelical truth.[407]

Petrus Lombardus

Amongst the Medieval theologians Petrus Lombardus is of great importance to Melanchthon, since he contrasts his own *Loci communes*

---

[402] See *supra*, 98.

[403] *Loci communes*, dating from 1559 (St.A. II), p. 258, *Explic. Symb. Nic.* (CR 23), p. 403: (Sicut Hugo inquit:) Peccatum originis est ignorantia de Deo in mente, et inobedientia in voluntate et corde.

[404] *De Sacramentis* I, pars VII, cap. xxvi: Originale peccatum dupliciter intelligi potest, sive videlicet prima illa inobedientia hominis quae prima omnium peccatorum fuit et subsequentium origo omnium exstitit, sive vitium illud cum quo ab illo traducto universi oriuntur, qui ab illo per carnis propagationem traducuntur.

[405] *Summa Sententiarum*, Tract. III, cap. xi: Alii dicunt quod originale, peccatum sit inobedientia, et haec inobedientia in omnibus est antequam renascantur. Sed non videtur quod puer inobediens sit; quia nihil unquam fuit ei imperatum. Et qui nondum potest ratione uti, quomodo aut obediens aut inobediens potest dici? Inobedientia namque voluntatis est ut obedientia, sed peccatum originale non est voluntarium.

[406] See *supra*, 29.

[407] *Conf. Saxon.*, dating from 1551 (St.A. VI), p. 95, Preface to the second Volume of Luther's works, dating from 1546 (CR 6), p. 167, *Declamatio in funere Lutheri* (CR 11), p. 728.

with the *Libri Sententiarum* of Petrus Lombardus.[408] His objection against Petrus Lombardus is that he is too speculative. So the *Libri Sententiarum* are to a large degree an example of what ought not be discussed in sound Christian theology.[409]

The doctrine of Christ and grace

The accusation of futile speculation becomes apparent in certain references to Petrus' expositions of the person of Christ:

The exposition in *Sent.* III, dist. x, cap. 3: Utrum persona vel natura praedestinata sit (and the speculations by later Commentators of Petrus Lombardus on this subject) are rejected as 'labyrinthi', i.e. endless speculations.[410]

There is a reference to *Sent.* I, dist. vi, cap. 1: Utrum Pater voluntate genuit Filium an necessitate,[411] the reference is made without any comment, but since Melanchthon nowhere shows any interest in this question, he obviously regarded it as an example of useless speculation.[412]

Melanchthon is also very critical of Petrus Lombardus when he says (quoting Augustin as his authority) that Christ was the Mediator in His human, not in His divine nature:[413]

> Nec his antiquis testimoniis anteferatur mutilatum dictum in Longobardo distinctione 19, tertio libro, quod ex Augustino citatur, quod ait, Christum esse Mediatorem secundum humanitatem, non secundum divinitatem. Et tamen in eodem loco pugnantia mox citantur, unde nata est otiosa distinctio de Medio et Mediatore. Fatentur Christum secundum utramque naturam medium esse, sed Mediatorem secundum humanam.

This is an abbreviated quotation from *Sent.* III, dist. xix, cap. 6-7. That Christ is *Mediator* as man is demonstrated from Augustin's *Sermo* 293, 7: Mediator est igitur in quantum homo,—that Christ is *medius* as God and man is demonstrated from Vigilius, *Contra Eutychen* V 15: Si

---

[408] *Loci communes*, dating from 1521 (St.A. II), p. 5, Letter of dedication to the *Loci communes*, dating from 1535 (CR 2), p. 921. In the *Loci communes*, dating from 1559 (St.A. II), p. 176, he says that his Scriptural approach to God's being and will is to be preferred to the idle speculations provided by the commentators of Petrus Lombardus.

[409] Cf. the list of subjects discussed in speculative theology which Melanchthon gives in the beginning of the *Loci communes*, dating from 1521 (St.A. II), p. 6.

[410] *Explic. Symb. Nic.* (CR 23), p. 520.

[411] *Chronicon Carionis*, Pars II (CR 12), p. 986, cf. *supra*, 61.

[412] As we have seen, Erasmus regarded this question as an expression of curiosity, see *supra*, 15f.

[413] *Responsio de controversiis Stancari*, dating from 1553 (St.A. VI), p. 274, *Dictata*, dating from 1551 (CR 7), pp. 884f., *Enarratio Epist. Pauli ad Col.*, dating from 1559 (CR 15), p. 1271, *Postilla Melanchthoniana* (CR 24), p. 861, letter to E. Schnepfius (CR 7), p. 1134, letter to Hardenbergius (CR 7), p. 1148.

ergo Christus secundum vos, o haeretici, unam tantum habet naturam,
unde medius erit? Nisi ita sit medius ut Deus sit propter divinitatis, et
homo propter humanitatis naturam, quomodo humana in eo reconcilian-
tur divinis? (The quotation is given with considerable freedom.)

These critical remarks about Petrus Lombardus' christology are made
in later writings, from which it becomes clear that not only as a young
Reformer Melanchthon opposed Petrus Lombardus because of his
speculations. But Melanchthon also repeatedly refers with approval to
one of Petrus Lombardus' christological statements (which he makes on
Augustin's authority):[414]

> Sic Augustinus loquitur, et citantur verba in Longobardo, libro 3, dist. 22.
> Non dimisit Patrem Christus, cum venit in virginem, ubique totus, ubique
> perfectus. Deinde additur forma sermonis: Ubique totus est, sed non
> totum.

The young Reformer Melanchthon contrasts his *Loci communes* with the
Sententiae of Petrus Lombardus. Nevertheless there is in the first edition of
the *Loci communes* also occasional praise of Petrus Lombardus in the context of the doctrine of grace. Melanchthon opposes the Thomistic doctrine that grace is a quality in the souls of the saints,[415] and says that
Petrus Lombardus preferred to call grace the Holy Spirit rather than
such a quality, and that he thereby showed to have a better understanding of this matter than his later commentators who treated him with
arrogance:[416]

> Petrum Longobardum quod alicubi spiritum sanctum potius gratiam
> vocarit, quam Parisiensem, hoc est, fictitiam illam qualitatem, mirum est,
> quo supercilio tractent sophistae, qui tamen quanto rectius quam isti sentit.

This is a reference to *Sent.* I, dist. xvii, cap. 1, 2:

> ... ipse idem Spiritus Sanctus est amor sive caritas, qua nos diligimus Deum
> et proximum, quae caritas cum ita est in nobis ut nos faciat diligere Deum
> et et proximum, tunc Spiritus Sanctus dicitur mitti vel dari nobis.

Later on Melanchthon expresses some criticism of the questions raised
in and by these expositions of Petrus Lombardus, *viz.*, whether there is
an effect of the Holy Spirit in our hearts, an effect which is not the Holy
Spirit Himself. Melanchthon then expresses as his view that both are
true, the Holy Spirit is in the hearts of the reborn, and love is an effect or

---

[414] *Dictata* (CR 7), pp. 884f., *En. in Epist. Pauli ad Col.* (CR 15), p. 1271, *Post. Mel.* (CR 24), p. 861, — see *Sent.* III, dist. xxii, cap. 3.

[415] Cf. *infra*, 107.

[416] *Loci communes* (St.A. II), p. 87. Erasmus regards such expositions as given by Petrus Lombardus as rejectable curiosity, see *supra*, 16.

quality given by the Holy Spirit with the assent and obedience of the human will. But he still says that this whole question is irrelevant.[417]

Petrus Lombardus' definition of original justice, which lies in the fact that man is created in God's likeness, is quoted with approval. (Melanchthon appoves of this, since it implies that man has lost this justice after the fall):[418]

> (Nec novi quidquam diximus. Vetus definitio recte intellecta prorsus idem dicit, Cum ait peccatum originis carentiam esse iustitiae originalis. Quid est autem iustitia?) ... Nec Longobardus veretur dicere, quod iustitia originis sit ipsa similitudo Dei, quae homini indita est a Deo.

Although Melanchthon regarded Petrus Lombardus as one of the writers whom he wanted to oppose in principle, he nevertheless feels free to praise certain statements made by him, and he expresses such praise in all periods of his life, just as he criticizes him in all periods of his life. It seems arbitrary that Hugo of St. Victor is regarded, because of his definition of original sin, as one of the Medieval witnesses to the Evangelical truth, and that Petrus Lombardus, who also provides a definition of original sin of which Melanchthon approves, is portrayed in much darker colours. The reason could be that criticism of Petrus Lombardus also implied criticism of his later commentators.

Melanchthon's view on Petrus Lombardus was similar to those of Luther. They acknowledge his intellectual capacities, but criticize the fact that he does not base his doctrine on Scripture.[419]

---

[417] See *Enarratio in Evang. Joannis* (edited by Cruciger in 1546, but dating from 1536/37) (CR 15), p. 349: ... quaestiones ... Longobardi ... volens praetereo, an sit effectus aliquis dilectio in corde accensa, qui non sit ipsa persona Spiritus sancti. Dixi utrunque affirmandum esse, quod adsit in cordibus renatorum Spiritus sanctus, et quod dilectio sit effectus, seu qualitas accensa in corde per Spiritum sanctum, assentiente et optemperante voluntate. Sed libenter abrumpo has quaestiones, de quibus inerudite et frigide in commentariis Longobardi disputatur. Melanchthon here may have in mind the question of whether, if the Holy Spirit is in the hearts of the believers, the Spirit Himself can grow or diminish in the hearts, *Sent.* I, dist. xvii, cap. 5, 1, to which the answer is given in 5, 3: His ita respondemus, dicentes quod Spiritus Sanctus sive caritas penitus immutabilis est, nec in se augetur vel minuitur, nec in se recipit magis vel minus, sed in homine vel potius homini augetur et minuitur, et magis vel minus datur vel habetur. — But here, too, the criticism is directed more against the commentators of Petrus Lombardus than against Petrus Lombardus himself. On this particular doctrine of Petrus Lombardus and its interpretation in later times see J. Auer, *Die Entwicklung der Gnadenlehre in der Hochscholastik, I: Das Wesen der Gnade*, Freiburg i.B. 1942, pp. 86ff.

[418] *Apol. Conf. Aug.* B (CR 27), pp. 424f. See Petrus Lombardus, *Sent.* III, dist. xvi, cap. 3, 5: Factus est ergo homo ... ad similitudinem secundum innocentiam et iustitiam quae in mente rationali naturaliter sunt.

[419] See e.g. *Tischreden* 1, p. 85: Petrus Lombardus satis placet pro theologo, es thuts yhm keiner nach. Est quasi methodus theologie. Legit Hilarium, Augustinum,

WILLIAM OF OCCAM

Melanchthon is obviously much more often implicitly in opposition against William of Occam and his followers[420] than the few explicit quotations we give in connection with the doctrine of sin and grace indicate.[421]

The doctrine of sin and grace

Occam's definition of original sin is criticized as being too mild:

> Occam mavult dicere peccatum originis tantum esse reatum, sine ullo vicio.[422]

> Recentes, ut Occam et multi alii, nomen retinent peccati originalis, sed rem extenuant. Negant illa malla esse res pugnantes cum Lege Dei, caliginem in mente, contumaciam in voluntate et corde, quae vocatur concupiscentia.[423]

Melanchthon here ignores that Occam does give a definition of original sin of which he approves:[424] it is *de facto* (though not *de possibili*) a *carentia iustitie originalis*.[425] But Melanchthon may have in mind other passages where Occam discusses the possibility that man can be saved without first having received grace.[426] There he does say that sin does not take away anything from the human soul, there are only actual sins which disappear after having been committed so that God does not find anything in the sinner which is in opposition to his grace and glory.[427] So

---

Ambrosium, Gregorium item omnia concilia. Ist ein gross man gewest; wenn er in die bibel geraten wäre, fuisset sine dubio summus, — cf. what Melanchthon says at the beginning of the first edition of the *Loci communes* (St.A. II), p. 5: Longobardus congerere hominum opiniones quam scripturae sententiam referre maluit. On Luther and Petrus Lombardus see further E. Schäfer, *op. cit.*, p. 445.

[420] Melanchthon criticizes the fact that the followers of Occam (and Duns Scotus and Thomas Aquinas) call themselves after their teacher, not after Christ: see *Did. Fav. adv. Th. Placentinum* (St.A. I), p. 126: Nemo enim Theologorum iam Christianus dicebatur, sed aut Thomista, aut Scotista, aut Occamista. A similar objection is made in the early church against the heretics, see e.g. Athanasius, *Contra Arianos* 1, 1-2.

[421] We leave out Melanchthon's evaluation of William of Occam's views on the authority of the Pope, church and state, cf. *Did. Fav. adv. Th. Placentinum* (St.A. I), p. 98.

[422] *Disputationes* (CR 12), p. 438.

[423] *Loci communes*, dating from 1559 (St.A. II), p. 262.

[424] See *supra*, 94.

[425] *In Sententiarum libros IV*, II dist. xxvi U.

[426] *In Sent. lib. IV*, I dist. xvii, IV dist. ix, *Quodlibeta* VI 1-4, see on this whole matter (and on the inconsistencies between what is said in this passage and what is said on original sin) E. Iserloh, *Gnade und Eucharistie in der philosophischen Theologie des Wilhelm von Ockam. Ihre Bedeutung für die Ursachen der Reformation*. Wiesbaden 1956, pp. 89ff.

[427] See e.g. *In Sent. libros IV*, IV 9 M: Sed in peccatore nihil invenitur repugnans gratiae et gloriae, quia actus iam transit et ex illo actu non oportet, quod aliquis habitus derelinquatur. — Occam does speak here about God's *potentia absoluta*, which could mean

sin does not take away anything from the human soul. Melanchthon may also have this passage in mind when he says that according to Occam man can obey God's law,[428] and that according to Occam grace is not necessary in order to receive justification.[429]

Melanchthon's utter dislike of Occam's doctrine of sin and grace obviously made him regard Occam as one of the rejectable Scholastic theologians.[430]

DUNS SCOTUS

The doctrine of grace

Melanchthon opposes his doctrine that mortal sins can be avoided without help by the Holy Spirit.[431] Similarly Melanchthon rejects his doctrine that human will can fulfill God's commandments.[432]

Duns Scotus is one of the rejectable Scholastics, since he transforms the Gospel into philosophy,[433] as appears from his moralism and his speculations.[434]

J. TAULER

There is one statement about God's goodness which Melanchthon likes to quote:[435]

---

that his expositions are to a certain degree hypothetical, — see E. Iserloh, *op. cit.*, pp. 99f., in *Quodlibeta* VI 4 he denies that God can forgive sins without grace according to *leges ordinatae*. (These expositions are meant primarily to underline God's freedom to grant forgiveness without grace, rather than to underline man's goodness which needs no grace.)

[428] *En. Symb. Nic.* (CR 23), p. 283.

[429] *Did. Fav. adv. Th. Plac.* (St.A. I), p. 96: Gratia opus esse ad iustificationem, neque scripturam neque experientiam testari, cf. Occam, *Quodlibeta* VI 1: ergo potest (sc. deus) dare vitam aeternam alicui facienti bonum opus sine tali gratia que est principium merendi.

[430] See e.g. *Did. Fav. adv. Th. Plac.* (St.A. I), p. 75, p. 148.

[431] *Did. Fav. adv. Th. Plac.* (St.A. I), p. 96: Scilicet obnoxiam fecistis rationem Evangelio, delire Thoma et tu somniator Scote, cum docuistis, citra divini Spiritus auxilium posse singula letalia peccata vitari. — Duns Scotus does say that, but with clear qualifications, and he also says the opposite, see the quotations given by J. Auer, *op. cit.*, II: *Das Wirken der Gnade*, Freiburg i.B. 1951, pp. 31f.

[432] *En. Symb. Nic.* (CR 23), p. 283, cf. *supra*, 103f. Duns Scotus does say that, see J. Auer, *op. cit.*, p. 42.

[433] See the Preface to the second volume of Luther's works, dating from 1546 (CR 6), p. 168.

[434] *Did. Fav. adv. Th. Plac.* (St.A. I), p. 75, p. 126. Because of his subtleties he deserves the name Scotus, which Melanchthon brings into connection with σκότος, p. 86: Scotus, vir hoc nomine longe dignissimus, p. 94: subtilitatem Scoto (sc. tribuis), adeo non explicanti sua, ut et a tenebris nomen meruerit, nullius enim confusior quam huius doctrina est; cf. P. Fraenkel, *Testimonia Patrum*, p. 104, note 269.

[435] *Loci communes*, dating from 1559 (St.A. II), p. 657 (the quotation already appears in the edition, dating from 1535), *Postilla Melanchthoniana* (CR 25), pp. 74f. and (CR 24), p. 838.

Praeclare igitur Taulerus inquit animum hominis nunquam avidum esse ad accipiendum, quin Deus multo avidior sit ad dandum. — Menschlich hertz ist nimmermehr so begierig gnade zu begeren, Gott is viel begierlicher zu geben.

This is an abbreviated quotation from Tauler's sermon *Von Beten aus dem Grunde*:[436]

Wie mag aber nun das zugehen, dass so mancher Mensch bittet, und bittet all seine Lebtage, und doch wird ihm das lebendige Brot nicht zuteil, während doch Gott so unaussprechlich milde ist *und ohne alles Mass über all Weise gibt und vergibt und tausendmal bereiter zu geben ist als der Mensch zu nehmen?*

There is a fairly general reference to Tauler's sermons about *affectus spirituales*:[437]

Sapientia est experientia rerum spiritualium, cuiusmodi est sermo Taulerii iudicantis de affectibus spiritualibus.

This is meant as praise, since Melanchthon continues:

Haec intelligit quid sit fides, quid spes, quid peccatum, quarum rerum nihil prorsus intelligunt hypocritae.

One may here think of the sermon "Von den sieben Gaben des Geistes" and the sermon "Vom Wandeln im Geiste."[438]

Tauler is praised time and again by Melanchthon as one of the witnesses to the evangelical truth.[439] This high esteem of Tauler was also held by Luther.[440]

THOMAS AQUINAS

Even more than William of Occam and Duns Scotus Thomas Aquinas is the target of Melanchthon's attack, often without Thomas' name being given. Again we confine ourselves to explicit quotations in the context of the doctrine of *Christ and grace*:

---

[436] See *Johannes Tauler, Predigten II, übertragen eun eingeleitet* von W. Lehmann, Jena 1923, p. 85.

[437] *Annotationes in priorem epist. Pauli ad Corinthios*, dating from 1522 (St.A. IV), p. 69.

[438] See W. Lehmann, *op. cit.* I, pp. 108ff., II, pp. 7ff.

[439] *Conf. Saxonica* (St.A. VI), p. 95, Preface to the edition of *De spiritu et littera*, dating from 1545 (CR 5), p. 805, *Declamatio in funere Lutheri*, dating from 1546 (CR 11), p. 728, *Disputationes* (CR 12), p. 676, *In Danielem Prophetam comm.*, dating from 1543 (CR 13), p. 956, *En. in Epist. Pauli ad Rom.*, dating from 1556 (CR 15), p. 803, *Postilla Melanchthoniana* (CR 25), p. 80, p. 609, p. 862. (Often he is mentioned in the same breath with Irenaeus, Augustin and Hugo of St. Victor.)

[440] See e.g. his *Epistola gratulatoria super inventione et editione lucubrationum Joannis Tauleri ord. praedicatorum*, dating from 1522 (W.A. 10, 2), p. 329: Prodiit nuper vernacula lingua Johannes Taulerus quondam Thomista, ut libere pronunciem, talis qualem ego a saeculo Apostolorum vix natum esse scriptorem arbitror.

Thomas is attacked for the distinction he makes between counsels and precepts.[441] As an example is quoted what he says on the giving of alms:[442]

> Non omnis necessitas obligat ad praeceptum, sed illa sola, sine qua is, qui necessitatem patitur, sustentari non potest. In illo enim casu locum habet, quod Ambrosius dicit: Pasce fame morientem, si non paveris, occidisti. Sic ergo dare Eleemosynam de superfluo est in praecepto, et dare Eleemosynam ei, qui est in extrema necessitate, alias dare Eleemosynas est in consilio.

This is an almost literal quotation from *Summa Theologica* II 2, qu. 32, art. 5. Thomas' doctrine that Christ brought a new law, which differs from the old law given by Moses, since the old law applied to outward actions and the new law to internal disposition is criticized:[443]

> Dic Thoma, quid in mentem venerit cur doceres Mosaica lege nihil exigi praeter pharisaismum, hoc est externa opera, cum toties etiam Moses exigat nihil obscuris verbis affectus?

This is a reference to *Summa Theologica* II 1, qu. 108, art. 1.[444]

Thomas is quoted as saying that human reason can avoid mortal sins without the help of justifying grace:[445]

> Antequam ratio, in qua est peccatum mortale, reparetur per gratiam iustificantem potest singula peccata mortalia vitare.

The quotation is misleading, since Thomas does not say that man can avoid singula peccata mortalia, but that he can acquire a certain *habitus virtutis* and can avoid sins which are contrary to reason, and since Thomas explicitly says that there are "quaedam peccata mortalia," which man cannot avoid without divine grace, see *Summa Theologica* II 1, qu. 63, art. 2:

> Et ideo, licet sine gratia homo non possit peccatum mortale vitare ita quod numquam peccet mortaliter, non tamen impeditur quin possit habitum virtutis acquirere, per quam a malis operibus abstineat ut in pluribus, et praecipue ab his quae sunt valde rationi contraria. — Sunt etiam quaedam

---

[441] Cf. *supra*, 60, 66.

[442] *Did. Fav. adv. Th. Plac.* (St.A. I), p. 80.

[443] *Loci communes*, dating from 1521 (St.A. II), pp. 70f.

[444] ... omnes exteriores actus pertinere intelliguntur ad manum, sicut interiores actus pertinent ad animum. Sed haec ponitur differentia inter novam legem et veterem, quod vetus lex cohibet manum, sed lex nova cohibet animum, cf. the explicative note by H. Engelland in St.A. II, p. 71. — It should be noted that this distinction between the Old and the New Testament is already to be found in Irenaeus, *Adv. Haer.* 4, 24, 2: Etenim lex quippe servis posita, per ea quae foris erant corporalia animam erudiebat, velut per vinculum attrahens eam ad oboedientiam praeceptorum, uti disceret homo servire Deo: Verbum autem liberans animam, et per ipsam corpus voluntarie emundari docuit.

[445] *Did. Fav. adv. Th. Plac.* (St.A. I), p. 96.

peccata mortalia quae homo sine gratia nullo modo potest vitare, quae scilicet directe opponuntur virtutibus theologicis, quae ex dono gratiae sunt in nobis.

The distinction which is made here between theological and philosophical virtues is rejected by Melanchthon:[446]

Nec est, quod virtutum genera et formas distinguamus philosophorum et scholasticorum more in morales, theologicas, dona, fructus, quemadmodum Aquinas ineptiit cum suis.

Melanchthon is strongly opposed to Thomas' doctrine that justification takes place through faith which has been formed by these theological virtues, especially love. This means, according to Melanchthon, that man is in fact justified through his own virtues.[447]

Melanchthon may here have in mind *Summa Theologica* III 49, 1:

Fides autem per quam a peccato mundamur, non est fides informis, quae potest esse etiam cum peccato, sed est fides formata per caritatem.

In the same context Thomas' doctrine is rejected that the eucharist earns remission of sins:[448]

opinio est Thomae ... quod missa sit opus quod exhibetur Deo ac meretur gratiam vivis ac mortuis. Nam hoc proprie vocatur sacrificium, opus Deo exhibitum ad placandum Deum, seu meritorium.

All these critical remarks lead to the harsh general verdict on Thomas that he was in fact a Pelagian.[449] His theology is an example of rejectable speculation.[450] But despite this very harsh and negative judgement on Thomas he is also sometimes quoted with approval:

Melanchthon quotes his definition of original sin:[451]

---

[446] *Loci communes*, dating from 1521 (St.A. II), p. 114, cf. H. Engelland's explicative note which refers to *Summa Theologica* II 1, qu 68 art. 2, see also *Did. Fav. adv. Th. Plac.* (St.A. I), p. 83.

[447] See e.g. *Loci communes*, dating from 1521 (St.A. II), p. 89, *Loci communes*, dating from 1559 (St.A. II), p. 380, *Comm. in Epist. Pauli ad Rom.*, dating from 1532 (St.A. V), p. 99, letter to U. Mordeisen (CR 8), p. 739, *Explic. Symb. Nic.* (CR 23), p. 457, letter to Luther, dating from 1541 (CR 4), p. 572, *Conf. Saxonica*, dating from 1551 (St.A. VI), p. 104. For Luther's opposition against the *fides formata* see Th. Harnack, *Luthers Theologie* II, p. 342. — Similar opposition is expressed against Thomas' view on *latria* as a cultus seu opus, quo proprie agantur gratiae, et laudetur Deus, see letter to Luther, dating from 1530 (CR 2), p. 230, Thomas, *Summa Theologica* II 2, qu. 94, art. 1.

[448] *Iudicium de Missa et coelibatu*, dating from 1526 (CR 1), p. 840, cf. *Propositiones de Missa*, dating from 1521 (St.A. I), pp. 166f., *Iudicium de Missa*, dating from 1530 (CR 2), p. 209. — These could be references to *Summa Theologica* III qu. 52, art. 8 and III qu. 49, art. 1.

[449] See ee.g. *Enarratio in Epist. Pauli ad Rom.* (CR 15), p. 813.

[450] *Did. Fav. adv. Th. Plac.* (St.A. I), p. 75, p. 86, p. 126, the Preface to the second volume of Luther's works, dating from 1546 (CR 6), p. 168, *De Luthero et de aetatibus ecclesiae*, dating from 1548 (CR 11), p. 786.

[451] *Apol. Conf. Aug.* B (CR 27), p. 425.

Peccatum originis habet privationem originalis iusticiae, et cum hoc inordinatam dispositionem partium animae, unde non est privacio pura, sed quidam habitus corruptus.

This is a literal quotation from *Summa Theologica* II 1, qu. 82, art. 1.

Melanchthon's attitude towards Thomas can be compared with his view on Origen. Origen was his most important target in his criticism of the corruption of the truth which began in the early church, Thomas Aquinas is his most important target when he attacks the almost total corruption of the truth in Scholastic theology. But in both he finds also statements which suit him and to which he freely draws attention.

Melanchthon's attitude towards Medieval theology in principle does not differ from his view on Patristic theology. On the surface there seems to be a great difference, since he sometimes claims to oppose Scholastic theology with Scripture and the *consensus* of the Fathers. But we have seen that Melanchthon does not work with any Patristic *consensus*, but that he picks out as an eclectic those statements from the writings of the Fathers which suit him, because they seem to say the same as what he wants to say, and he ignores those which do not suit him (and sometimes explicitly criticizes them).[452] With a different emphasis he does the same with Medieval theologians: He picks out those statements which suit him for his attack and those statements which suit him because they confirm his views. There is less praise for Medieval theologians than there is for the Fathers, and there is more criticism of them than there is of the Fathers. But he approaches both the Fathers and the Scholastics as an eclectic who has his preconceived ideas which he wants to see confirmed. He sees less light in Medieval theology than in Patristic theology and more darkness than he sees in Patristic theology. His theory of the small number of witnesses of the truth which always existed therefore applies to Medieval and not to Patristic theology.[453] So according to Melanchthon the original truth revealed in the Bible was gradually more and more corrupted in the course of time and known by fewer and fewer people, until it was restored again in the Reformation. This view is typical of a new movement which wants to show that it has roots in history and thereby wants to escape the accusation of coming forward with audacious novelties.[454]

---

[452] See *supra*, 84f.

[453] See on this theory P. Fraenkel, *Testimonia Patrum*, pp. 100ff.

[454] In the early church this view was held by Justin Martyr, see J. C. M. van Winden, *An Early Christian Philosopher*, pp. 111ff., cf. also *supra*, 10f., note 43 and *infra*, 143, note 8.

CHAPTER THREE

CONTINUITY AND DISCONTINUITY IN THE THOUGHT OF MELANCHTHON

The young Reformer Melanchthon strongly opposes in the first edition of the *Loci communes* speculations about the ways in which the incarnation took place and about the divine and the human nature of Christ and states that to know Christ means to know His *beneficia*.[1] As clearly appears from other statements made by Melanchthon around the same time he does believe in the fact of the incarnation and in the pre-existence of Christ. God sent His Son down in human flesh, Melanchthon says.[2] God came down in flesh in order to be known.[3] In the *Loci communes* he speaks of Christ's incarnation[4] and declares that he believes the Nicene Creed about the divinity of Christ, because he believes Scripture.[5] In his defence of the doctrine of the Trinity against the anti-trinitarians he will later on compare the anti-trinitarian Servet with Paul of Samosata,[6] but already in the first edition of the *Loci communes* he (indirectly) opposes Paul of Samosata's christology. He refers to the fact that Paul of Samosata, who denied the divinity of Christ, was condemned by an Antiochean Synod without the Pope exerting his authority.[7] He produces this as an argument against the authority of the Pope, but such an argument can only be used if one believes that Paul of Samosata was rightly condemned. Similarly he refers to the fact that the Romans believe the Synod at Nicaea rather than the (Semi-Arian) one at Rimini, although

---

[1] (St.A. II), pp. 6f.: Proinde non est, cur multum operae ponamus in locis illis supremis de trinitate dei, de mysterio creationis, de modo incarnationis ... hoc est Christum cognoscere beneficia eius cognoscere, non, quod isti docent, eius naturas, modos incarnationis contueri. Cf. for the following: S. Wiedenhofer, *op. cit.*, pp. 401ff.

[2] *Declamatiuncula in Divi Pauli doctrinam*, dating from 1520 (St.A. I), p. 31: Dimisit igitur in terras opt. max. deus filium carne nostra.

[3] *Did. Fav. adv. Th. Placentinum*, dating from 1521 (St.A. I), p. 75: Voluit sane cognosci se deus, sed ut cognosceretur delapsus est in carnem, cf. *Declamatio de studio doctrinae Paulinae* (CR 11), p. 36: Imo, si per sese hominum animi ad virtutem erigi potuere, quid erat, cur carne Filius Dei, adeoque aeternus sermo, vestiretur.

[4] (St.A. II), p. 82.

[5] (St.A. II), p. 61: De divinitate filii credo Nicaeno concilio, quia scripturae credo, quae Christi divinitatem tam clare nobis probat ...; cf. for the following: K. Haendler, *op. cit.*, pp. 44ff.

[6] See *supra*, 64, 80

[7] (St.A. II), p. 58: Cur enim Antiochenam synodum probas, quae Paulum Samosatenum negantem Christi divinitatem damnavit, cum res omnis citra Romani pontificis auctoritatem gesta sit?

the former one was not proved to be right by the authority of the Pope.[8]
Again such an argument can only be produced if one believes that the
Romans are right in believing that the Synod at Nicaea ought to be
preferred to the one at Rimini.

One may ask: If Melanchthon clearly believes in the divinity of Christ,
which kinds of speculation about the natures of Christ and the ways of the
incarnation does he oppose? Does he only attack the Scholastic
theologians or perhaps also the Fathers? The latter seems highly unlikely
to us: The reason for the incarnation is that man is unable to contemplate
God's majesty, God came down in human flesh as an adaptation to and
as a reminder of human weakness: being unable to contemplate God's
majesty, man could know God in the act of the incarnation.[9] In a similar
statement made in another piece of writing around the same time he
explicitly adds that all Fathers are agreed that men could not see God and
live.[10] It was indeed almost a commonplace in Patristic theology to
describe the revelation given in the incarnation as an adaptation to
human weakness. It appears in Augustin and Ambrose (of whom
Melanchthon claims to have a thorough knowledge at that time) and
others.[11]

It is important, Melanchthon continues, to know the usefulness of the
incarnation. In this connection he makes the following comparison: Is it
enough for a doctor to know the species, colours and features of herbs and
does it not matter whether he knows their natural potency? In the same
way we must know Christ who is given to us as a remedy or, to use a
Scriptural term, as a salvation, in another way than the Scholastics show
Him to us. The incarnation is here compared with the imparting of a
medicine and Melanchthon knows that this is not a Scriptural term,

---

[8] (St.A. II), p. 58: Quaeso te, cur Nicaenae Synodo potius quam Ariminensi credis?
Num quia eam Romani pontificis comprobavit auctoritas? On Melanchthon's views on
the Synod at Rimini see further *supra*, 38f., 61

[9] (St.A. II), p. 6: Et carne filium deus Optimus Maximus induit, ut nos a contempla-
tione maiestatis suae ad carnis adeoque fragilitatis nostrae contemplationem invitaret.

[10] *Did. Fav. adv. Th. Plac.* (St.A. I), p. 75: Nam cum immensa illa maiestas comprehen-
di non posset, eam induit personam, quam complecti mens humana utcunque potuit;
vulgaris enim patrum sententia fuit, non victuros, qui deum vidissent. This is a Biblical
thought, so Melanchthon refers to the Fathers when they express Biblical doctrines.

[11] See e.g. Augustin, *Tractatus in Joannem* 2, 16: Ideo *factum est Verbum caro, et habitavit in
nobis*: sanavit oculos nostros: et quid sequitur? *Et vidimus gloriam eius*. Gloriam eius nemo
posset videre, nisi carnis humilitate sanaretur. Ambrose, *De fide* 5, 7, 99: Unde si sobrie
de Dei Filio quae digna sunt, opinemur, ideo missum intelligere debemus, quia ex illo
incomprehensibili inenarrabilique secreto maiestatis profundae dedit se comprehenden-
dum pro captu nostro mentibus nostris Dei Verbum. See further Irenaeus, *Adv. Haer.* 4,
62, Tertullian, *Adversus Marcionem*, 2, 27, 1, Athanasius, *De Incarnatione Verbi* 43.

hence the words "or—to use a Scriptural term—as a salvation". This comparison is very popular in Patristic writings.[12]

It seems to us that the opening chapter of the first edition of the *Loci communes* is an attack on Scholastic speculations about Christ, an attack in which Melanchthon replaces these speculations by Scriptural and Patristic terminology and arguments. The divinity of Christ is presupposed by Melanchthon, but not speculated upon. In his adherence to the doctrine of the divinity of Christ he is in line with both Luther[13] and Erasmus.[14] There is a reference by the young Melanchthon to Erasmus' views on this matter, *viz.*, in his comment on *Matthew* 19:16, where Melanchthon approves of the interpretation that Christ does not want to be called 'good' by somebody who does not believe Him to be God. Here he refers to Erasmus' explicative note in which this usual Patristic interpretation is cautiously approved of.[15]

The divinity of Christ is presupposed by the young Melanchthon, but he focuses his attention on the work of Christ, His *beneficia*. These *beneficia* are in fact Christ's saving grace, the forgiveness of sins.[16]

---

[12] See e.g. Augustin, *Tract. in Joann.* II 16: Verbum caro factum est: medicus iste tibi fecit collyrium, Tertullian, *Adversus Marcionem* 1, 22, 9, Athanasius, *De Incarnatione Verbi* 43, Cyril of Alexandria, *Adversus Anthropomorphitas* 24. Although it says nowhere in Scripture that the incarnation is a medicine against sin, the Scriptural background could be a word like *Luke* 5:31: It is not those who are well who need a doctor but those who are ill (Irenaeus quotes this word in connection with the preaching of the Gospel, *Adv. Haer.* 3, 5,2).

[13] See the quotations (from all periods of Luther's life) given by Th. Harnack, *Luthers Theologie* II, pp. 126ff., see especially *Operationes in Ps.* 2, 7, 1519-1521 ((W.A. 5), p. 59: "Das ist der Grund und die Meinung des ganzen Evangelii Christum erkennen, dass er Gottes Sohn sei ... Allda ist auch nicht die rechtschaffene christliche Gemeinde, da Christus Christum (den Sohn Gottes) nicht aufs Allerreinste lehret und prediget. Denn es hat sich etwas Grosses, dass er sagt: Der Herr hat zu mir gesagt: Du bist mein Sohn."

[14] See Erasmus' views on the Trinity, *infra*, 120ff.

[15] See *Annotationes in Evangelium Matthaei* (St.A. IV), p. 192, which came out in 1523, but are based on lectures given in 1519/1520 (see P. Barton's introductory notes, p. 133): Alii et melius eo referunt quasi dicat Christus: cur me bonum dicis? quem Deum non credis? Agit in pluribus in Annotationibus Erasmus. See *Erasmi opera omnia*, t. VI, ed. J. Clericus, p. 101: Imo Christus subindicat se esse Deum, et ob id iuxta quorundam interpretationem obiurgat hominem quod ei tribueret cognomen *boni*, quam nondum crederet Deum, quod haud scio an quisquam apostolorum adhuc perfecte crediderat. Erasmus explicitly rejects as heretical the view that the word 'good' in the proper sense only applies to the Father. This is the usual Patristic interpretation of this text, see e.g. Hilary of Poitiers, *De Trinitate* 9, 17, Augustin, *De Trinitate* 1, 13, 31.

[16] *Loci communes*, dating from 1521 (St.A. II), p. 7: Certe de lege, peccato, gratia, e quibus locis solis Christi cognitio pendet, see also *Declamatiuncula in Divi Pauli doctrinam* (St.A. I), pp. 28ff., cf. T. Schäfer, *Christologie und Sittlichkeit in Melanchthons frühen Loci*, Tübingen 1961, pp. 59f. In his commentary on the Gospel according to St. Matthew (St.A. IV), pp. 184f., he makes a distinction between a human opinion about Christ and a divinely inspired one. The former one speculates about His nature and majesty, the latter one is held by those who confess Christ as the Son of the living God and are free from sin, death and an accusing conscience. Here the divinity of Christ is clearly confessed, but all

Later on Melanchthon refers more explicitly to Patristic writers in his defence of the divinity of Christ. But we also detect some speculation on the natures of Christ which is backed up by Patristic authorities. Christ died in His human nature, not in His divine nature, Melanchthon says.[17] The doctrine of the *communicatio idiomatum* is explained and approved of. This doctrine makes it clear why it can be said of Christ "God has died", whilst it has been established that Christ died in His human nature and that divinity as such is immortal: In the hypostatical union proprieties of one nature can also be attributed to the other one. In this sense it can be said "God has died", but not "The divinity has died".[18] Is Melanchthon here making statements about the natures of Christ which he rejected as idle curiosity in the first edition of the *Loci communes*? There seem to be some reasons to answer this question affirmatively. The definition he gives of the *communicatio idiomatum* shows great similarity with statements made on this matter by Scholastics whom Melanchthon opposes.[19] Melanchthon himself would presumably not have acknowledged a change of mind in this respect. He does not explicitly refer to Scholastic authorities in this context, but to Fathers like Irenaeus, Athanasius,

---

attention is given to the usefulness of this confession: a liberated life. See on this subject further O. Ritschl, Die Entwicklung der Rechtfertigungslehre Melanchthons bis zum Jahre 1527, *Theologische Studien und Kritiken* (85), 1912, pp. 522ff.

[17] See *supra*, 31, 68, 70.

[18] See *Explicatio Symb. Nic.* (CR 23), p. 371, p. 508, *Postilla Melanchthoniana* (CR 24), p. 132, p. 561, pp. 923f., *Responsio de controversiis Stancari* (St.A. VI), pp. 261ff., *Disputationes* (CR 12), p. 593. The definition which Melanchthon gives of the *communicatio idiomatum* is (see *Explic. Symb. Nic.*, CR 23, p. 371): est forma loquendi, qua proprietas conveniens uni naturae tribuitur personae in concreto, propterea quia unica est persona, ut dicimus, Homo numerat, etiamsi tantum mente numerat. Ac diligenter retinenda est forma loquendi gravi autoritate recepta: nequaquam dicitur in abstracto: Divinitas est mortua, quia in abstracto significatur natura secundum se considerata, et tribuitur uni naturae hoc quod contrarium est huic naturae, ut cum dicerem: Sanguis numerat aut nasus. See further *Loci communes*, dating from 1559 (St.A. II), p. 199 (and also the edition of 1535, CR 21, p. 363), letter to Musculus, dating from 1553 (CR 8), p. 68, *En. Symb. Nic.* (CR 23), pp. 342f., *Explic. Symb. Nic.*, p. 509, *Postilla Melanchthoniana* (CR 24), p. 861, *Examen ordinandorum* (CR 23), p. 6. — For Luther's views on this doctrine see Th. Harnack, *Luthers Theologie* II, pp. 157f.

[19] See e.g. John of Damascus, *De fide orthodoxa* III 4 (Migne PG 94, 998f.), Thomas Aquinas, *Summa Theologica* III qu. 16, art. 5: In mysterio autem incarnationis non est eadem divina natura et humana: sed est eadem hypostasis utriusque naturae. Et ideo ea quae sunt unius naturae, non possunt de alia praedicari secundum quod in abstracto significantur. Nomina vero concreta supponunt hypostasim naturae. Et ideo indifferenter praedicari possunt ea quae ad utramque naturam pertinent, de nominibus concretis ... Et ideo quaedam dicuntur de Filio Dei quae non dicuntur de divina natura: sicut dicimus quod Filius Dei est genitus, non tamen dicimus quod divina natura sit genita ... Et similiter in mysterio incarnationis dicimus quod Filius Dei est passus, non autem dicimus quod natura divina sit passa, — cf. Melanchthon's definition of the *communicatio idiomatum* quoted in the previous note.

Jerome, Ambrose, and Augustin.[20] But rather interestingly the quotations he gives from the Fathers in order to back up the (Scholastic) doctrine of the *communicatio idiomatum* only partly say what this doctrine says, *viz.*, say that Christ died in His human nature so that His death does not contradict His divinity, these quotations are at the utmost a part of the later, elaborated doctrine of the *communicatio idiomatum* which Melanchthon provides. So Melanchthon explains the doctrine of the *communicatio idiomatum* with Patristic texts which in reality have little to do with this doctrine. It could be that Melanchthon wanted (consciously or unconsciously) to give the impression that the doctrine of the *communicatio idiomatum* cannot be idle speculation, since it is testified to by the Fathers.[21] Melanchthon comes forward with these expositions when he wants to refute the tenet: "The divinity cannot die, Christ died, so Christ cannot be God." He will have had the feeling that as he first attacked futile speculation on the natures of Christ with the sound Patristic doctrine about Christ's work,[22] he now refutes attacks on the divinity of Christ with the sound Patristic doctrine about the two natures of Christ. The fact that Servet, whose doctrine about the Trinity Melanchthon opposes right from the beginning, attacked the doctrine of the *communicatio idiomatum*[23] may have been a reason for Melanchthon to defend his views on the Trinity with the help of just this doctrine. (It is not uncommon that a theologian starts liking a doctrine as soon as he notices that his theological opponent dislikes it).—Closely connected with all this is that later on Melanchthon also reflects on the way in which the two natures of Christ are united. He likes to compare this union with the union of the soul and the body.[24] This Patristic comparison is given in order to maintain the divinity of Christ and to mark the clear difference between God's presence in Christ and other ways in which God's presence becomes

---

[20] See the quotations from these Fathers in the previous chapter under the heading of christology.

[21] If our assumption that Melanchthon ascribes Scholastic doctrines to the Fathers and thereby gives these doctrines authority is right, then Melanchthon certainly goes a big step further than the young Luther who only accepts Scholastics doctrines when they have clear backing of the Fathers, see H. Jürgens, Die Funktion der Kirchenväterzitate in der Heidelberger Disputation Luthers (1518), *Archiv für Reformationsgeschichte* (66) 1975, pp. 71ff. (in connection with Petrus Lombardus and Augustin).

[22] See *supra*, 109, 110.

[23] See *De Trinitatis erroribus libri septem*, per Michaelem Serveto, alias Reves, ab Aragonia, Hispanum, 1521, p. 9, p. 11, p. 59, pp 76ff., *Dialogorum de Trinitate libri duo*, per Michaelem Serveto, alias Reves, ab Aragonia Hispanum, 1532, p. A 7, p. B 3. On Servet and Melanchthon see the study referred to *supra*, 67, note 250, by H. Tollin. Tollin's thesis that Servet first wanted to be Melanchthon's pupil and later on for a while positively influenced Melanchthon(*op. cit.*, pp. 88ff.), has been correctly refuted by I. K. F. Knaake, *Theologische Studien und Kritiken* (54), 1881, pp. 317ff.

[24] See *supra*, 35f., 55, 79.

manifest.[25] Again Melanchthon may have had the feeling that a return to the Patristic doctrine on this matter was a sound way of refuting attacks on the divinity of Christ.[26]—Similarly Melanchthon approves of the Scholastic doctrine "Opera trinitatis ad extra sunt indivisa, scilicet servata cuiusque personae proprietate" with the (usual) reference to Augustin.[27]

There is, however, one aspect in which there seems to be a considerable development in the thought of Melanchthon in the sense that he later on does himself what he initially rejected. Initially Melanchthon insists that man should refrain from speculation about God's being and concentrate on God's manifest will, and that he should not enquire into the motives of God's will.[28] As we have seen,[29] later on Melanchthon discusses extensively the reasons why the Son of God became man. Melanchthon himself may have had the feeling that he did not deviate from his initial positions, since he once introduces his enumeration of the reasons for the incarnation with the remark that he does not want to detract from God's free decree which is the final cause of the incarnation.[30] Furthermore, the reasons he gives centre to a large degree around the divine victory over human sin and death. In the third place he once says, before enumerating the reasons for the incarnation, that these reasons are given by the Fathers.[31] All this could still be regarded as an elaboration of what is said in the wake of the Fathers in the first edition of the *Loci communes*, *viz.*, that the goal of the incarnation is that man should

---

[25] See e.g. *Responsio de controversiis Stancari*, dating from 1553 (St.A. VI), pp. 265f., where God's presence in Christ is distinguished from His presence in all creatures, in the angels, in the saved in heaven, and in the reborn in this life, cf. *Explic. Symb. Nic.* (CR 23), pp. 368f., *Postilla Melanchthoniana* (CR 24), pp. 129f., — a similar distinction appears in Petrus Lombardus, *Sent.* I, dist. xxxvii, cap. 1, 2: Quod deus in omni re est potentia, praesentia, et in sanctis per gratiam, et in homine Christo per unionem.

[26] See *Responsio de controversiis Stancari* (St.A. VI), p. 266: Reverenter considerandum est consilium Dei, et gratiae Deo agendae sunt, quod misit Filium et hac miranda assumptione foedus nobiscum fecit et ostendit ingentem amorem erga nos. Ac pium est uti modis loquendi usitatis et non procul quaerere profanas quaestiones et modos loquendi inusitatos.

[27] *Explic. Symb. Nic.* (CR 23), p. 374, cf. e.g. *Enchiridion symbolorum definitionum et declarationum de rebus fidei et morum*, edd. Denzinger/Schönmetzer, Herder Freiburg i.B., 1968[32], p. 177, the usual reference is to Augustin, *De Trinitate* 1, 4.

[28] See *supra*, 5.

[29] See *supra*, 94.

[30] *En. Symb. Nic.* (CR 23), p. 338: Decretum hoc factum est liberrimo consilio Dei, nec ita recitabimus causas, quasi aliquid de libertate voluntatis in Deo detrahatur, sed certum est miranda sapientia, et servato ordine iustitiae et misericordiae hoc decretum factum esse.

[31] *Responsio de controversiis Stancari*, dating from 1553 (St.A. VI), p. 273: Vetustas causas quaesivit, quare Salvator non tantum sit homo, et causae recensentur ...

know the *beneficia* of Christ, i.e. the forgiveness of sins. Here we have the same picture as in connection with the doctrine of the *communicatio idiomatum*: typically Scholastic speculations are adopted, but presented as Patristic ones. But things are different when Melanchthon wants to answer the question why the Son and not the Father or the Holy Spirit became man.[32] The reasons which Melanchthon gives have little to do with man's salvation, but are meant as an explanation of why this way of revealing Himself was becoming to God. This question was asked and dealt with in Scholastic theology.[33] Melanchthon does not refer to Scholastics in this context, but to Augustin (who does not, however, provide the answer Melanchthon ascribes to him). Melanchthon may have had the idea that if the answer given to this question can be found in Augustin it no longer falls under the verdict of speculation,—but this does not alter the fact that Melanchthon here does himself what he initially rejected as futile speculation: God's will is manifest in the incarnation of the Son, but Melanchthon asks whether this revelation is becoming to God's being as Father, Son and Holy Ghost.—Something similar can be found in Melanchthon's assertion that God would be the Father of the Son even if no world had been created. Melanchthon says this when he answers the question "What is God?" with a reference to the eternal Father, Son and Holy Ghost. He defines the Son as God's eternal λόγος and εἰκών. The Son is called εἰκών with respect to the Father, since He is generated by the thought of the Father through selfcontuition of the Father. Since this takes place in eternity, this title εἰκών not only applies to the Son's work, but is also an indication of the order of the eternal divine Persons, and the Son would therefore be the Father's λόγος and εἰκών even if no world had been created.[34] Again Melanchthon immediately refers to the Fathers as supporters of this doctrine,[35] and perhaps he had the feeling that, since this doctrine has Patristic backing, it is not idle speculation, but this, too, does not alter the fact that here statements are made about God's being which are not the immediate consequence of God's actual revelation, but which are the result of human reflections on what lies behind actual revelation. The very fact

---

[32] See *supra*, 20f.

[33] See apart from the passage in Petrus Lombardus quoted *supra*, 21, also Thomas Aquinas, *Summa Theologica* III qu. 3, art. 5.

[34] *Postilla Melanchthoniana* (CR 24), p. 74: Neque tamen prior enarratio illa, cur Filius nominetur λόγος et εἰκών respectu Patris aspernanda est: Quia monstrat ordinem personarum, ac docet, filium esse verbum et imaginem Patris, etiamsi numquam conditus esset mundus. — On the connection between this statement and Melanchthon's later views on creation see *infra*, 132.

[35] Melanchthon continues: Ideo veteres scriptores Graeci ac Latini plurimum usi sunt hac explicatione vocabulorum respectu Patris, ut est apud Basilium, Nazianzenum, Augustinum et alios. See for this doctrine also Athanasius, *Contra Arianos* 2, 31.

that Melanchthon makes in this context statements about how the Son
was eternally generated by the Father, also falls in the same category of
statements which the young Reformer Melanchthon described as
speculation. The Son is generated because the Father in selfcontuition
thinks an Imago of Himself. The earliest example of this doctrine we
could find dates from 1527.[36] Later on it appears repeatedly and in a
more elaborated way.[37] Melanchthon draws support for this doctrine
from the Fathers, especially Basil and Augustin,[38] but again this does not
alter the fact that he speculates here about the mystery of the Trinity
without being able to demonstrate the clear connection between what is
said here and forgiveness of sins through Christ, and such speculation
was rejected by the young Reformer Melanchthon.[39]—In the same context Melanchthon repeatedly answers the question why the Son is
generated and the Holy Ghost procedes and what the difference between
these two is.[40] To begin with he shows less hesitation in dealing with this
question than e.g. Augustin and Petrus Lombardus.[41] Melanchthon
makes the distinction between the generation of the Son and the procession of the Holy Spirit quite clear: Man has two faculties, *viz.*, to think
and to will. By thinking he creates images, by willing he is driven. These
faculties can be used as examples: The Son is generated by the thought as

---

[36] *Scholia in Epistulam Pauli ad Colossenses* (St.A. IV), p. 285: Vocatur enim ideo filius
verbum quia sicut in cogitando rei de qua cogitamus, simulacrum concipimus, ita
substantialis imago Patris Filius est, sic in epistula ad Hebraeos scriptum est: "Character
substantiae eius".

[37] *Liber de anima*, dating from 1553 (St.A. III), p. 335: Ibi crebri motu et spiritibus for-
mantur cogitationes quae sunt imagines rerum, quae cogitantur seu aspiciuntur. Eodem
modo et mente pingimus imagines, ut unusquisque cogitans suos parentes, in ea ipsa
actione format eorum imagines ... Mirando autem consilio Deus notitias voluit esse
imagines, quia in nobis umbras esse voluit significantes aliquid de ipso. Aeternus Pater
sese intuens gignit Filium cogitando, qui est imago aeterni Patris, cf. pp. 308f., pp. 361ff.,
Postilla Melanchthoniana (CR 24), pp. 910f., *Explic. Symb. Nic.* (CR 23), p. 367, *Annotationes
in Evangelia* (CR 14), p. 281.

[38] See *supra*, 29f., 42.

[39] We agree with K. Haendler, *op. cit.*, pp. 131ff., that there is more continuity
between the late and the young Melanchthon in this respect than has often been thought,
but doubt whether one can say that the trinitarian views of the later Melanchthon were
only 'heilsgeschichtlich' and essentially unspeculative. A certain element of speculation
cannot, it seems to us, be denied.

[40] See *Examen ordinandorum* (CR 23), pp. 3f., *Explic. Symb. Nic.* (CR 23), pp. 380ff., p.
500, *Postilla Melanchthoniana* (CR 24), p. 871, *Enarratio Evang. Joan.* (CR 15), p. 348.

[41] In *En. in Ev. Joann.* (CR 15), p. 348, he makes the following qualification: Si
hominum natura incorrupta esset, consideratio eius magis nos erudisset de Deo. But he
immediately goes on to say: Sed sumamus tamen aliquo modo exempla ab hominum
natura. Augustin shows much more restraint, see *De Trin.* 9, 12, 17-18 and 15, 27, 50:
Sed ad hoc dilucide perspicueque cernendum, non potes ibi aciem figere; scio, non potes.
Verum dico, mihi dico, quid non possim scio. Petrus Lombardus says, *Sent.* I, dist. xiii,
cap. 3: Inter generationem vero Filii et processionem Spiritus sancti, dum hic vivimus,
distinguere non sufficimus.

the Image of the Father. The Father and the Son look at each other and thereby will and love each other, out of this mutual love the Holy Spirit procedes.[42] This is obviously a brief summary of the tentative expositions put forward by Augustin,[43] and what is said here shows great similarity with statements made by Thomas Aquinas on this matter.[44]—In later times Melanchthon still opposes futile speculations about the Trinity, as appears from his assertion that what he says about the Trinity is not futile speculation, but that his words must lead to an understanding of human weakness and the need for divine help.[45] This remark proves that Melanchthon always opposed speculations which had nothing to do with a life which wants to receive God's grace, but what he sometimes says about the Trinity shows that he (consciously or unconsciously) did change his mind on what should be regarded as futile speculation and what should not. It cannot be denied that there is an element of discontinuity between the young Reformer and the later Melanchthon in what he actually says about Christ in the context of the doctrine of the Trinity. But the statements about the Trinity which Melanchthon later on makes and which he would have rejected in the beginning as speculative are relatively small in number and his initial insistence on the work of Christ, which is the forgiveness of sins, remains important in later times. In the latest edition of the *Loci communes* he still calls the doctrine of grace and justification the *summa evangelii* and explains this with a reference to the *beneficium* of Christ.[46] He still insists that faith is not only knowledge in

---

[42] *Enarratio in Evang. Joannis* (CR 15), pp. 348f.: Duae sunt facultates animae, facultas intelligens, et facultas volens. Intelligens gignit imagines cogitando, volens habet impetus ... Ab his exemplis sumitur declaratio, cum filius vocetur λόγος, gignitur cogitando. Est autem cogitatio imago rei cogitatae, λόγος igitur dicitur filius, quia filius est imago patris. At spiritus sanctus dicitur procedere, quia voluntatis est amor. Intuens igitur Pater Filium, vult et amat eum, ac vicissim Filius intuens Patrem, vult et amat eum. Hoc mutuo amore, qui proprie est voluntatum, procedit Spiritus sanctus, qui est agitator ab aeterno Patre, et filio coaeterna imagine Patris. See further the passages quoted in note 40.

[43] See the passages from the *De Trinitate* given in note 41.

[44] *Summa Theologica* I, qu. xxvii, art. 4: ... processio amoris in divinis non debet dici generatio. Ad cuius evidentiam, sciendum est quod haec est differentia inter intellectum et voluntatem quod intellectus fit in actu per hoc quod res intellecta est in intellectu secundum suam similitudinem: voluntas autem fit in actu, non per hoc quod aliqua similitudo voliti sit in voluntate, sed ex hoc quod voluntas habet quandam inclinationem in rem volitam.

[45] *Postilla Melanchthoniana* (CR 24), pp. 874f.: Haec sunt observanda, et discenda in quotidianis exercitiis verae poenitentiae, et invocationis: ibi enim experimur hanc doctrinam non esse speculationes otiosas: et sicut caeterae artes non discuntur sine usu: ita hae tantae res tantum discuntur usu et experientia. Ibi etiam intelligimus, oportere in nobis esse agnitionem nostrae infirmitatis, et desiderium auxilii divini, et luctam certantem cum infirmitate, cf. also *supra*, 109, note 4.

[46] (St.A. II), p. 353: Hic locus continet summam Evangelii. Monstrat enim proprium Christi beneficium. S. Wiedenhofer, *op. cit.*, pp. 182ff., rightly stresses the continuity in

one's mind, but also trust in one's heart and will and as such gives consolation to man in his anxiety.[47] These and similar statements occur much more often in the later writings of Melanchthon than the typically speculative ones (from Melanchthon's initial point of view). His speculations on God's being are an addition in later times to the original theme which Melanchthon never abandoned. In later times he does not contrast the doctrine of the *beneficia* of Christ with the doctrine of Christ's person, but he puts these two doctrines beside each other.[48] This can nicely be illustrated with the mild criticism he later on sometimes makes of Patristic christology and with the development in his thought on God's will and God's being:

According to Melanchthon certain Biblical texts speak about the essence of the Son, other texts about the work of the Son. As examples of the latter category he lists *John* 14:28 "The Father is more than I am" and *John* 17:5 "Father glorify Me". Melanchthon observes that the Arians want to show with these texts that the Father is in His being more than the Son. The usual orthodox reply is that these texts refer to the human and not to the divine nature of Christ. Melanchthon rejects the Arian assertion, but also says that there is a more simple (i.e. less speculative[49]) solution than the one which is put forward by the orthodox Fathers, and that solution is that the Son here does not speak about His essence, but about His work which is to speak with the authority of one who has been sent by the Father.[50] Although the criticism he makes of the

---

the thought of Melanchthon on the following points: Knowledge of God has a christological basis, it is soteriological, it implies knowledge of Christ's *beneficia*, it is caused by Scriptural revelation which is testified by the Holy Spirit.

[47] *Postilla Melanchthoniana* (CR 24), pp. 81f.: Est enim fides non tantum notitia in mente, sed simul est fiducia in voluntate et corde, et sic consolationem affert, quando in seriis pavoribus homo sustentat se voce Evangelii, et intuetur filium.

[48] See e.g. *Loci communes*, dating from 1559 (St.A. II), p. 213: In tali invocatione quotidie de essentia Dei, de patefactione, de beneficiis, de promissionibus.

[49] See *supra*, 66.

[50] *Explic. Symb. Nic.* (CR 23), p. 375: Ariani citabant hoc dictum: Pater maior est me, inde ratiocinabantur, Filium non esse ὁμοούσιον Patri, non omnipotentem. Responsio usitata est, Maior me est, scilicet quam ego sum, secundum naturam humanam, ita plerumque decurrunt veteres ad hanc responsionem sumtam ex communicatione idiomatum. Sed simplicior responsio est: alia dicta de essentia loquuntur, alia de officio personae. Manifestum est autem hoc dictum, Pater maior me est, loqui de officio huius personae missae et praedicantis, et obedientis in passione, non loquitur de inaequalitate essentiae. Cum enim Iudaei accusarent Christum, quod doceret contra autoritatem Dei, necesse fuit Christo allegare autoritatem Patris, a quo affirmat se missum esse, et traditam sibi doctrinam et mandatum docendi, ac Patrem maiorem esse dicit, tanquam mittentem, fontem doctrinae, cf. p. 511, *Enarratio Symb. Nic.* (CR 23), p. 228, *Loci communes*, dating from 1559 (St.A. II), pp. 200f. — For this Patristic exegesis see e.g. Augustin, *Tractatus in Joannem* 78, 3, Hilary of Poitiers, *De Trin.* 9, 51ff. (although Hilary stresses that Christ here speaks about Himself in the state of obedience in the flesh, which is close to what Melanchthon wants to say). John Calvin is in this respect much harsher in his criticism of the orthodox Fathers than Melanchthon, see E. P. Meijering, *Calvin wider die Neugierde*, pp. 88ff.

Fathers is less harsh than the one he makes of the Arians, the orthodox clearly do not escape criticism, and this criticism shows that also in his later years Melanchthon was interested in the orthodox doctrine about Christ's nature only in so far as it was necessary to understand Christ's work as a Redeemer.

As we have seen,[51] the young Reformer Melanchthon stresses that man should not speculate about God's being, but concentrate on God's manifest will. This does not, of course, mean that Melanchthon denies that there is a being of God, but he insists that faith should not focus on it, since it remains God's secret, and that instead faith should focus its attention on God's will, i.e. His revelation given to us. God's being is to the young Reformer Melanchthon the mysterious background of God's will. Here we can observe a clear shift of emphasis in Melanchthon's thought, since he later on stresses that the Christians must know *God's essence and God's will*, and that this knowledge of both God's being and God's will distinguishes the Christian from Jews and Pagans. God's being is that He is Father, Son and Holy Ghost, God's will appears in the history which leads to the incarnation of Christ through whom forgiveness of sins is received. This is repeated by Melanchthon time and again.[52] It is understandable that when Melanchthon was confronted

---

[51] See *supra*, 4ff., to the examples given on p. 4, note 2 can be added *Loci communes*, dating from 1521 (St.A. II), p. 118: Vult cognosci voluntatem suam deus, vult gloriari nos de voluntate sua. Quid est igitur magis impium quam negare vel non debere vel non posse cognosci voluntatem divinam. Nempe cum eam expresserit verbo suo? See also H. Engelland, *Melanchthon, Glauben und Handeln*, pp. 10ff., pp. 73ff.

[52] See e.g. *Annotationes in Evangelia* (CR 14), p. 279: Invocant Turci et alii impii, sed aberrant a Deo dupliciter. Primum quod de essentia Dei falsam opinionem mordicus retinent. Secundo quod voluntatem ignorant. Turci enim et similes, etsi dicunt hunc esse Deum, qui condidit caelum et terram, tamen negant esse verum Deum, hunc, qui se per Filium patefecit, qui tradidit nobis Evangelium, negant Filium et Spiritum sanctum esse de essentia Patris. Ita primum de essentia errant. Postea et de voluntate, quia verbum revelatum a Patre abiecerunt, ignorant promissionem gratiae nec possunt credere se respici et exaudiri ... Seiungenda est igitur ab illorum opinionibus nostra invocatio, ac primum cogitandum, quis sit Deus, is videlicet ac talis, qui se in verbo suo patefecit ab initio, post conditionem et lapsum Adae. Sic autem patefecit se Deus in Evangelio suo: Unus est omnipotens et aeternus Pater, qui cum Filio suo, qui est coaeterna imago Patris, et Spiritu sancto, condidit omnes res bonas, et patefecit se dato verbo et misso Filio. Deinde, quia obstrepit tibi indignitas ... propone animo promissiones Evangelii: Cogita Deum mandasse, ut invocemus, et credamus placere et recipi nostras preces propter Filium. See further the following places where this view is expressed briefly or in lengthy expositions: *Loci communes*, dating from 1559 (St.A. II), pp. 175f., pp. 654f., *Annotationes et conciones in Evang. Matthaei* (CR 14), p. 966, *Enarratio in Evang. Joannis* (CR 15), p. 301, p. 331, *Explic. Symb. Nic.* (CR 23), pp. 355ff., p. 497, p. 525, *Postilla Melanchthoniana* (CR 24), p. 252, p. 475, pp. 762f., pp. 826f. (CR 25), pp. 15f., *Conf. Saxonica* (St.A. VI), p. 123, *Declamatio de Dei invocatione* (CR 11), pp. 662f., *Disputationes* (CR 12), p. 529, pp. 560f., cf. F. Hübner, *Natürliche Theologie und theokratische Schwärmerei bei Melanchthon*, Gütersloh 1936, pp. 58f.

with Jews, Muslims and anti-trinitarians who rejected the doctrine of the Trinity which he took for granted, he felt obliged to state explicitly that faith in the three Persons who are the one divine Being is an integral part of Christianity. It should not, however, be overlooked that Melanchthon does not speculate on the relationship between God's being and God's will. As Melanchthon probably knew[53] such speculations existed not only in Scholastic, but also in Patristic writings. Melanchthon ignores these speculations, since he is not interested in the relation between God's being and God's will, but wants to make sure that his readers know about God's saving will in Christ and about God as the triune God (the latter being the necessary background of the former). In this development one aspect should not be overlooked: The young Melanchthon says that the mystery of the Trinity should be adored rather than speculated upon. When Melanchthon later on defends the doctrine of the Trinity it is often because he wants to make clear what distinguishes the Christian *invocation* of God from the Pagan one.[54] This shows that the adoration of the Trinity always was of primary importance to Melanchthon both in earlier and later years. This certainly betrays a good deal of continuity in his thought on this matter. Melanchthon even wants to make us believe that there is much more continuity: At the outbreak of Servet's attack on the Trinity he says in a letter to Camerarius that Camerarius knows that Melanchthon had always been afraid that this would happen.[55] This should certainly be taken *cum grano salis*: If he really had been afraid of this at the time of the first edition of the *Loci communes*, he would certainly not have dismissed expositions on the Trinity, since he would have been afraid that this could be misinterpreted as a rejection of the Trinity.

Finally it seems fruitful to compare Melanchthon's views on christology and the Trinity with certain aspects of Erasmus' views on this matter.

Erasmus often expresses his faith in the orthodox doctrine of the Trinity: There is one divine substance and there are three divine Persons, about which he speaks in a typically Patristic way.[56] The *filioque*

---

[53] See *supra*, 61, 100, his reference to the problem of whether the Son was generated by free will or by necessity and *infra*, 131, his statement about God's will to create.

[54] See the passages quoted *supra*, 119, note 52.

[55] Letter to Camerarius, dating from 1533 (CR 2), p. 630: Περὶ τῆς τριάδος scis me semper veritum esse, fore ut haec aliquando erumperent.

[56] See e.g. *Explanatio Symboli* (ed. J. N. Bakhuizen van den Brink), p. 215: esse unum Deum, quae tamen appellatio complectitur tres personas, Patrem qui solus a nullo est, Filium a Patre sine tempore genitum, Spiritum sanctum ab utroque procedentem ... Tres sunt proprietatibus distincti, sed trium eadem est substantia sive natura aut, quod verbum quidam arbitrantur aptius, essentia, *De ratione concionandi* IV (*Erasmi opera omnia* t. V, ed. J. Clericus), p. 1073.

is affirmed.[57] The work of the creation is the work of the three divine Persons.[58] He claims always to have adhered to the ecclesiastical doctrine of the Trinity and to have rejected Arianism.[59]

So far Erasmus' views on the Trinity will certainly have been welcome to Melanchthon. But there are also some difficulties here. In his explanation of the Apostolic Creed Erasmus does say that the number of Scriptural texts which confirm the doctrine of the Trinity is countless.[60] But in his *Annotationes* he is much more cautious. There he says that *John* 20:28 is the only place where Christ is plainly called 'God'.[61] In explaining the texts which seem to call Christ 'God' he leaves the possibility open that those texts do not say this.[62] He admits that the term ὁμοούσιος is not a Biblical one, but asserts that it is a legitimate conclusion on the authority of the Fathers from Biblical texts.[63] Erasmus does not mind the fact that

---

[57] *Explanatio Symboli*, pp. 268ff.

[58] *Explanatio Symboli*, p. 230: Est quidem omnibus personis mundi creatio communis. Siquidem Pater universam creaturam condidit per Filium cooperante Spiritu sancto, sic tamen ut hic nec instrumentum imagineris nec ministrum.

[59] *Apologia adversus Monachos quosdam Hispanos* (*Erasmi opera omnia* t. IX, ed. J. Clericus), p. 1023: Cum meae Lucubrationes tam numerosae, locis innumeris, ingenue dilucide, vivideque profiteantur de sacrosancta Triade, quod tradit Ecclesia Catholica, hoc est, divinae naturae aequalitatem in tribus Personis, imo ut expressius dicam, eandem individuam essentiam in tribus Personis, proprietatibus distinctis, non natura divisis: cumque toties detester Arianorum dogmata, insignis cuiusdam impudentiae videtur, mihi tam exsecrandae impietatis suspicionem impingere, quasi cum Arianis sentiam. — The number of times Erasmus opposes the Arians is indeed considerable, se e.g. *Enarratio Psalmi I* (*Erasmi opera omnia* t. V, ed. J. Clericus), p. 176, *De amabili ecclesiae concordia* (*Erasmi opera omnia* t. V, ed. J. Clericus), p. 475, and further the places in his writings which Erasmus himself lists when he wants to show that he always believed in the full divinity of the Son, *Apologia adversus Monachos quosdam Hispanos*, pp. 1023-1029, *Apologia ad Sanctum Caranzam* (*Erasmi opera omnia* t. IX), pp. 402ff., cf. *Apologia ad Stunicam* (*Erasmi opera omnia* t. IX), pp. 351ff. We have seen that Erasmus does defend the (Semi-) Arians as well, but then he does so, because he believes them to be less heretical than the orthodox opponents claim, see *supra*, 39.

[60] *Explanatio Symboli*, p. 223: Sed ex innumeris scripturae locis liquido patet unam et eandem trium esse divinitatem.

[61] (*Erasmi opera omnia* t. VI, ed. J. Clericus), p. 417: Hic est unus locus, in quo palam Evangelista Christo *Dei* vocabulam tribuit. In explaining the first epistle to Timothy he says (*Erasmi opera omnia* t. VI, ed. J. Clericus), pp. 930f.: Verum id rarum est in litteris Apostolicis, Christo aut Spiritui sancto tribuere vocabulam *Dei*.

[62] See his annotations on *Romans* 9:5, *Titus* 2:13, *First Epistle of John* 5:7 (*Erasmi opera omnia* t. VI), pp. 610f., p. 971, pp. 1079ff.

[63] *De ratione concionandi III* (*Erasmi opera omnia* t. V, ed. J. Clericus), pp. 1044f.: ... Filius dicitur homousios Patri, Pater ingenitus ac ἄναρχος, quum nihil horum expressum sit in sacris litteris, sed hinc certa ratiocinatione colliguntur, IV, p. 1090: Veluti quod dicitur homousios, tametsi vox haec in Scripturis canonicis non invenitur, est tamen a priscis orthodoxis magno consensu recepta. The Scriptural place which provides the strongest basis is *John* 1:2 "And the Word was God", see his annotation to this verse in *Erasmi opera omnia* t. VI, ed. J. Clericus, p. 337: ... hoc est particeps Essentiae divinae, sive ut melius dicam Graece, ὁμοούσιον τῷ Πατρί, on the importance of this see also the annotation on *Titus* 2:13 (*Erasmi opera omnia* t. VI), p. 971: Si Filius Dei tantum in principio Evangelii Joannis adeo clare pronuntiatus esset Deus, nonne sufficeret adversus universos Arianos?

the doctrine of the Trinity is not directly expressed in Scripture, since he believes it on the authority of the Church. The authority of the Church is so important to him that he is prepared to accept an exegesis of texts with which he himself does not agree, if the church prescribes it.[64] This is the exact opposite of Melanchthon's attitude, since Melanchthon in this matter only wants to believe what the (ancient) Church and the Fathers say in so far as they are clearly expressing Scriptural doctrines.[65] Melanchthon feels obliged to provide direct Scriptural proof for the doctrine that the Son is God.[66]

Furthermore it is interesting to see that Erasmus rejects as meaningless curiosity some questions about the Trinity which Melanchthon later on treats seriously, *viz.*, whether any other divine person could have assumed any nature in the way in which the Son assumed human nature,[67] or why the Holy Ghost procedes and is not generated.[68] To Erasmus it is enough to say that there are the Father, the Son and the Holy Ghost.[69]

The doctrine of the Trinity was obviously a less urgent problem to Erasmus than it was to Melanchthon. The anti-trinitarian movement did

---

[64] See his annotation on *Romans* 9:5 (*Erasmi opera omnia* t. VI, ed. J. Clericus), p. 611: Caeterum si Ecclesia doceat hunc locum non aliter interpretandum quam de divinitate Filii, parendum est Ecclesiae, and the annotation to the *First Epistle of John* 5:3 (*Erasmi opera omnia* t. VI), p. 1081: Totus hic locus de consensu caritatis ac testimonii tractat, et velimus nolimus cogimur illud *unum* aliter interpretari de nobis quam de personis divinis. Non igitur constringit locus nisi compellat Orthodoxorum auctoritas et Ecclesiae praescriptio, docens hunc locum aliter exponi non posse. Pium autem est nostrum sensum semper Ecclesiae iudicio submittere, simul atque claram illius sententiam audierimus. Nec interim tamen nefas est citra contentionem scrutari verum, ut Deus aliis alia patefacit.

[65] See *supra*, 7ff.

[66] See e.g. *Loci communes*, dating from 1559 (St.A. II), pp. 194ff., where *inter alia Romans* 9:5 (a text about which Erasmus expresses doubts whether it says that Christ is God) is quoted as a clear Scriptural proof that Christ is God.

[67] See his annotation on *I Timothy* 1:6 (*Erasmi opera omnia* t. VI, ed. J. Clericus), p. 927: Quid autem nunc loquar de quaestiunculis, non solum supervacaneis, sed pene dixerim impiis quas movemus de potestate dei ... An quaelibet persona divina possit quamlibet naturam assumere, quomodo Verbum humanam assumpsit. Melanchthon does not discuss the question whether another divine Person could have assumed *any* nature, but whether another divine Person could have assumed human nature, see *supra*, 20, 115.

[68] *Hyperaspistae Diatribes I* (*Erasmi opera omnia* t. X), p. 1259: Caeterum circa materiam hanc multa quaesita sunt olim ab Augustino, plura a recentioribus ... Erasmus admits that such curious questions are already to be found in Augustin (cf. *supra*, 14ff.), later on in the same treatise he says that the Fathers like Hilary, Augustin and Athanasius only with great reluctance dared to speak about God's mystery which is beyond human comprehension, p. 1274: At quoties Hilarius disputaturus de mysteriis sacrae Triadis, deprecatur crimen irreligiositatis quod res supra vires humanae mentis audeat humanis verbis attrectare? Nec dissimilia praefatur Augustinus in libros eiusdem tituli, et Athanasius disputaturus adversus Arianos, — cf. E. P. Meijering, *Hilary of Poitiers on the Trinity*, pp. 67ff.

[69] *Op. cit.*, p. 1260.

not appear until the end of Erasmus' life, so he could regard Arianism as being dead,[70] whilst Melanchthon was obviously deadly afraid of it, because he thought it had come to life again in anti-trinitarians like Servet. Erasmus defends the doctrine of the Trinity with real vigour when he himself is accused to Arianism.[71]

Another article of faith which Melanchthon refuses to discuss in the first edition of the *Loci communes* dating from 1521 is *creation*. What he is particularly opposed to is the Scholastic distinction between an active and a passive creation.[72] This distinction appears in the *Summa Theologica* of Thomas Aquinas, who calls active creation the divine creation, which is God's essence in relation to creature and who says of passive creation that it is in creature and is creature. Melanchthon regards this distinction as speculation. More important is that Melanchthon also ignores what is discussed in the following *quaestio* of the *Summa Theologica*, *viz.*, the question of whether creation is eternal or has a beginning in time, and whether the creation of all things took place in the beginning of time. Here Thomas *inter alia* refers to questions raised by Augustin in the eleventh book of the *De civitate Dei*.[73] This is a question in which Melanchthon initially shows no interest, but with which he does deal in later times. Before we try to trace the development of his views on this matter, we first want to show what his views on creation are in the first edition of the *Loci communes*. Although he does not discuss this subject under a specific head, his views do become apparent. Discussions with the goal to prove the existence of God from creation are despite the revelation given through creation (*Romans* 1) more an expression of curiosity than of piety. In this context Melanchthon repeats his warning not to speculate about this matter.[74] Melanchthon is opposed to a faith which only asserts the

---

[70] Cf. Erasmus' annotation on *I Timothy* 1:17 (*Erasmi opera omnia* t. VI, ed. J. Clericus), p. 930: Sed nihil est quod in his anxie torqueamur, Arianorum haeresi sic radicitus emortua, ut ne vestigium quidem ullum supersit.

[71] See *supra*, 121, note 59.

[72] (St.A. II), p. 7: Paulus in epistola, quam Romanis dicavit, cum doctrinae christianae compendium conscriberet, num ... de creation activa et creatione passiva philosophabatur? See Thomas Aquinas, *Summa Theologica* I, qu. 45, art. 3, cf. the explicative note given by H. Engelland and E. Gilson, *Le Thomisme, Introduction à la Philosophie de Saint Thomas*, Paris 1965[6], p. 143, note 33.

[73] *Summa Theologica* I, qu. 46, art. 2, see Augustin, *De civitate Dei* 11, 4, where Augustin discusses the view of those Platonists who say that the world has been created, although not in time but eternally.

[74] (St.A. II), pp. 42f.: ... inquit (sc. apostolus) deum declarasse omnibus hominibus maiestatem suam conditione et administratione universitatis mundi. Sed ut possit syllogismo humano colligi esse deum, curiosi magis est quam pii disputare, maxime cum rationi humanae non sit tutum de tantis rebus argutari, ut huius compendii principio monui. For the views on creation expressed in the first edition of the *Loci communes* see also

existence of God and does not believe in His power and mercy (or goodness).[75] He explains *Romans* 1 (and *Hebrews* 11:3) as faith in the creation of all things, this faith is not a chilly rational opinion, but is a very vivid knowledge of God's power and goodness, who governs all creatures. Scripture testifies to this power of God who manifests Himself in His creation, human flesh cannot deal with this matter in the same way.[76] These statements are made by Melanchthon when he speaks about justification and faith. He denies that faith can be a historical opinion about the creation of the world.[77] In his commentary on *Genesis* dating from 1523 Melanchthon holds the same view. He begins by saying that apart from indicating the creation of all things *Genesis* is primarily useful in order to learn about the origin of sin and the first promise of grace (the creation of all things being expressed in the first chapter, sin and grace being discussed in the third chapter).[78] He says that the order of instructing faith requires to start with the creation of things, since the first question is: "Is God? Has this world been created by some divine Power?"[79] Then Melanchthon makes an interesting statement: The Fathers were content with providing the church with arms against philosophical doctrines about the origin of the world. But he wants to use Scripture against hypocrisy, so that when one speaks about the creation of things, God's living words and power are understood, so that faith in creation leads to trust in God.[80] So there are two errors: The denial of

A. Brüls, *op. cit.*, pp. 59ff. and H. Engelland, Der Ansatz der Theologie Melanchthons, *Philip Melanchthon, Forschungsbeiträge* ... (herausgegeben von W. Elliger), pp. 60f.

[75] (St.A. II), p. 124: ... nec credit qui esse deum tantum credit, nisi et potentiae credat et misericordiae, see also his Preface to Luther's Commentary on the Psalms which was written in 1519 (CR 1), p. 73: Quid enim prodest scire, mundum a Deo conditum esse, nisi conditoris misericordiam et sapientiam adores?, cf. E. Bizer, *Theologie der Verheissung. Studien zur Theologie des jungen Melanchthon*, Neukirchen 1964, p. 54.

[76] After quoting *Psalm* 104: 27f. Melanchthon asks: Quaeso te, ad eum modum mysterium creationis tractare potest caro? (St.A. II), p. 100.

[77] (St.A. II), p. 99: Hic vero sophistae obstrepunt inepte a nobis aliam requiri fidem praeter historicam, cum epistola ad Hebraeos hic de historia tantum, nempe conditi mundi, loquatur.

[78] *Commentarius in Genesin* (CR 13), p. 761: Praeterquam quod Genesis rerum conditionem indicat, ad hoc ea potissimum utendum est ut inde discas originem peccati, et primam gratiae promissionem, ex quibus duobus locis postea universa pendet scriptura.

[79] (CR 13), p. 761: Ut a conditione rerum ordiretur, non historiae tantum ordo postulabat, sed ipsa docendae pietatis ratio, quia hoc caput omnium quaestionum est: Sitne Deus: Sintne a divina aliqua vi haec condita: Reganturne aliquo divino numine?

[80] (CR 13), pp. 761f.: Et veteres quidem Theologi contenti fuerunt Ecclesiam contra philosophica dogmata armare: contra hypocrisin non item: Ita factum est, ut enervaretur Verbum spiritus. Nobis ea contra hypocrisin utendum est, ut quando de conditione rerum loquitur, intelligenda sint verba viva potentia etc. iuxta illud: Dixit, et facta sunt. Ita quando Deus tangit cor nostrum fide creationis, et ostendit quod ex se, in se, et per se sint omnia, erigitur cor fiducia erga Deum. K. Haendler, *op. cit.*, pp. 469f., observes that Melanchthon does not speak exclusively in a negative way about this 'hypocrisy', only when historical knowledge does not include faith of the heart it is rejectable.

creation and a hypocritical acceptance of creation. The Fathers refuted the first error. Here Melanchthon will have in mind the doctrine of the creation out of nothing which the Fathers established against the philosophers and Gnostics.[81] Although Melanchthon is not, of course, opposed to this doctrine, he regards the second error, *viz.*, the error of hypocrisy as a more serious one: Here one admits according to the letter of *Genesis* that the world has been created, but one does not have the spirit of the faith in God's goodness which spreads out over all creatures.[82] The hypocritical knowledge of creation is referred to in *Romans* 1 ("Knowing God they have not glorified Him as God"), the spiritual knowledge in *Hebrews* 11 ("Through faith we understand that the world has been created"), in this spiritual faith what is invisible becomes visible, and the power and divinity becomes apparent in the work of the Creator.[83]—So Melanchthon does not accuse the Fathers of the hypocritical view on creation, but he does criticize them for not providing arms against such hypocrisy (which he detects in the Scholastics). But it should be noted that Melanchthon's insistence on God's power and goodness which is revealed in creation also appears in Irenaeus, of whom Melanchthon had a certain knowledge at the time when he wrote the first edition of the *Loci communes* and his commentary on the book of *Genesis*, and of whom he says at that time that he was the only theologian in the West to be of the truly Apostolic spirit.[84] Irenaeus' statement on this matter is quoted by John of Damascus, whom Melanchthon also knew at that time.[85] It is, of course, possible that this escaped Melanchthon's attention when he read Irenaeus, but he may also have picked it up without saying so. Then he would tacitly back up his views on creation with Patristic authority as he probably did in the beginning of the *Loci communes* in the context of

---

[81] See on this subject G. May, *Schöpfung aus dem Nichts, Die Entstehung der Lehre von der creatio ex nihilo*, Berlin-New York 1978.

[82] (CR 13), p. 762: Litera sententiae de creatione est hypocrisis et opinio carnalis de conditione rerum. Spiritus autem est fides, hoc est, certa scientia cordi a Spiritu sancto indicata qua sentimus amplitudinem bonitatis divinae, effundentis se in omnes creaturas.

[83] (CR 13), p. 763: Literam norant illi de quibus Roman. primo: Cognoscentes Deum non sicut Deum glorificaverunt ... De spiritu ad Hebraeos loquitur: Fide intelligimus condita secula, verbo Dei, ut invisibilia visibilia adparerent, id est, ut potentia et divinitas appareret in opere Creatoris.

[84] See *supra*, 67, see Irenaeus, *Adv. Haer.* 4, 63, 1: Περὶ τὸν θεὸν δύναμις ὁμοῦ καὶ σοφία, καὶ ἀγαθότης δείκνυται· δύναμις μὲν καὶ ἀγαθότης, ἐν τῷ τὰ μηδέπω ὄντα ἑκουσίως κτίζειν τε καὶ ποιεῖν. Irenaeus also links creation with providence, see *Adv. Haer.* 3, 38, 2: ... qui fecit, et plasmavit, et insufflationem vitae insufflavit in eis, et per conditionem nutrit nos, he then goes on to attack the god of Epicure who extends no providence over the world, — see also Tertullian, *Adversus Marcionem* 2, 5, 3: opera creatoris utrumque testantur, et bonitatem eius, qua bona, sicut ostendimus, et potentiam qua tanta, et quidem ex nihilo.

[85] See *supra*, 56, see John of Damascus, *Sacra Parallela* (ed. Halloix), p. 484.

christology.—In his commentary on *Genesis* he also, as we have seen,[86] dismisses Patristic speculations about the *beginning* in which heaven and earth were created (speculations in which the beginning is explained as the Son), and merely says that in the beginning of time the eternal God created heaven and earth. Just as an eternity of things before the beginning is incomprehensible, so there are incomprehensible abysses for human mind after the world. For faith it is enough to know that God is before, in and after all things.[87]

Turning to the expositions on creation given by Melanchthon in later times we shall try again to detect the element of continuity and discontinuity in his thought. When he discusses the doctrine of creation in the latest edition of the *Loci communes* he begins by saying that God wanted to be known, therefore He created the world with such skill that He might convince men that things did not come into existence through chance, but that there is an eternal Mind, an Architect, good, just, observing and judging the actions of men.[88] All this is, of course, traditional material,[89] and this view is already clearly expressed in the Commentary on the Epistle to the Romans dating from 1532.[90] Melanchthon makes it clear straight away that this natural revelation is inferior to the revelation given in Scripture.[91] The main errors in the doctrine of creation are

---

[86] See *supra*, 72.

[87] (CR 13), p. 763: Principium significat exordium temporis et rerum. Ergo cum ait, In principio, significat ante rerum conditionem aeternum fuisse Deum, non enim in hoc principio Deus factus est. Porro sicut incomprehensibilis est rationi rerum aeternitas ante principium: ita et post finem incomprehensibiles abyssi sunt. Fides autem quae capit Deum, et sentit ante omnia in omnibus et post omnia esse Deum, abyssos hos ingreditur gestata verbo Dei. These remarks show that Melanchthon does not understand the background of the speculations he rejects: not the eternity of things was incomprehensible, but the temporal beginning of things caused difficulties, since it implied that the eternal God changed by creating a world which He had not created before, see *infra*, 130f.

[88] (St.A. II), p. 214: Voluit Deus innotescere et se conspici. Ideo et condidit omnes creaturas et miram artem adhibuit, ut convinceret nos non extitisse res casu, sed esse aeternam mentem, architectatricem, bonam iustam, spectantem hominum facta et iudicantem.

[89] On the revelation through creation see amongst early Christian writers e.g. Irenaeus, *Adv. Haer.* 2, 4, 5; 2, 8, 1, Tertullian, *Adversus Marcionem* 1, 10, 1; 2, 3, 1; 5, 16, 3, Athanasius, *Contra Gentes* 35ff. Opposition against the doctrine that things had come into being through chance was already briefly expressed in *Commentarius in Genesim* (CR 13), p. 761: ... quae (sc. impietas humana) comprehendere non potest rerum vel conditionem vel administrationem, sentitque res temere ferri, nasci, interire, redire etc. The Fathers used to attack this doctrine as well (usually ascribing it to Epicure), see e.g. Athanasius, *De Incarnatione Verbi* 2, Hilary, *De Trinitate* 1, 4. — The definition of God which is given here is according to Melanchthon a definition which natural man can accept, see *supra*, 7.

[90] (St.A. V), pp. 70ff., see also *Comm. in Epist. Pauli ad Rom.*, dating from 1544 (CR 15), pp. 564f. and *Enarratio in Epist. Pauli ad Rom.*, dating from 1556 (CR 15), p. 832.

[91] (St.A. II), pp. 214f.: Quamquam autem haec consideratio universae naturae admonet nos de Deo, tamen nos referamus initio mentem et oculos ad omnia testimonia,

refuted with Scripture. Against the creation out of an already existing matter, Melanchthon asserts (like the Fathers) the creation out of nothing.[92] The error that God created the world, but then withdrew from it leaving control over creation to His creatures, just as a shipbuilder leaves a boat to the sailors once it has been built, must also be rejected: For this error significantly no name is given.[93] The Epicurean denial of Providence is rejected (as the Fathers did): the Epicureans wrongly substitute creation by chance.[94] The Stoics deny God's free Providence by binding God to *causae secundae*, this, too, has to be rejected (as the Fathers did).[95] This insistence on God's free will in His Providence is in

in quibus se Deus Ecclesiae patefecit ... Ideo semper defixae sint mentes in horum testimoniorum cogitationem et his confirmatae articulum de creatione meditentur, deinde considerent etiam vestigia Dei impressa naturae. Cf. S. Wiedenhofer, *op. cit.*, pp. 189ff.

[92] (St.A. II), p. 215: Non igitur ex materia priore extructae sunt, ut Stoici duo aeterna fingebant, mentem et materiam, sed Deo dicente, cum res non essent, esse coeperunt. The Fathers more often link the creation out of matter with Plato and the Platonists than with the Stoics, see on this matter further *supra*, 125, note 81.

[93] (St.A. II), p. 215: Infirmitas humana, etiamsi cogitat Deum esse conditorem, tamen postea imaginatur, ut faber discedit a navi extructa et relinquit eam nautis, ita Deum discedere a suo opere et relinqui creaturas tantum propriae gubernationi. Melanchthon is obviously fond of this comparison, since he produces it repeatedly, see e.g. *Scholia in Epist. Pauli ad Col.*, dating from 1527 (St.A. IV), p. 222, p. 238, *Examen ordinandorum* (St.A. VI), p. 181, *Explic. Symb. Nic.* (CR 23), p. 386, p. 350. Early Christian writers accused Aristotle of holding this view, *viz.*, that he did not deny God's existence but that he denied God's providence, according to them Aristotle dared not deny God's existence, because of his fear of public opinion, see on this matter J. C. M. van Winden, *An Early Christian Philosopher. Justin Martyr's Dialogue with Trypho. Chapters 1-9*, Leiden 1971, p. 37, A. J. Festugière, *L'idéal religieux des Grecs et l'évangile*, 1932, E. P. Meijering, *Hilary of Poitiers on the Trinity*, p. 28. Melanchthon, who had a great admiration for Aristotle, does not link this view with Aristotle, but he, too, says that Aristotle's doctrine of providence is put forward cautiously and with human righteousness as its object, see *Initia doctrinae physicae* (CR 13), p. 205: Aristoteles Ethicorum decimo ait, esse providentiam, etsi timide adfirmat. Si inquit: curae sunt Deo res humane, ut videtur et consentaneum, est maxime ei curae sunt homines iustitia, et aliis virtutibus praediti. (On Melanchthon's views on Providence cf. further M. Büttner, *Regiert Gott die Welt? Vorsehung Gottes und Geographie. Studien zur Providentialehre bei Zwingli und Melanchthon*, Stuttgart 1975, pp. 49ff.) In 1521 he was much harsher in his criticism of Aristotle and accused him of being an atheist, see *Did. Fav. adv. Th. Placentinum* (St.A. I), p. 76: ἄθεος est et vester ille, Hirce, Aristoteles ...

[94] (St.A. II), pp. 215f.: Epicuraei, omnia casu volvi et confundi. For Patristic polemics against the Epicurean denial of providence see e.g. Tertullian, *Adversus Marcionem* 1, 27, Irenaeus, *Adversus Haereses* 3, 38, 2; 3, 39, Hilary, *De Trinitate* 1, 4, Augustin, *Sermo* 348, 2, 3.

[95] (St.A. II), p. 215: Stoici fingunt Deum alligatum causis secundis nec quicquam aliter posse fieri, quam ut causae secundae cient, — for Melanchthon's opposition against the limitation of God's freedom by the *causae secundae*, see also *Initia doctrinae physicae* (CR 13), p. 191, p. 210, p. 375, *Explic. Symb. Nic.* (CR 23), pp. 387ff., *Definitiones* (St.A. II), p. 784, — for the Fathers' opposition against the Stoic doctrine of Fate to which also God is subjected see e.g. Irenaeus, *Adv. Haer.* 2, 4, 4 and 2, 18, 4, for Irenaeus' insistence on God's free will see *Adv. Haer.* 2, 1, 1; 2, 1, 4; 2, 2, 1.2.3; 2, 9, 2; 2, 11, 1; 2, 47, 2; 3, 8, 3; 4, 34, 1; 5, 18, 2. Augustin is much more positive about the Stoic doctrine of the *connexio causaram*, see *De civitate Dei* 5, 8, he praises the fact that the Stoics ascribe this to God's will and power.

line with the emphasis the young Reformer Melanchthon put on the fact that the doctrine of creation primarily means that God now manifests His goodness and His power in man's life.[96] But unlike what he said in the beginning the later Melanchthon goes (just like the Fathers) to great lengths to refute erroneous doctrines about the origin of the world. He primarily bases his arguments on Scripture, after that he also gives arguments taken from revelation through creation.[97] He then lists nine proofs for the existence of God,[98] all of which stem from ancient, Patristic and Medieval sources:[99]

1) The order of nature points towards its Maker.[100]
2) An unreasonable being cannot produce man who has a reason, so man must have been created by a divine mind.[101]
3) Man can distinguish between good and evil, the possibility to do this cannot have been given by chance, but must have been given by God.[102]

---

[96] (St.A. II), p. 216: Adest Deus suae creaturae, sed non adest ut Stoicus Deus, sed ut agens liberrimum, sustentans creaturam et sua immensa misericordia moderans, dans bona, adiuvans aut impediens causas secundas. The Stoics deny that God can alter the *causae secundae.*

[97] (St.A. II), pp. 219f.: Postquam autem mens confirmata est vera et recta sententia de Deo et de creatione ac praesentia Dei in creaturis et moderatione causarum secundarum ex verbo Dei et illustribus testimoniis ... tunc etiam utile et iucundum est aspicere opificium mundi et in eo vestigia Dei quaerere et demonstrationes colligere.

[98] (St.A. II), pp. 220ff. Exactly the same arguments are given in *Initia doctrinae physicae* (CR 13), pp. 200f. In the *Commentarii in Epist. Pauli ad Rom.*, dating from 1544 (CR 15), pp. 566f., also nine proofs are given: the fourth proof from the *Loci communes* (1559) does not appear, the seventh and the eighth one are given as one proof, two further proofs are added: 1) murderers are punished, imperial powers are preserved or destroyed by God (CR 15), p. 567, 2) the heroic virtues which are gifts of God, — as appears from *Explic. Symb. Nic.* (CR 23), p. 432, Melanchthon found this argument in Seneca: Et haec gubernatio in aliis magis, in aliis minus adiuvatur, vel temperamento, vel motibus heroicis, qui sunt singulares motus insiti praestantibus viris a Deo, sicut inquit Seneca: Nulla magna virtus sine Deo est, — this could be a reference to Seneca, *Epist.* 73, 16: nulla sine Deo mens bona est.

[99] Cf. for the following: H. Plate, *Die Stellung Melanchthons und Gerhards zur Kantschen Kritik der Möglichkeit einer natürlichen Gotteserkenntnis*, Göttingen 1910, pp. 4ff., H. Engelland, *Melanchthon, Glauben und Handeln*, pp. 210ff., Cl. Bauer, Melanchthons Naturrechtslehre, *Archiv für Reformationsgeschichte* (42) 1951, pp. 65f., H.-J. Horn, Gottesbeweis, *Reallexicon für Antike und Christentum* XI, pp. 951ff.

[100] (St.A. II), p. 220: Prima ab ipso naturae ordine sumitur, id est, ab effectibus. This is one of Cleanthes' four proofs, see Cicero, *De natura deorum* II 15, cf. Irenaeus, *Adv. Haer.* 2, 37.

[101] (St.A. II), p. 221: Bruta res non est causa naturae intelligentis. Mentes hominum habent aliquam causam, quia homo non habet esse per se, sed incipit et aliunde oritur. Ergo necesse est aliquam intelligentem naturam causam esse mentis humanae. Necesse est igitur esse Deum, — cf. Cicero, *De natura deorum* 2, 6, 18: Et tamen ex ipsa hominum sollertia esse aliquam mentem et eam quidem acriorem et divinam existimare debemus. Unde enim hanc homo 'arripuit' (ut ait apud Xenophontem Socrates)?

[102] (St.A. II), pp. 221f.: Tertia a discrimine honestorum et turpium et aliis notitiis naturalibus ... Impossibile est discrimen honestorum et turpium in mente casu aut a

4) The argument *e consensu gentium.*[103]

5) The argument taken from the guilty conscience which criminals have. Men have been bestowed by God with this.[104]

6) The argument taken from the order of human society.[105]

7) The argument from the series of *causae efficientes.* There is no infinite progress of the causes, there must be a first cause.[106]

8) The argument from the *causae finales.* All things in nature have been

---

materia ortum esse ... Ergo necesse est aliquam mentem architectatricem esse, cf. John Chrysostomus, *De Anna Sermo* I 3 (Migne PG 54, 636): Εἷς μὲν οὖν θεογνωσίας τρόπος, ὁ διὰ τῆς κτίσεως ἁπάσης· ἕτερος δὲ οὐκ ἐλάττων, ὁ τοῦ συνειδότος ὄν ... ἐξεθέμεθα ... δεικνύντες πῶς αὐτοδίδακτος ἡμῖν ἐστιν ἡ τῶν καλῶν καὶ τῶν οὐ τοιούτων γνῶσις, καὶ πῶς ἔνδοθεν ἡμῖν τὸ συνειδὸς ἅπαντα ἐνηχεῖ ταῦτα. In the *Loci communes,* dating from 1559 (St.A. II), p. 316 he links this doctrine with Xenophon and Cicero, see e.g. Xenophon, *Memorabilia* 4, 4, 19ff. This passage from Xenophon is quoted extensively by Melanchthon in his letter to Burenius, dating from 1550 (CR 7), pp. 684f., — for a brief reference to Xenophon's proof of the existence of God see *Philosophiae moralis epitomes* I (St.A. III), p. 153.

[103] (St.A. II), p. 222: Notitiae naturales sunt verae. Esse deum naturaliter omnes fatentur. Ergo haec notitia vera est. Cf. Cicero, *De natura deorum* 2, 2, 5: Quod (sc. aliquod numen praestantissimae mentis esse) nisi cognitum comprehensumque animis haberemus, non tam stabilis opinio permaneret nec confirmaretur diuturnitate temporis nec una cum saeclis aetatibusque hominum inveterari potuisset. Etenim videmus ceteras opiniones fictas atque vanas diuturnitate extabuisse, and Tertullian's well known tenet of a natural knowledge of God in the human soul, e.g. *Apologeticum* 17, 5-6, *De testimonio animae* 2, 2, *Adversus Marcionem* 1, 10, see also *Ad Scapulam* 2: nos unum deum colimus, quem omnes naturaliter nostis, — on the originally Stoic background of the *sensus communes* see J. H. Waszink's edition of the *De anima,* pp. 454f.

[104] (St.A. II), p. 222: Constat homicidas et alios perpetratis magnis sceleribus horribiles animorum cruciatus sustinere, etiamsi nulla humana iudicia metuant. Est igitur aliqua mens, quae hoc iudicium in animis ordinavit. Melanchthon himself refers to Xenophon for this argument, see Xenophon, *Memorabilia Socr.* 1, 4, 7: οὕτω γε σκοπουμένῳ πάνυ ἔοικε ταῦτα σοφοῦ τινος δημιουργοῦ καὶ φιλοζῴου τεχνήμασι (see the edition of the *Loci communes,* dating from 1535 (CR 21), p. 370). Melanchthon obviously refers to this passage in Xenophon, but there this particular argument does not appear, — there does, however, appear something similar in John Chrysostomus, *De Anna Sermo* 1, 3 (Migne PG 54, 636): τό τε συνειδὸς ἔνδον ἐνηχοῦν, ἅπαντα ὑποβάλλει τὰ πρακτέα· καὶ τὴν δύναμιν αὐτοῦ, καὶ τῆς ψήφου τὴν κρίσιν διὰ τῶν τῆς ὄψεως πραγμάτων καταλαμβάνομεν. Ὅταν γὰρ ἔνδον κατηγορῇ τῆς ἁμαρτίας, συγχεῖ τὴν ὄψιν ἔξωθεν, καὶ πολλῆς τῆς ἀθυμίας πληροῖ.

[105] (St.A. II), p. 222: Politica societas non est concursus hominum fortuitus, sed certo ordine et iure consociata multitudo nec posset humana ope tantum retineri, sed experientia testatur aliquo numine ad poenam rapi eos ... Ergo est aliqua mens aeterna, cf. Cicero, *De natura deorum* 2, 31, 78: Atqui necesse est cum sint di ... animantis esse, nec solum animantis sed etiam rationis compotes inter seque quasi civili conciliatione et societate coniunctos, unum mundum ut communem rem publicam atque urbem aliquam regentis, (Ps.-) Aristotle, *De mundo* 400 b 13ff., Athanasius, *Contra Gentes* 38, 43.

[106] (St.A. II), p. 223: Non est processus in infinitum in causis efficientibus. Ergo necesse est resistere in una prima causa. According to Melanchthon this has been discussed lucidly by natural philosophers. We regard it as most likely that he found this argument in Thomas Aquinas, *Summa Theologica* I qu. 2, art. 3 (Non autem est possibile quod in causis efficientibus procedatur in infinitum ... Ergo est necesse ponere aliquam causam efficientem primam: quam omnes Deum nominant), that he recognized the Aristotelian background and therefore preferred to ascribe it to natural philosophers.

destined for some utility. This cannot have happened by chance, but must have been ordered by a divine Architect.[107]

9) The argument from the prediction of future events.[108]

After the enumeration of the proofs for the existence of a Creator Melanchthon again emphasizes that the arguments taken from Scripture are more important than these rational ones. But these rational arguments had been ignored by the young Reformer Melanchthon.

Similarly he later on sometimes discusses a question which he initially briefly dismissed: How can the eternal God at a certain moment decide to create a world? What is the relation between the world which has a temporal beginning and the eternal and unchangeable Creator?[109] This was a question in which Fathers and Scholastics showed interest.[110] Melanchthon somewhere lists several Aristotelian arguments against the temporal beginning of the world. For our subject the most important one is: The most perfect cause cannot have been infinitely idle, so God cannot have been idle in loneliness in the eternity before He created the world.[111] In

---

[107] (St.A. II), p. 223: Octava a causis finalibus. Omnes res in natura destinatae sunt ad certas utilitates. Hanc distributionem finium impossibile est aut extitisse casu aut casu manere, sed necesse est consilio architecti factum esse, — cf. Cicero, *De natura deorum* 2, 14, 37 where Chrysippus is quoted as saying: praeter mundum cetera omnia aliorum causa esse generata, for further examples see E. Zeller, *Die Philosophie der Griechen in ihrer geschichtlichen Entwicklung* 3, 1, Darmstadt 1963[6], pp. 175ff. So Melanchthon here reproduces in Aristotelian language a Stoic doctrine.

[108] (St.A. II), p. 223: Certo monstrantur futuri eventus ... Necesse est igitur aliquam mentem esse praevidentem eas mutationes et praemonstrantem, cf. Cicero, *De natura deorum* 2, 3, 7: Praedictiones vero et praesensiones rerum futurarum quid aliud declarant nisi hominibus ea quae futura sint ostendi monstrari portendi praedici.

[109] Melanchthon deals with this question in *Disputationes* (CR 12), pp. 585ff., *Initia doctrinae physicae* (CR 13), pp. 221f., 377ff.

[110] See e.g. Augustin, *Confessiones* 11, 10, 12ff., Thomas Aquinas, *Summa Theologica* I qu. 46.

[111] *Initia doctrinae physicae* (CR 13), p. 377: Perfectissima causa non est in infinitum otiosa. Prima causa est perfectissima. Igitur non fuit in tam longa aeternitate retro otiosa ... Miramur enim quid in illis infinitis saeculorum spatiis egerit prima causa, si fuit sola, si nullum obiectum fuit, circa quod exerceret suam potentiam aut sapientiam. This argument does not appear in Aristotle, it could be that Melanchthon here ascribes to Aristotle the argument which is quoted by Augustin, *Conf.* 11, 10, 12; 11, 13, 15 (Melanchthon betrays knowledge of the eleventh book of the *Confessions*, since he freely quotes Augustin's famous words that he does not know what is time when he has to explain it, *Conf.* 11, 14, 17, see *Initia doctrinae physicae* (CR 13), p. 369, *Erotemata Dialectices* (CR 13), p. 559, in both cases Melanchthon denies that there are great difficulties and gives Aristotle's definition of time: Tempus est numerus seu mensura motus secundum prius et posterius, see Aristotle, *Phys.* IV 10, 219 b1-2: τοῦτο γάρ ἐστιν ὁ χρόνος, ἀριθμὸς κινήσεως κατὰ τὸ πρότερον καὶ ὕστερον). The other arguments which Melanchthon quotes (Heaven knows no changes and is therefore not subject to generation and corruption, time and motion have no beginning, circular movement has no beginning) do appear in Aristotle, see *Phys.* 219 b, 251 b 10ff., *Metaphys.* 1071 b 3ff.

answering this critical question he first refers to God's free will.[112] Then he refers to the belief that there has been an eternal communication of Wisdom between the Father, Son and Holy Ghost.[113] Similar to this one is another argument which he gives elsewhere: The act of creation is *ad extra* an act in time, but *ad intra* it was eternally in God.[114]

At first sight there seems to be a great difference between the young and the later Melanchthon in his attitude towards the doctrine of creation. First he does not give any proofs for the existence of God taken from creation, first he does not elaborate on the natural revelation through creation, and first he dismisses any questions about the beginning in which heaven and earth were created, questions which are caused by the fact that it is extremely difficult to think of a moment in which God's eternity and time coincide. Later on all these problems are discussed in Melanchthon's writings. But the similarity between the young and the later Melanchthon should not be overlooked in this context. The reason why he initially rejects speculations about creation is that he is primarily interested in God's free and powerful will to rule the world and human lives. This insistence on God's free will is still dominant in Melanchthon's later expositions. Natural revelation through creation is not denied by the young Reformer Melanchthon, since it is testified to by Paul in *Romans* 1. In the beginning he does not want to prove the existence of God on account of creation, later on he does provide a list of such proofs, but he gives these proofs after the proofs based on Scripture and insists that these proofs are inferior to the Scriptural ones. In this respect he still differs significantly from Thomas Aquinas who begins with such rational proofs.[115] As Melanchthon first refused to speculate about God's being without denying it, and later on produces statements about God's being which show some similarity with statements made by

---

[112] *Initia doctrinae physicae* (CR 13), p. 377: Haec propositio non est vera de agentibus voluntariis, ut architectus etiam praestantissimus diu potest suspendere actionem. Ita de prima causa dicimus, volens et liberrime condidit mundum, non effudit necessitate aliqua. For this insistence on free will in connection with creation see also *Disputationes* (CR 12), p. 585, *Enarratio Symb. Nic.* (CR 23), p. 214, p. 249, *Explic. Symb. Nic.* (CR 23), p. 383, p. 398. Amongst the Fathers Irenaeus particularly stresses God's free will as the cause of creation, see *supra*, 127, note 95. Augustin does so as well, but refers to God's free will as the final answer to the question why God created the world at all, and does not refer to it when he tries to answer the question why God created the world at the moment He did, see E. P. Meijering, *Augustin über Schöpfung, Ewigkeit und Zeit. Das elfte Buch der Bekenntnisse.* Leiden 1979, pp. 40ff.

[113] (CR 13), p. 377: Deinde nobis in Ecclesia responsio de solitudine proposita est: Quid in illa tam longa aeternitate egerit Deus, hic divina revelatio adfirmat communicationem sapientiae esse aeternam inter Patrem, Filium et Spiritum sanctum.

[114] *Disputationes* (CR 12), p. 586: Haec actio (ut aliae ad extra) etsi ab aeterno semper fuit in Deo, ut proprium, tamen actu coepit in principio a Mose descripto.

[115] See *Summa Theologica* I, qu. 2, art. 3, cf. F. Hübner, *op. cit.*, pp. 59ff.

Scholastics, so Melanchthon first refuses to speculate on God's creation without denying it and later on produces statements on creation which not only resemble statements made by the Fathers, but also by Scholastics. The development of his thought in connection with God's being can perhaps be explained by the emergence of the anti-trinitarian movement: the anti-trinitarians forced him to make his belief in the Trinity more explicit. No such reason can be given for the development in his thought on creation, since there was no need to attack living people who denied the creation. The explanation could be that having developed in his thought on God's being this implied a development in the thought on creation. One cannot insist that God is from all eternity Father, Son and Holy Ghost and at the same time refuse to answer the question (which was often put in the course of history) how the relation is between the temporal creation and the eternal triune Creator. If one asserts the former, then one must answer this latter question. But Melanchthon does not give the impression of dealing with these questions *contre coeur*, on the contrary, when he deals with these questions, we see the learned humanist[116] in him, who likes to show that he knows about the problems put forward in ancient philosophy and Patristic theology and who knows the appropriate solutions to these problems. We see the learned humanist rather than the Scholastic, compared with the Scholastics also the later Melanchthon shows only occasional interest in speculative questions about God's being and about creation. He did not have the solution he offers to the problem of temporal creation and an eternal Creator constantly in mind, otherwise he could not have said, in dealing with God's being and God's will, that creation was a *contingent* act of God.[117] The word 'contingent' certainly needs qualification if one also says that God wanted to be the Creator from all eternity.

In the context of the doctrine of grace there are relatively few references to Patristic sources to be found in the writings of the young Reformer Melanchthon. There are a few references to Augustin and other Latin Fathers.[118] Later on the Greek Fathers Basil, John

---

[116] There is certainly an element of truth in what R. Scharlemann, *Thomas Aquinas and John Gerhard*, Yale 1964, p. 23, observes on the double character of Melanchthon's theology: "It comes from the difference between theology as academic or scientific and theology as kerygmatic ... or personal."

[117] See *supra*, 131, *Enarr. Symb. Nic.* (23), p. 249.

[118] See *supra*, 23, 52, 66. H. G. Geyer, *op. cit.*, pp. 186f., notices some differences between the young Melanchthon and Augustin in connection with the doctrine of predestination: the young Melanchthon does not want to make a distinction between 'praedestinatio' and praescientia, he does not accept the Augustinian tenet of the 'certus numerus sanctorum', and unlike Augustin he is primarily interested in the denial of free will, not in the emphasis on God's omnipotence.

Chrysostomus and Gregory Nazianzen are quoted fairly often by Melanchthon in connection with the doctrine of grace and free will, although the number of passages referred to is limited.[119] This broadening of support from Patristic writings goes together with a certain development in Melanchthon's views on this matter.

It is interesting to see that Melanchthon starts his attack on the Scholastic doctrine of free will by calling it speculative, as appears from his claim that it crept into Christian theology under the influence of philosophy.[120] This doctrine obscures the *beneficia* of Christ. He intends to put forward his own doctrine *simplicissime et planissime*, i.e. in a completely unspeculative and clear way.[121] Melanchthon does not deny that man has a free will in outward actions, like whether or not man greets another person, what clothes he wears and what food he eats.[122] But this is not what Christian theology is interested in, it focuses on the internal motives of the human heart. Aristotle makes the mistake of basing his doctrine of free will on the freedom in external actions.[123] Christian theology knows that in the human heart there is no free will, since will is subjected to the *affectus*.[124]

If we now look at the end of Melanchthon's development in his thought on free will, *viz.*, the latest edition of the *Loci communes*,[125] we see that he is

---

[119] See *supra*, 40f., 46, 59. In the first edition of the *Loci communes* there is only the general remark that there are only occasional references to man's free will in the writings of the Greek Faters, (St.A. II), p. 8: Sunt hac de re etiam apud Graecos quaedam, sed sparsim. It is hardly conceivable that Melanchthon did not know that there are numerous lengthy expositions on free will in the writings of the Greek Fathers, so he must mean that amongst the Greek Fathers only a few statements can be found which support his own position.

[120] *Loci communes*, dating from 1521 (St.A. II), p. 8: Et in hoc quidem loco, cum prorsus christiana doctrina a philosophia et humana ratione dissentiat, tamen sensim irrepsit philosophia in christianismum, et receptum est impium de libero arbitrio dogma et obscurata Christi beneficentia per profanam illam et animalem rationis nostrae sapientiam, — this influence is primarily the one of Aristotle, see p. 15.

[121] *Op. cit.*, p. 8: ... non sequar hominum opiniones et simplicissime et planissime rem exponam.

[122] *Op. cit.*, pp. 12f.: negari non potest iuxta rationem humanam, quin sit in ea libertas quaedam externorum operum, ut ipse experiris in potestate tua esse, salutare hominem aut non salutare, indui hac veste vel non indui, vesci carnibus aut non vesci.

[123] *Op. cit.*, p. 15: Vocabat quidem Aristoteles voluntatem delectum illum rerum in externis operibus, qui fere mendax est. Sed quid ad christianam disciplinam externa opera, si cor sit insincerum.

[124] *Op. cit.*, p. 15: At ego nego vim esse ullam in homine quae serio affectibus adversari possit.

[125] Cf. for the following: H. Engelland, *Melanchthon, Glauben und Handeln*, pp. 237ff., pp. 359ff., pp. 403ff., R. Stupperich, *Melanchthon*, Berlin 1960, pp. 76ff., P. Schwarzenau, *Der Wandel im theologischen Ansatz bei Melanchthon von 1525-1535*, Gütersloh 1956, pp. 10ff., E. Bizer, *Theologie der Verheisung*, pp. 77f., A. Sperl, *Melanchthon zwischen Humanismus und Reformation*, p. 123ff., H. Bornkamm, Humanismus und Reformation im Menschenbild Melanchthons, *Das Jahrhundert der Reformation. Gestalten und Kräfte*, Göt-

still opposed to speculations on this matter which obscure the *beneficia* of Christ. But now he has another enemy in mind: He does not begin with an attack on the Scholastic doctrine of free will, but with an attack on the Stoic doctrine of necessity.[126] Melanchthon still maintains the distinction between outward and inward actions and states again that in outward actions man does have a free will.[127] He extends the kind of works which belong to this category and says that man has the free will to abstain from murder and theft. But in the inward actions free will is, although not completely, largely denied. Free will cannot obey and love God completely.[128] These spiritual acts man cannot do without (the help of) the Holy Spirit.[129] Here there is the most important shift in Melanchthon's views on free will: these spiritual acts are not *the work of* the Holy Spirit, but they are done *with the help of* the Holy Spirit. The Holy Spirit, when it is at work in man, needs the Word of God through which it speaks and it needs the consent of human will.[130] In support of this doctrine Melanch-

---

tingen 1961, pp. 73ff., R. Bring, *Das Verhältnis von Glauben und Werken in der lutherischen Theologie*, München 1955, pp. 67ff., E. Mühlenberg, Humanistisches Bildungsprogramm und reformatorische Lehre beim jungen Melanchthon, *Zeitschrift für Theologie und Kirche* (65), 1968, pp. 434ff. (according to Mühlenberg it was also Erasmus' view that human will is subjected to the *affectus*). On Melanchthon's views on predestination as expressed in his earliest commentary on the Epistle to the Romans see R. Schäfer, Zur Prädestinationslehre beim jungen Melanchthon, *Zeitschrift für Theologie und Kirche* (63), 1966, pp. 352ff.

[126] (St.A. II), pp. 236f.: Valla et plerique alii detrahunt voluntati hominis libertatem ideo, quia fiant omnia decernente Deo. Haec imaginatio orta ex Stoicis disputationibus deducit eos ad tollendam contingentiam bonarum et malarum actionum ... cum de voluntate hominis et de ceteris humanis viribus quaeritur, tantum de humana infirmitate disseritur, non de omnibus motibus in tota natura. Nos ipsos, mentis nostrae caliginem et voluntatis et cordis imbecillitatem consideremus. Hanc doctrinam de nostris morbis proponit Ecclesia, non ut Stoicas opiniones serat, non ut mentes implicet perplexis et inextricabilibus disputationibus, sed ut monstret nobis beneficia Filii Dei.

[127] *Op. cit.*, p. 238: ... reliquus est etiam delectus externorum operum civilium. Quare voluntas humana potest suis viribus sine renovatione aliquo modo externa legis opera facere.

[128] *Op. cit.*, p. 240: Non potest voluntas exuere nascentem nobiscum pravitatem nec potest legi Dei satisfacere, qui lex Dei non tantum de externa disciplina et de umbra operum concionetur, sed postulat integram obedientiam cordis.

[129] *Op. cit.*, p. 241: Ingens et inenarrabile beneficium Dei est quod promittitur nobis auxilium Spiritus sancti ... Voluntas humana non potest sine Spiritu sancto efficere spirituales effectus.

[130] *Op. cit.*, p. 243: Sciendum est autem Spiritum sanctum efficacem esse per vocem Evangelii auditam seu cogitatam ... Cumque ordimur a verbo, hic concurrunt tres causae bonae actionis, verbum Dei, Spiritus sanctus et humana voluntas assentiens nec repugnans verbo Dei, cf. *Ethicae doctrinae elementa* (CR 16), p. 193: ... cum promissio sit universalis, nostram aliquam adsensionem concurrere oportere, cum quidem iam et Spiritus sanctus accenderit mentem, voluntatem et cor, cf. p. 240, *Explic. Symb. Nic.* (CR 23), pp. 435f., p. 544 (in all these cases there is a reference to Augustin, Basil and Chrysostomus), *Loci communes*, dating from 1559 (St.A. II), pp. 598f., *Definitiones* (St.A. II), p. 784. Because of this doctrine of the three *causae* which must cooperate Melanchthon

thon refers to the Fathers.[131] The reference to (Ps.-) Basil is in this context the most interesting one. As we have seen,[132] (Ps.-) Basil's words Μόνον θέλησον καὶ θεὸς προαπαντᾷ are often quoted by Melanchthon and he once says that Basil makes this statement in a sermon about the prodigal son. This is not enirely correct, since the sermon Melanchthon has in mind is about penitence, and not about the prodigal son, but in that sermon the parable of the prodigal son is referred to by (Ps.-) Basil and the words Μόνον θέλησον καὶ θεὸς προαπαντᾷ are a kind of a conclusion from this parable. Melanchthon agrees with this conclusion and this is an interesting indication that he changed his position in this respect since the first edition of the *Loci communes*. Already at the *Leipzig Disputation* in the interpretation of the parable of the prodigal son was controversial. Eck referred to it as a proof that man does have a free will which can receive its rewards even in such religious matters like conversion,—Luther denied this. According to Eck the parable proves that conversion starts with the hope of reward and the fear of punishment.[133] Eck draws from this the (synergistic) conclusion that there is no conversion without grace and no grace without conversion.[134] Luther states that the conversion of the prodigal son does not stem from his own fragility. It is caused by the Father who draws him from inside and inspires him with the love of the

---

has often been accused of synergism. But K. Haendler, *op. cit.*, pp. 551ff. has shown that these are not three *causae efficientes* besides each other, but that God's Spirit is the only *causa efficiens*, the Word of God is the *causa instrumentalis* and human will the *causa materialis*, that which is worked upon, — see also L. C. Green, The Three Causes of Conversion in Philip Melanchthon, Martin Chemnitz, David Chytraeus, and the "Formula of Concord", *Lutherjahrbuch* (47) 1980, pp. 92-98. In connection with the doctrine of predestination Stoic determinism is rejected because it prevents faith and the invocation of God, see e.g. *Loci communes*, dating from 1559 (St.A. II), p. 602: Removeamus igitur a Paulo Stoicas disputationes, quae fidem et invocationem evertunt.

[131] *Loci communes*, dating from 1559 (St.A. II), p. 244: Veteres dixerunt: Praecedente gratia, comitante voluntate bona opera fieri. (This is a quotation from Augustin, see *supra*, 27). Sic et Basilius inquit: Μόνον θέλησον καὶ θεὸς προαπαντᾷ ... Deus antevertit nos, vocat, movet, adiuvat, sed nos viderimus, ne repugnemus. Constat enim peccatum oriri a nobis, non a voluntate Dei. Chrysostomus inquit: ὁ δὲ ἕλκων τὸν βουλόμενον ἕλκει. *Op. cit.*, p. 245: Ideo veteres aliqui sic dixerunt: Liberum arbitrium in homine facultatem esse applicandi se ad gratiam. H. O. Günther, *op. cit.*, pp. 108f., rightly observes that Melanchthon only produces these quotations from Augustin, Basil and Chrysostomus, whilst Erasmus produces many more quotations from the Fathers and Scholastics, which shows that the notion of free will had even in the later Melanchthon another function than in Erasmus: Unlike the Scholastics and Erasmus Melanchthon does not make distinctions in the notion of grace, but merely maintains some freedom of man's natural will.

[132] See *supra*, 41.

[133] O. Seitz, *Der authentische Text der Leipziger Disputation*, p. 189: Hic Dominus Christus modum poenitentis describens, exponit primo motum poenitentem praemiorum magnitudine ... et timore poenae ... quibus gradibus evectus poenitentiam veram coepit meditari, scilicet: "et dicam: Pater, peccavi", this is followed by a reference to Basil.

[134] *Op. cit.*, p. 190: Neque ergo poenitentia sine gratia, neque gratia sine poenitentia.

father's house.[135] Eck constantly corroborates his views with quotations from the Fathers. When Melanchthon in the first edition of the *Loci communes* makes hardly any effort to seek support from the Fathers (with the exception of Augustin and some general references to Cyprian and Ambrose), this could mean that Eck had made him doubt whether the Fathers shared his view on grace and free will. (In the *Adversus furiosum Parrisiensium Theologastrorum decretum*, also written in 1521, there are only a few references to Ambrose, Cyprian and Chrysostomus as supporters of Melanchthon's doctrine of grace.[136]) It could be that under the influence of Erasmus Melanchthon turned to the Fathers again in order to seek support for his doctrine of grace and human will. When the later Melanchthon says that the Fathers taught that man has the ability to turn towards grace he repeats what Erasmus had said before him.[137] Erasmus supports this view with many quotations from the Fathers, amongst others from Augustin and Chrysostomus, to whom Melanchthon also refers in this context.[138] From all the quotations which Erasmus provided on this matter Melanchthon obviously drew the conclusion that, if only the assent of human will was added, the Lutheran doctrine that grace draws man to salvation could be brought into harmony with the views of the Fathers, and that it was very difficult to defend this doctrine against the Romans with support of the Fathers, if the assent of human will was not added.[139]

---

[135] *Op. cit.*, p. 193: Hanc autem conversionem sui in se ipsum non habuit ex fragilitate sua aut ex timore poenae ... Habuit autem eam ex trahente intus patre et dilectionem inspirante paternae domus. Eck is not convinced by this, see *op. cit.*, p. 197.

[136] See *supra*, 31, 48. See also the fairly critical remarks he makes on Origen, Jerome, and even Cyprian and some statements of Augustin in *De Erasmo et Luthero elogion* etc. (CR 20), pp. 704ff.

[137] Cf. the quotation given *supra*, 135, note 131, with Erasmus, *Hyperaspistae diatribes lib. I* (*Erasmi opera omnia* t. X, ed. J. Clericus), p. 1328: Certe cum nostra voluntas operatur cum operante gratia, applicat sese ad gratiam, naturae vires ad gratiam operantem accommodans. See on this matter also K. Haendler, *op. cit.*, pp. 544ff., who points out that according to Melanchthon the 'homo renatus' has the 'facultas se applicandi ad gratiam', and that therefore this formula cannot be interpreted in a synergistic way and is not a concession to Pelagianism. On Erasmus' possible influence on Melanchthon in this respect see also G. Hoffmann, Luther und Melanchthon. Melanchthons Stellung in der Theologie des Luthertums, *Zeitschrift für systematische Theologie* (15) 1938, p. 123.

[138] We could not find a reference to Chrysostomus' ὁ θεὸς μὲν ἕλκει τὸν βουλόμενον δὲ ἕλκει in Erasmus' piece of writing quoted in the previous note, but there is a reference to a similar statement made by Chrysostomus, *Hyperasp. diatr.* II, p. 1511: Verba Chrysostomi sic habent: Verum hoc nostrum non tollit arbitrium, sed divino egere auxilio ostendit, nec invitum, sed omni conatu contendentem venire. — Melanchthon's reaction to Erasmus' *Hyperaspitae diatribes libri* was fairly favourable, see his letter to Erasmus, dating from 1528 (CR 1), p. 946. (In the first edition of the *Loci communes* Melanchthon accuses Bernardus of Clairvaux of inconsistencies in the doctrine of grace, later on he refers to him with approval, see *supra*, 95f. (just like Erasmus did, the statement by Erasmus quoted in note 137 is made with reference to Bernardus).)

[139] W. Maurer, Melanchthon als Humanist, *Melanchthon-Studien*, Gütersloh 1964,

In the doctrine of grace we find the same widening of perspective as in the doctrine of the person of Christ and the Trinity, and in the doctrine of creation. Melanchthon does not fundamentally contradict his original position, but there are certain corrections and additions. He becomes less harsh in his judgement on what is futile speculation and does not refuse to answer the question how God's grace and free will of man are related. This widening of perspective puts him more in line with the mainstream of Patristic thought and makes him see light also in some of those Medieval theologians in whom he originally only saw darkness.[140]

---

pp. 29f. also supposes the influence of Erasmus in this shift of position. But he adds the following qualifications: "An dem 'Gratis' and 'Sola fide' ist damit nichts Grundsätzliches geändert; nicht das Heilshandeln Gottes, sondern das Wesen des Menschen wird anders verstanden als es 1521 der Fall war." And: "Die Trennung zwischen evangelischer Gnadentheologie und einer rein auf den menschlichen Fähigkeiten beruhenden Philosophie hat Melanchthon nicht erst nach 1525 unter dem Eindruck von Luthers *De servo arbitrio* vollzogen, sie ist vielmehr in seinen Loci von 1521 schon angelegt und seit 1519 vorbereitet. Sie ist gegeben mit der Ablösung der evangelischen Gnadenreligion von der ethischen Religion des Erasmus, mit der Unterscheidung von Heilsglauben und Ethik." We entirely agree with the former statement, the latter statement needs correction in so far as the distinction which is rightly referred to does not necessarily imply a substitution of 'Gnadenreligion' by 'ethische Religion'; see also Maurer's paper, Melanchthons Anteil am Streit zwischen Luther und Erasmus, *Melanchthon-Studien*, pp. 137ff.

[140] Cf. P. Fraenkel, *Testimonia Patrum*, pp. 100ff.

CHAPTER FOUR

CONCLUSIONS AND SOME FINAL OBSERVATIONS

a) *Conclusions*[1]

Melanchthon wanted to be an anti-speculative theologian who based his doctrine primarily on Scripture and in the second place on the Fathers. This applies to all periods of his life. In his anti-speculative attitude he proves to be a Reformer and a Humanist. In the actual contents of his theology a development is apparent. The late Melanchthon makes statements which he at the time regarded as Scriptural and not speculative, but which the young Reformer Melanchthon would have rejected as speculative. The difference between the late and the young Melanchthon should on the whole be regarded as the result of a *development* rather than a *break*. He never became unfaithful to the core of his faith as a young Reformer, *viz.*, that only God's grace can save. While a young Reformer he put forward this faith exclusively, later on he placed it into a wider context. There are several factors which caused this widening in his theology, the most important ones being the emergence of the anti-trinitarian movement[2] and his humanistic learning which could not be suppressed for the whole of his life.[3] The Reformers had been accused of being innovators right from the beginning, and right from the beginning they rejected this accusation by referring to Scripture and the Fathers. The anti-trinitarians must have made it clear to Melanchthon how dangerous innovators could be, and they also gave him the opportunity to prove with Patristic material that he himself was not an innovator at all. This fight against the anti-trinitarians also gave him the opportunity to show that he was a learned humanist who knew his Patristic sources well.[4]

---

[1] As background of the comparisons made between Melanchthon and several Fathers the reader is referred to the author's studies listed on p. 146.

[2] Cf. P. Fraenkel, *Testimonia Patrum*, pp. 45ff., H. Römer, *Die Entwicklung des Glaubensbegriffes bei Melanchthon*, p. 34.

[3] On Melanchthon's humanism as background for his interest in Patristic theology cf. A. Sperl, *Melanchthon zwischen Humanismus und Reformation*, pp. 175ff.

[4] Cf. R. Stupperich, *Melanchthon*, p. 79: "Im Vergleich zu Luther ist in Melanchthons Büchern ein intellektualistischer Zug zu bemerken. Manches mutet geradezu scholastisch an. Aber das ist nicht das Wesentliche. Die Grundauffassung ist bei ihm unverändert geblieben, nur sind einzelne Lehrstücke gegenüber älteren Fassungen erweitert und ausgestaltet. Dabei zieht Melanchthon an vielen Stellen Verbindungen zur Tradition." See also H. Maier, Melanchthon als Philosoph, p. 47. The continuity in the thought of

If one asks whether the Fathers really influenced Melanchthon or whether he used the Fathers as supporters of views which he already held, there can be little doubt that the latter was the case. He had a number of quotations from the Fathers in store which he had either found himself in their writings or to which contemporaries drew his attention, and he used these quotations wherever it suited im, and he merely ignored what did not suit him. Not seldom he—consciously or unconsciously—twisted his quotations in such a way that they suited him even more. When in the course of his life there was a development in his thought on various matters, he obviously looked for more and other quotations from the Fathers which could support his views.

In Melanchthon we find two somewhat contradictory positions: on the one hand he claimed to reproduce the *consensus* of the Fathers and on the other hand he picked from the Fathers what seemed attractive to him. Usually he gives his quotations in such a way that the readers must get the impression that he does the former, only occasionally he admits *disertis verbis* that he does the latter. In all his writings he shows that the latter is true. But nevertheless looking back as historians we must admit that the former is not entirely untrue. Of course, there was no *consensus* amongst the Fathers, they contradicted each other and even sometimes themselves on all important issues. But this does not mean that Melanchthon's claim that he reproduces their *consensus* is entirely fictitious. He does not reproduce their *consensus*, but he certainly does stand in their tradition, and therefore his references to the Fathers are to a certain degree legitimate and not arbitrary. If these references were arbitrary, the quotations from the Fathers could be substituted by quotations from e.g. the Scholastics as well. But this is, it seems to us, not the case. There is a certain degree of continuity between the theology of the Fathers and the thought of the Reformer Melanchthon (and in the case of Melanchthon this continuity is greater than e.g. in the case of the Reformer John Calvin). His doctrine of grace does not altogether exclude free will and therefore does find support in Augustin, though to a much lesser degree in the Greek Fathers who have to be called Semi-Pelagians, a fact of which Melanchthon was not unaware.[5] His doctrine of the Trinity is in

---

Melanchthon is also stressed by K. Haendler, see his final conclusions given in *op. cit.*, pp. 563ff., and by S. Wiedenhofer, *op. cit.*, pp. 182ff., — where Wiedenhofer speaks of 'Variablen' (e.g. in the doctrine of creation), he qualifies these as 'Erweiterung', *op. cit.*, p. 185.

[5] See e.g. *Postilla Melanchthoniana* (CR 25), p. 425 where Melanchthon after a qualified praise of Augustine's doctrine of grace (see *supra*, 28) indirectly criticizes the Greek Fathers: Certe qui nobis noti sunt Athanasius, Chrysostomus, Basilius, non sunt meliores Augustino. Augustinus magis perspicue docet et pertinentiora, cf. *Loci communes*, dating from 1559 (St.A. II), p. 386.

line with Nicene orthodoxy, although he develops his doctrine in a less speculative way than the Fathers. This can be explained by the fact that to Melanchthon the doctrine of the Trinity was *inter alia* the border line between the Christian concept of God and the concept of God which man has on account of natural revelation. This was only to a certain degree the case in the orthodox Patristic Trinitarian thought. They regarded the revelation of the Father, Son and Holy Ghost as the specifically Christian revelation, but in their speculations about it they made use of the Triadic speculations in Neo-Platonism, so there was an element of natural theology even in their doctrine of the Trinity. — In his doctrine of creation Melanchthon was more speculative than e.g. Irenaeus, who simply referred the act of creation to God's will and refused to answer further questions, but less speculative than e.g. Augustin, who often deals in lengthy discussions with the question of what the relation is between the eternal Creator and temporal creation.

If we look at the amount and level of speculation in the thought of Melanchthon we can perhaps best compare him with Hilary of Poitiers (whom he probably did not know very well). Like Hilary he is certainly more speculative than e.g. Irenaeus and Tertullian, but less speculative than e.g. Origen, the Cappadocians and Augustin. With Hilary he shares his formal Biblicism, which in itself is incompatible with speculation, but like Hilary he does not maintain his Biblicism consistently and does cautiously deal with speculative questions when it seems necessary. Like Hilary he has one important central theme, to Hilary that is the infinity of God, to Melanchthon it is the doctrine of grace, both develop this theme in a systematic way. Around their central theme they place the other articles of faith which are primarily interpreted in the light of this main theme. Both can afford being systematicians who keep their heads cool in the raging of the theological controversies, because both can have the feeling that whilst the war is still on, the first battle has already been won by somebody else: Athanasius and Luther.

b) *Some Final Observations*

The strength and weakness of Melanchthon's theology coïncide in one aspect of it: its great *lucidity*. He seldom leaves his readers in doubt about his intentions. This lucidity was striven after by Melanchthon in order to distinguish himself from the Scholastics who in his view came forward with lengthy, obscure and complex expositions. But lucidity is constantly in danger of being superficial and dismissing too easily as unimportant what may not quickly be understood but ought to be taken seriously.[6] It is interesting that in the course of his life Melanchthon changed his position in as much as he showed interest in questions which he had at first refused to deal with, since he had regarded them as speculative, but that at the same time he always expressed opposition to speculation. He did not change in his rejection of speculation, but he did change his view on what actually is speculation. From his own point of view this is understandable: In the discussions with his Roman opponents he could simply not afford to make any concessions in his theological principle that Scripture is the exclusive norm of theology. But from our point of view it must be called arbitrary to reject speculation about the person of Christ at one stage and to engage in such speculation at a later stage and to accuse those who do not agree with these speculations of being speculative in an unscriptural way,—or to reject the affirmation of free will as unscriptural speculation at one stage and to reject the negation of free will as unscriptural speculation at a later stage. Such an attitude can now receive approval from different corners at the same time. The theological 'right' of our time will certainly welcome the fact that Melanchthon became more explicit in his doctrine of the Trinity and in doing so became more speculative (judged by his early standards), the theological 'left' will certainly approve of the fact that he later on gave more room to man's free will than he initially did and in doing so became (judged by his early standards) more speculative. This arbitrariness can only be overcome if we take a more favourable view of speculation and admit that as a theologian one has to be speculative. *Faith is not speculative, theology which reflects upon faith must be speculative.* Faith begins somewhere, it can certainly begin where Melanchthon began: God's incomprehensible grace which accepts the in himself unacceptable sinner. This faith has in itself little to do with intellectual curiosity. But theology has the task to set this faith into a wider context and to explore the ground around this beginning. Theology cannot be content with God's relation to the individual believer, but must ask questions about God's relation to the world of which the individual believer is a part. Here faith in God's grace must be connected with thoughts about God as the Creator of the world. When faith in God's grace is specified as faith in God's grace which appears in Christ, then questions must be raised about Christ's position in history and about the relation between the eternal God and

---

[6] Cf. W. Schenk, Erasmus and Melanchthon, *The Heythrop Journal of Theology* (8) 1967, p. 258: "... Melanchthon's was not a first rate mind. He even had something of the half touching, half ridiculous pedantry not unknown among schoolmasters and professors: he disliked loose ends and tried to tie them up wherever possible." We believe this statement to be unfair, but it is significant that it is made at all.

what happens in time. Here faith in God's grace leads to further speculations about the Trinity (however understood).

So far the speculation, i.e. the reasonable reflection about faith, takes
place within the framework of Biblical material. But speculation goes
beyond this when it takes into account that God is not only the God of
history and the Father of Jesus Christ (the predominant theme of the
Biblical writers), but also the ground of being (a theme not entirely
absent in the Bible, but developed much more in Greek philosophy). A
theologian who realizes that God is also the ground of being must take
(the history of) Greek philosophy much more seriously than Melanchthon did. When Melanchthon concedes that Plato and his followers had a
vague knowledge of God, this can hardly be called a concession:
Melanchthon needs this vague knowledge of the philosophers in order to
hold them (and natural man in general) responsible for their sins. This
way of approaching Greek philosophy must be abandoned. Greek
philosophy can make a positive contribution to theology in teaching us
how to speak about God as the ground of being. When we realize that
God is not only the God of history and the Father of Jesus Christ, but also
the ground of being, then not only is something 'added' to Christian
theology, but this addition has a clear impact on our speech about God as
the God of history and the Father of Jesus Christ. Faith in God as the
ground of being makes us use our words for God as the God of history
and the Father of Jesus Christ much more tentatively, it forces us to place
the famous Plotinian «οἶον» before every statement about God.

Melanchthon is an example of a faith which begins somewhere and is
then gradually placed in a wider theological, speculative context. Such a
development is inevitable in every believer who also is a theologian. We
believe Melanchthon's development towards being a more speculative
theologian to be a change for the better and not for the worse. In this he is
an example which ought to be followed. But here we should at once add a
qualification: In following the example set by Melanchthon we ought at
the same time to be more traditional and less traditional than he was. We
ought to be more traditional: Traditionalism is not something we should
be ashamed of, it is not a theological vice but a virtue. Lucidity may be in
danger of becoming superficial, theological novelties, if they claim to
express what has never been expressed before, are always superficial.[7] In
this respect we should even try to surpass Melanchthon in traditionalism:
He singled out certain elements of tradition as authoritative, *viz.*, the
Bible, the Fathers in so far as they expressed Biblical doctrines, and the

---

[7] The Dutch theologian I. van Dijk once observed: "He who wants to say things which
have never been said before him has a good chance that they will never be said again after
him."

few Medieval theologians who remained faithful to the Bible and the Fathers. Such a confinement was understandable and perhaps necessary in Melanchthon's days, but it would be arbitrary to maintain it. We should broaden our tradition to the whole history of Christian theology and to the tradition of religious philosophy ever since the Pre-Socratics.[8] Having broadened the tradition and thus having become even more traditionalist than Melanchthon was we should also become less traditional, *viz.*, in the sense that no period in tradition, whether Biblical, Patristic, Neo-Platonic or Scholastic has *absolute authority* for us. The various parts of the tradition which are equally valuable to us make each other relatively important and cancel out any absolute authority.

What then are our norms, do we not expose ourselves to the danger of arbitrary eclecticism? We are indeed constantly in danger of becoming arbitrary and superficial eclectics, and Christian theology has often experienced this. The protection against such arbitrary eclecticism is not the absolute authority of one part of tradition, but the serious effort to take seriously as much as possible and to combine only the best. In determining what should be taken seriously and what is the best there is inevitably a subjective and arbitrary element. But if rashness in the making of statements is avoided this arbitrariness can be checked. There is no absolute norm for our speculations, but the barrier against uninhibited and rash speculations is our desire not to fall too short of the level of theological and philosophical speculations offered by the great thinkers of the past.

We should seek as many thinkers as possible who can make a meaningful contribution to our theological discussion, and in seeking these thinkers in the past we are thorough traditionalists. But we are aware that nobody speaks the final word in the theological discussion, since it goes on endlessly.[9] In admitting that the theological discussion is endless we

---

[8] If Maurer's interpretation of Melanchthon's view on tradition is right (see *supra*, 10f., note 42), *viz.*, that one of its roots is Neo-Platonic universalism later on put into a Biblical framework, then the difference with the view presented here is that we advocate a universalism of all Christian theology and Greek philosophy, one of which roots is the Biblical tradition.

[9] The continuity with the past can be expressed from rather different angles, see e.g.: A. H. Armstrong, Negative Theology, Myth and Incarnation, *Néoplatonisme. Mélanges offerts à Jean Trouillard*, Les Cahiers de Fontenay, 1981, p. 57: "And accepting a myth is not like accepting a creed. It leaves room for free reinterpretation, imaginative and intellectual development, and plenty of criticism of details and variation of emphasis (even the most orthodox and conformist Christianity allows, and has always allowed, for plenty of all these, though theologians have sometimes pretended otherwise). But, in the end, I can think of no better representations of the faith I hold, if they are interpreted in the free and universal way I have suggested, than the great theological and artistic 'icons' of traditional Christianity." H. J. Heering, Het theïstisch godsgeloof afgedaan?, *Theologie en Praktijk* (27), 1967, p. 144: "In general liberal theology has made its most valuable con-

are much less traditionalist than Melanchthon was, and we even try to come forward with something new, but not new in the sense that what is being said has never been said before, but that we combine what never has been combined before. But once a 'new' position has been established the discussion goes on. Melanchthon thought that what is true has been expressed in the Bible and by the Fathers. The Fathers to him do no more than provide him with quotations which testify the Biblical truth, these quotations are not really interpreted from a historical context. He collected these quotations from a fairly great number of writers. When we similarly try to have a discussion with a great number of thinkers in the past, it is not that we look for quotations which suit our purpose. We look for human beings who can enrich our minds, who can open perspectives which we on our own would not have seen. We look for people who were in the same position as Melanchthon was and as we are: who want to say what is already known in a new way so that it can have a new impact, and who want to say something new what nevertheless can be generally understood because it is explained in terms which are generally known. Melanchthon was understandably fond of an ancient saying: τὰ μὲν κοινὰ καινῶς, τὰ δὲ καινὰ κοινῶς.[10]

---

tributions not in critical rejection but in listening reinterpretation". J. N. Bakhuizen van den Brink, Melanchthon: De ecclesia et de autoritate Verbi Dei (1539) und dessen Gegner, p. 106: "Und doch hatte Melanchthon den Glauben, dass die Frommen des Alten und Neuen Testamentes mit den orthodoxen Christen aller Zeiten eine innerlich zusammenhängende und niemals unterbrochene Reihe darstellen ... Das ist für die Kirche und sollte auch für den Kirchenhistoriker selbstverständlich sein. Heisst das aber formaler Traditionalismus? Meine Antwort lautet: Keineswegs, und bestimmt nicht im 'traditionellen' Sinne. Zugrunde liegt vielmehr die Überzeugung, dass Christus seine Kirche wirklich nicht verlässt, dass der heilige Geist sie in der Wahrheit leitet."

[10] See e.g. the letter to Anhaltinus (CR 6), p. 452, but it is telling that Melanchthon finds the former half more important and even wants to express τὰ κοινὰ κοινῶς: Magna haec ars est. Sed utinam ego communia et nota possim communi et facili genere sermonis explicare. Id quoque magnum decus est ... Utinam unam Evangelii vocem incorruptam, semper iisdem verbis, etiam delectis optimis et propriis maxime, omnes sonarent ubique.

BIBLIOGRAPHY

Auer, J., *Die Entwicklung der Gnadenlehre in der Hochscholastik, I: Das Wesen der Gnade,* Freiburg i.B. 1942.

Bakhuizen van den Brink, J. N., De ecclesia et de autoritate Verbi Dei (1539) und dessen Gegner, in: *Reformation und Humanismus. Robert Stupperich zum 65. Geburtstag.* Herausgegeben von M. Greschat und F. G. Goeters, Witten 1969.

——, Traditio in de Reformatie en in het Katholicisme in de zestiende eeuw, in: *Mededelingen der Koninklijke Nederlandse Academie van Wetenschappen,* Afd. Lett. N.R. 2, Amsterdam 1952.

Bauer, Cl., Die Naturrechtsvorstellungen des jüngeren Melanchthon, in: *Festschrift für Gerhard Ritter zu seinem 60. Geburtstag,* Tübingen 1950.

——, Melanchthons Naturrechtslehre, in: *Archiv für Reformationsgeschichte* (42) 1951.

Béné, Ch., *Erasme et Saint Augustin ou l' influence de Saint Augustin sur l' humanisme,* Geneva 1969.

Bizer, E., *Theologie der Verheissung, Studien zur Theologie des jungen Melanchthon,* Neukirchen 1964.

Bornkamm, H., Humanismus und Reformation im Menschenbild Melanchthons, in: *Das Jahrhundert der Reformation. Gestalten und Kräfte,* Göttingen 1961.

Breen, Q., *Christianity and Humanism. Studies in the History of Ideas,* Grand Rapids 1968.

Bring, R., *Das Verhältnis von Glauben und Werken in der Lutherischen Theologie,* München 1955.

Brink, J. A. B. van den, Bible and Biblical Theology in the Early Reformation, in: *Scottish Journal of Theology* (14) 1961.

Brüls, A., *Die Entwicklung der Gotteslehre beim jungen Melanchthon, 1518-1535,* Bielefeld 1975.

Büttner, M., *Regiert Gott die Welt? Vorsehung Gottes und Geographie. Studien zur Providentialehre bei Zwingli und Melanchthon,* Stuttgart 1975.

Dress, W., Gerson und Luther, in: *Zeitschrift für Kirchengeschichte* (52) 1933.

Engelland, H., *Melanchthon, Glauben und Handeln,* München 1931.

Fraenkel, P., *Testimonia Patrum. The Function of the Patristic Argument in the Theology of Philip Melanchthon,* Geneva 1961.

——, Revelation and Tradition, in: *Studia Theologica* 1959.

Fredouille, J.-C., *Tertullien et la conversation de la culture antique,* Paris 1972.

Friedler, R., Zum Verhältnis Luthers und Melanchthons zu Platon, in: *Das Altertum* (13) 1967.

Geyer, H. G., *Von der Geburt des wahren Menschen. Probleme aus den Anfängen der Theologie Melanchthons,* Neukirchen 1965.

——, Zur Rolle der Prädestinationslehre beim jungen Melanchthon, in: *Studien zur Geschichte und Theologie der Reformation.* Festschrift für Ernst Bizer. Herausgegeben von Luise Abramowski und J. F. Gerhard Goeters, Neukirchen 1969.

Gilson, E., *Le Thomisme, Introduction à la Philosophie de Saint Thomas,* Paris 1965[6].

Green, L. C., The Influence of Erasmus upon Melanchthon, Luther and the Formula of Concord in the Doctrine of Justification, in: *Church History* (43) 1974.

——, The Three Causes of Conversation in Philip Melanchthon, Martin Chemnitz, David Chytraeus, and the "Formula of Concord", in: *Lutherjahrbuch* (47) 1980.

Günther, H. O., *Die Entwicklung der Willenslehre Melanchthons in der Auseinandersetzung mit Luther und Erasmus* (Diss. Erlangen) 1963.

Haendler, K., *Wort und Glaube bei Melanchthon. Eine Untersuchung über die Voraussetzungen und Grundlagen des melanchthonischen Kirchenbegriffs,* Gütersloh 1968.

Harnack, Th., *Luthers Theologie mit besonderer Beziehung auf seine Versöhnungs- und Erlösungslehre, I-II,* 1862 and 1886 (reprint 1927).

Hausschild, W.-D., Die Confessio Augustana und die altkirchliche Tradition, in: *Kerygma und Dogma* (26) 1980.

Hoffmann, G., Luther und Melanchthon. Melanchthons Stellung in der Theologie des Lutherthums, in: *Zeitschrift für systematische Theologie* (15) 1938.

Hübner, F., *Natürliche Theologie und theokratische Schwärmerei bei Melanchthon,* Gütersloh 1936.

Iserloh, E., *Gnade und Eucharistie in der philosophischen Theologie des Wilhelm von Ockam. Ihre Bedeutung für die Ursachen der Reformation,* Wiesbaden 1956.

Jürgens, H., Die Funktion der Kirchenväterzitate in der Heidelberger Disputation Luthers (1518), in: *Archiv für Reformationsgeschichte* (66) 1975.

Kantzenbach, F. W., *Das Ringen um die Einheit der Kirche im Jahrhundert der Reformation*, Stuttgart 1957.

——, *Evangelium und Dogma. Die Bewältigung des theologischen Problems der Dogmengeschichte im Protestantismus*, Stuttgart 1959.

Maier, H., Philip Melanchthon als Philosoph, in: *An der Grenze der Philosophie*, Tübingen 1909.

Maurer, W., Der Einfluss Augustins auf Melanchthons theologische Entwicklung, in: *Kerygma und Dogma* (9) 1959.

——, Melanchthons *Loci communes* on 1521 als wissenschaftliche Programmschrift, in: *Lutherjahrbuch 1960*, Berlin 1960.

——, Melanchthon als Humanist, in: *Philip Melanchthon. Forschungsbeiträge zur vierhundertsten Wiederkehr seines Todestages dargeboten in Wittenberg*, herausgegeben von W. Elliger, Göttingen 1960.

——, Die geschichtliche Wurzel von Melanchthons Traditionsverständnis, in: *Zur Auferbauung des Leibes Christi (Festgabe Peter Brunner)*, herausgegeben von E. Schlink und A. Peters, Kassel 1965.

——, *Der junge Melanchthon zwischen Humanismus und Reformation. I-II*, Göttingen 1967 and 1969.

——, *Historischer Kommentar zur Confessio Augustana. Band 2. Theologische Probleme*, Gütersloh 1978.

Meijering, E. P., *Orthodoxy and Platonism in Athanasius. Synthesis or Antithesis?*, Leiden 1974².

——, *God Being History. Studies in Patristic Philosophy*, Amsterdam/Oxford 1975.

——, *Tertullian contra Marcion. Gotteslehre in der Polemik (Adversus Marcionem I-II)*, Leiden 1977.

——, *Augustin über Schöpfung, Ewigkeit und Zeit. Das elfte Buch der Bekenntnisse*, Leiden 1979.

——, *Calvin wider die Neugierde. Ein Beitrag zum Vergleich zwischen patristischem und reformatorischem Denken*, Nieuwkoop 1980.

——, *Hilary of Poitiers on the Trinity. De Trinitate 1,1-19,2,3*, Leiden 1982 (in close cooperation with J. C. M. van Winden).

Mühlenberg, E., Humanistisches Bildungsprogramm und reformatorische Lehre beim jungen Melanchthon, in: *Zeitschrift für Theologie und Kirche* (65) 1968.

Oberman, H. A., *Contra vanam curiositatem. Ein Kapitel der Theologie zwischen Seelenwinkel und Weltall*, Zürich 1974.

——, *Werden und Wertung der Reformation*, Tübingen 1977.

Pauck, W., Luther und Melanchthon, in: *Luther und Melanchthon. Referate des zweiten internationalen Lutherkongresses*, Göttingen 1961.

Petersen, P., Aristotelisches in der Theologie Melanchthons, in: *Zeitschrift für Philosophie und philosophische Kritik* (164) 1917.

Plate, H., *Die Stellung Melanchthons und Gerhards zur Kantschen Kritik der Möglichkeit einer natürlichen Gotteserkenntnis*, Göttingen 1910.

Posthumus Meyjes, G. H. M., *Jean Gerson. Zijn Kerkpolitiek en Ecclesiologie*, The Hague 1963.

Ritschl, O., *Dogmengeschichte des Protestantismus I*, Leipzig 1908.

Römer, H., *Die Entwicklung des Glaubensbegriffs bei Melanchthon nach dessen dogmatischen Schriften*, Bonn 1902.

Schäfer, E., *Luther als Kirchenhistoriker*, Gütersloh 1897.

Schäfer, E., Zur Prädestinationslehre beim jungen Melanchthon, in: *Zeitschrift für Theologie und Kirche* (63) 1966.

Schäfer, T., *Christologie und Sittlichkeit in Melanchthons frühen Loci*, Tübingen 1961.

Schirmer, A., *Das Paulusverständnis Melanchthons*, Wiesbaden 1967.

Schmitt, C. B., *Cicero Scepticus: A Study of the Influence of the Academia in the Renaissance*, The Hague 1972.

Schwarzenau, P., *Der Wandel im theologischen Ansatz bei Melanchthon von 1525-1535*, Gütersloh 1956.

Seitz, O., *Der authentische Text der Leipziger Disputation*, Berlin 1903.

Sperl, A., *Melanchthon zwischen Humanismus und Reformation. Eine Untersuchung über den Wandel des Traditionsverständnisses bei Melanchthon und die damit zusammenhängenden Grundfragen seiner Theologie*, München 1959.

Stead, G. C., *Divine Substance*, Oxford 1977.

Stege, H., Beneficia Christi. Das Zeugnis der Reformation in den *Loci communes* Philip Melanchthons, in: *Evangelische Theologie* (21) 1961.

Stupperich, R., *Melanchthon*, Berlin 1960.

Tecklenburg Johns, C., *Luthers Konzilsidee in ihrer historischen Bedingtheit und ihrem reformatorischem Neuansatz*, Berlin 1966.

Tollin, H., *Ph. Melanchthon und Servet. Eine Quellenstudie*, Berlin 1876.

Tracy, J. D., *Erasmus, The Growth of a Mind*, Geneva 1972.

Waszink, J. H., *Q. S. F. Tertulliani De anima, Edited with Introduction and Commentary*, Amsterdam 1947.

Wiedenhofer, S., *Formalstrukturen humanistischer und reformatorischer Theologie bei Philipp Melanchthon*, Bern/Frankfurt a.M./München 1976.

Winden, J. C. M. van, *An Early Christian Philosopher. Justin Martyr's Dialogue with Trypho. Chapters 1-9*, Leiden 1971.

INDICES

Quotations

Clear quotations of and references to ancient, Patristic and Medieval sources in the works of Melanchthon have been set in bold type, possible references in italic.

AESCHYLUS

Persae
742   27

AMBROSE

Expositio in Lucam
6, 93   86
6, 98   86
8, 32   32

Commentarii in Pauli Epist. ad Cor. I
(Migne PL 17)
195   31
205   31

Commentarius in Epistulam I ad Timotheum
(Migne PL 17)
493   30f.

Epistulae
73, 10f.   32

De fide
2, 13, 83   31
5, 7, 99   110

Liber de incarnatione
5, 37   31

De poenitentia
2, 9, 80   32

Sermones
23, 3   33

De spiritu sancto
1, 9, 107   31

PS.-AMBROSE

Epistula ad Demetriam
3   32

De vocatione gentium
17   31
23   31

ANSELM

Cur deus homo
I 19f.   94
II 1-4   94
II 6-7   94

De conceptu virginali et originali peccato
3   94f.

ARISTOTLE

Metaphysica
1071b   130

Physica
219b   130
251b   130

PS.-ARISTOTLE

De mundo
400 b 13ff.   129

ATHANASIUS

Ad Serapionem
1, 4   43
1, 17   12
1, 18   12
1, 30   37
3, 5   38
4, 5   12

Contra Arianos
1, 1-2   103
1, 14   43
1, 16   37
2, 31   115
2, 36   12
3, 1   12
3, 59-67   16, 61

Contra Gentes
35ff.   126
38   36, 129
43   129

De Decretis Nicaenae Synodi
25   36
28   9

De Incarnatione Verbi
2   126
5ff.   94
6ff.   35
9   34f., 94
13   35
17   36
18   37
43   110, 111

De sententia Dionysii
18   36
19   36
22   36

De Synodis
51   43

Ps.-ATHANASIUS

De incarnatione Domini nostri Jesu Christi contra Apollinarium
1, 4   36

AUGUSTIN

Confessiones
7, 9, 13-15   22
9, 13, 34   22
11, 3, 5   13
11, 9, 11   30
11, 10, 12   130
11, 13, 15   130
11, 14, 17   130
12, 1, 1   13
13, 22, 32   13

Contra epistulam Manichaeorum
5, 6   88

Contra Faustum Manichaeum
19, 10   23

Contra Julianum
2, 4, 8   24f.
5, 3, 8   25

Contra duas epistulas Pelagianorum
4, 10, 27   52

Epistulae
139   23
186, 3, 10   27

De baptismo contra Donatistas
II 3, 4   87

De civitate Dei
5, 8   127
11, 4   123

De Genesi ad litteram liber imperfectus
1, 1   13

De Genesi ad litteram
1, 19, 38   13
1, 19, 39   13
1, 20, 40   13
7, 1, 1   13
11, 4, 6ff.   15
12, 1, 1   13

De unitate ecclesiae
(Migne PL 43)
392   88

In Ioannem
2, 16   110, 111
41, 10   26
41, 12   26
78, 3   118

De gratia et de libero arbitrio
9, 21   28

De peccatorum meritis et remissione
2, 5   24
3, 6, 12   24

De gestis Pelagii
3, 7   26

Enarrationes in Psalmos
30, 2, 1, 6   27
31, 2, 7   27
130, 10   21

De vera religione
14, 27   29

Retractationes
I 13, 5   29

Sermones
76, 1, 1   87
293, 7   100
348, 2-3   127

De sermone Domini in monte
I 19, 56-57   23
II 10, 37   26

De spiritu et littera
4, 6   23
9, 15   23
29, 50   23
29, 50ff.   28
30, 52   23

De Trinitate
1, 13, 31	111
4, 20, 27	20
6, 10, 11	65
9, 12, 17-18	116
14, 6, 8	30
15, 26, 47	21
15, 27, 50	116

Ps.-Augustin

Liber Meditationum
14	22

Hypognosticon
III 4, 5	25

De praedestinatione et gratia
9, 10	25

Basil

Epistulae
8, 2	44
52, 1-2	43
204, 6	89
210, 3	89
223, 3	89

Homilia de fide
2	42

Homilia II in Hexaemeron
6	43f.

Homilia de humilitate
(Migne PG 31)
529	40

Homilia XVI, In illud "In principio erat Verbum"
3	42

Homilia de spiritu sancto
(Migne PG 31)
1429	43

Regulae brevius tractatae
288	41

Sermo de legendis libris genitilium
3	85

Liber de spiritu sancto
24	42
43	42
67	13
68	44
71ff.	89
72	44
75	42

Ps.-Basil

De poenitentia
2	42
3	41

Bernardus of Clairvaux

De libero arbitrio
	95

Sermo in festo Annuntiationis beatae virginis
1	96
3	96

Sermones
105	97

Sermones in Cantica Canticorum
32, 3	96
68, 6	96

Bonaventura

Breviloquium
1, 6, 1, 3	65

Dominica II Post Pascha Sermo I
(Opera omnia IX)
295	97

In Sententias
II, dist. xxviii, art. 1, qu. 1	98
II, dist. xxx, art. 2, qu. 1	98
II, dist. xxx, art. 2, qu. 2	98

John Chrysostomus

Contra eos qui subintroductas habent vigines
(Migne PG 47)
511	60

De ferendis reprehensionibus
(Migne PG 51)
143	46

De incomprehensibili Dei natura
5, 7	47

Expositio in Psalmum CXL
7	47

Homiliae
46, 258	46
51, 283	46

De poenitentia homiliae
2, 2ff.	49

In Matthaeum Homilia XVIII
(Migne PG 57)
265ff. 48

In Ioannem Homiliae
(Migne PG 59)
73 46
254 46

In Epistulam ad Romanos Homiliae
8, 1 47
13, 1 49

In Epist. primam ad Timotheum, cap. II
Homilia VII
(Migne PG 62)
537 45f.

De Anna Sermo
(Migne PG 54)
1, 3 129

In Epist. ad Hebr. cap. XII Homilia
31, 3 48

PS.-CHRYSOSTOMUS

In Psalmum L
(Migne PG 55)
581 47

Sermo I in Pentecosten
(Migne PG 52)
806 90

CICERO

De natura deorum
2, 2, 5 129
2, 3, 7 130
2, 6, 18 128
2, 14, 37 130
2, 15 128
2, 31, 78 129

CLEMENT OF ALEXANDRIA

Stromata
2, 20, 116, 3-4 51
3, 2, 6, 1 50
3, 9, 63-64 51
4, 12, 81 51
6, 2, 10, 5 50f.

CYPRIAN

Epistulae
63, 18 52f.
64, 5 53
69 90

De lapsis
13ff. 53
18 53
35 53

De opere et eleemosynis
(CSEL 3, 1)
p 374 53

De oratione dominica
22 52

Orationes
(CSEL 3, 3)
150ff. 52

PS.-CYPRIAN

De clericorum singularitate
54

CYRIL OF ALEXANDRIA

Adversus Anthropomorphitas
13 15
24 111

Adversus Nestorium
3, 1 55f.

Epistulae
45 55

Thesaurus
(Migne PG 75)
504 55

Dialogus de Trinitate
V 582ff. 55

JOHN OF DAMASCUS

De fide orthodoxa
3, 4 112
3, 9 56
3, 17 56
3, 27 56

DIDYMUS OF ALEXANDRIA

De Trinitate
1, 30 36

EPIPHANIUS

Adversus Haereses
II i, 61, 6 57f.
II i, 62 58
II i, 64, 5 58
III i, 74 58

Eusebius

Historia ecclesiastica
5, 20, 3-8   91
7, 25   64

Gerson

Contra curiositatem studentium
(ed. Glorieux)
    p. 230   14
    p. 233   14
    p. 238   14
    p. 244   14

Gregory Nazianzen

Carminum liber
(Migne PG 37)
    908   59
    1577   59

Epistulae
    130   84

Orationes
    5, *Contra Julianum* II 60
    30, 20   62
    37, 13   59
    39, 18-19   60
    40, 26   60
    44, 4   63

Orationes theologicae
    III 6   61
    IV 20   62
    V 3   62

Gregory of Neocaesarea
(quoted by Eusebius)

Historia ecclesiastica
    7, 25   64

Hilary of Poitiers

De Trinitate
    1, 4   126, 127
    1, 18   66
    2, 1   12, 65
    3, 14   65
    4, 14   12
    5-6   65
    6, 23   63
    6, 36   90
    7, 1ff.   9
    7, 16   12
    9, 17   111
    9, 32ff.   65
    9, 36   65
    9, 42   12
    9, 44   12

9, 51ff.   118
11, 1   12
12, 26   12
12, 53   12

In Matthaeum
    4, 25   66
    20, 10   12

In Psalmos
    1, 3   12

Hugo of St. Victor

De sacramentis
    I, pars vii, cap. 26   99
    I pars VII, cap. 28   99

Summa Sententiarum
    III 11   99

Irenaeus

Adversus Haereses
    2, 1, 1   127
    2, 1, 4   127
    2, 2, 1-3   127
    2, 4, 4   127
    2, 4, 5   126
    2, 8, 1   126
    2, 8, 2   9
    2, 9, 2   127
    2, 11, 1   127
    2, 18, 1   9
    2, 18, 4   127
    2, 37   128
    2, 40, 1   12
    2, 41, 1   11
    2, 41, 4   12
    2, 42, 2   12
    2, 42, 3-4   12
    2, 47, 2   127
    3, 3, 4   91
    3, 5, 2   111
    3, 6, 1   63
    3, 8, 3   127
    3, 16ff.   91
    3, 19, 1   68
    3, 19, 6   69
    3, 20, 3   68
    3, 38, 2   125, 127
    3, 39   9, 127
    3, 41   9
    4, 24, 2   106
    4, 34, 1   127
    4, 46   15
    4, 55   69
    4, 56, 1   69
    4, 61ff.   15

4, 62	110
4, 63, 1	125
5, 18, 2	127

JEROME

Adversus Jovianum
1, 1	72
1, 26	91

Confessio ad Damasum
(Migne PL 45)
1717	70f.

Dialogus contra Pelagianos
1, 4	71
1, 19	72
2, 7	72

Epistulae
22, 8	72
146, 1	91f.

Liber Hebraicarum quaestionum in Genesim
(Migne PL 23)
985ff.	73
987f.	73

Ps.-JEROME

Epistula ad Demetriam
3	71
16	71

Ps.-JUSTIN

Expositio rectae confessionis
11	73f.

PETRUS LOMBARDUS

Sententiae
I, dist. vi, cap. 1	100
I, dist. xiii, cap. 1	21
I, dist. xiii, cap. 3	116
I, dist. xvii, cap. 1, 2	101
I, dist. xvii, cap. 5, 1	102
I, dist. xvii, cap. 5, 3	102
I, dist. xxxi, 2	65
I, dist. xxxvii, cap. 1, 2	114
III, dist. i, cap. 1, 3	21
III, dist. x, cap. 3	100
III, dist. xvi, cap. 3, 5	102
III, dist. xix, cap. 6-7	100
III, dist. xix, cap. 7, 2	82
III, dist. xxii, cap. 3	101

LUCRECE

De rerum natura
3, 11-12	85

MELANCHTHON

Adversus Anabaptistas iudicium
(St.A. I)
p. 281	24, 75

Alloquia et breves conciones
(CR 10)
p. 1005	89, 91

Liber de anima
(St.A. III)
pp. 308f.	116
p. 317	7
p. 334	7
p. 335	116
p. 341	7
p. 354	46
pp. 361ff.	116
p. 362	29, 30

Apologia Confessionis Augustanae A
(CR 27)
pp. 277f.	24
p. 278	28

Apologia Confessionis Augustanae B
(CR 27)
pp. 424ff.	102
p. 425	98, 107
p. 426	24, 98
p. 445	32
p. 505	22, 28, 52
p. 508	32
p. 549	95
p. 553	32, 81
pp. 567f.	49
p. 633	95, 96

Chronicon Carionis
(CR 12)
p. 924	68
p. 961	73
p. 986	38, 61, 100
p. 1015	48, 58
pp. 1016f.	7
p. 1017	71
p. 1019	73
p. 1029	35, 68, 82

Commentarii (Explicationes, Enarrationes, Annotationes, Conciones, Scholia)

In Genesim
(1523) (CR 13)
p. 761	124, 126
pp. 761f.	124
p. 762	125
p. 763	30, 72f., 125, 126

p. 766	43, 73
p. 769	63
p. 783	4

In Danielem
(CR 13)
| p. 867 | 11 |
| p. 956 | 97, 105 |

In Psalmos
(CR 13) (1553-1555)
| p. 1228 | 37, 38 |

In Proverbia
(1529) (St.A. IV)
p. 318	4
p. 408	5
p. 431	24
p. 444	5
p. 446	11
p. 459	5

(1557) (CR 14)
| p. 80 | 7 |

In Ecclesiasten
(1550) (CR 14)
| p. 120 | 5 |

In Evangelia
(1544) (CR 14)
p. 177	31, 42, 65, 68
p. 217	96
p. 279	119
p. 281	116
p. 296	78
p. 311	40

In Matthaeum
(1523) (St.A. IV)
pp. 150f.	6
p. 184f.	111
p. 185	5
p. 192	111

(1558) (CR 14)
pp. 561ff.	5
p. 576	38
p. 880	33
p. 903	5
p. 966	119
p. 991	97

In Ioannem
(1523) (CR 14)
p. 1050	65
p. 1062	5
p. 1205	65

(CR 15)
| p. 10 | 42 |

pp. 56f.	89
p. 57	68, 79
p. 81	68
p. 240	68
p. 265	4
p. 280	68
p. 301	119
p. 331	119
p. 289	11
pp. 348f.	117
p. 348	116
p. 349	102
p. 373	68
p. 420	68

In Ad Romanos
(1532) (St.A. V)
pp. 33f.	28
p. 44	28
pp. 45f.	28
p. 51	28
p. 52	28
pp. 70ff.	126
p. 72	4
p. 99	107
p. 100	28
pp. 118f.	76
p. 121	28
p. 128	76
p. 156	76
p. 172	25, 94
p. 216	76
p. 251	5
p. 254	25
p. 266	28
pp. 280f.	5
p. 327	28
pp. 340ff.	33

(1540) (CR 15)
p. 466	58
p. 495	97
pp. 505f.	5
pp. 520f.	76
p. 520	46, 95
pp. 564f.	126
pp. 566f.	128
p. 623	94
p. 668	28

(1556) (CR 15)
p. 803	97, 105
p. 813	107
p. 832	126
p. 857	50
pp. 860f.	78
pp. 877f.	40

p. 877   22
pp. 882f.   28
p. 917   94
p. 935   95
p. 951   37
pp. 978ff.   5
p. 980   41
p. 998   5

In Ad Corinthios
(1522) (St.A. IV)
p. 20   6
p. 44   72
p. 56   29
p. 69   105
p. 97   39, 41

In Ad Cor. I
(CR 15) (1551)
p. 1068   97
p. 1112   52
p. 1168   92

In Ad Coloss.
(1527) (St.A. IV)
p. 222   127
pp. 230ff.   6
p. 230   6
pp. 232ff.   7
p. 238   127
p. 260   72
p. 285   4, 29, 116

(1559) (CR 15)
p. 1239   35
pp. 1247ff.   7
p. 1258   14
p. 1271   36, 100, 101

In Ad Tim. I
(1550) (CR 15)
p. 1298   5
pp. 1321f.   94
p. 1350   38

Confessio Augustana
(CR 26)
p. 276   31
p. 286   31
p. 303   48
p. 324   87
p. 407   87

Confessio Augustana (*Variata*)
(ST.A. VI)
p. 15   31
p. 24   25
pp. 29f.   31
p. 30   23

pp. 32f.   27
pp. 49f.   48
p. 50   47
pp. 51ff.   33
p. 52   14
p. 67   41
p. 74   87

Confessio Saxonica
(St.A. VI)
p. 95   78, 97, 99, 105
p. 102   40, 95
p. 104   107
p. 123   119
p. 127   75
p. 151   14
p. 152   41
p. 164   11

Declamationes
(CR 11)

De Ambrosio
p. 570   33
p. 571   38
p. 598   84

De Basilio episcopo
pp. 675ff.   45
pp. 678f.   64
p. 682   84
p. 683   40

De cura recte loquendi
p. 219   58

De dicto: Sermo Christi habitet...
p. 899   57

De dignitate studii theologiae
pp. 326ff.   89
p. 326   91
p. 327   89

De dono interpretationis
p. 646   33

De dei invocatione
pp. 662f.   119

De Luthero et de aetatibus ecclesiae
p. 786   107

In funere Lutheri
p. 728   70, 97, 99, 105

De maxilla Simsonis
p. 745   70

De nativitate Christi
p. 1036   67

De odio sophistices
p. 546   38

De Platone
p. 425   9

De precatione
p. 988   40

De studio doctrinae Paulinae
p. 36   109

De vita Augustini
p. 451   21
p. 453   78

De vita Hieronymi
p. 741   72, 84

Encomium formicarum
p. 150   33
(CR 12)

De Gregorio Nazianzeno
p. 279   50
pp. 282f.   84
p. 283   59, 62, 84

De iudiciis ecclesiae
p. 141   38

Declamatiuncula in Divi Pauli doctrinam
(St.A. I)
pp. 28ff.   111
p. 31   109
p. 40   4f.
p. 44   10
p. 50   10, 87

Defensio Phil. Melanchthonis contra Joh. Eckium (St.A. I)
p. 17   8
p. 18   8
p. 19   8, 20, 86
p. 20   10, 90, 91, 92

Definitiones multarum appellationum quarum in ecclesia usus est
(St.A. II)
p. 782   7
p. 784   127, 134
p. 792   50
p. 806   7
p. 811   51

Didymi Faventini adversus Thomam Placentinum pro Martino Luthero theologo oratio
(St.A. I)
p. 72   6
p. 74   11

p. 75   4, 104, 107, 109, 110
p. 76   127
p. 77   9
p. 80   106
p. 83   107
pp. 86f.   6
p. 86   17, 104, 107
p. 87   5
p. 94   104
p. 95   5
p. 96   104, 106
p. 98   103
p. 107   8
p. 117   67
p. 126   103, 104, 107
p. 133   85f.
p. 148   104

Disputationes
(CR 12)
p. 438   97, 98, 103
p. 442   26
pp. 445f.   42
p. 466   46
pp. 482ff.   88
p. 491   40
p. 505   81
p. 522   7
p. 529   119
p. 532   40
p. 545   95
p. 553   47
pp. 560f.   119
p. 585   131
pp. 585ff.   130
p. 586   131
p. 591   58
p. 593   36, 55, 73, 94, 112
p. 610   62
p. 613   37
p. 616   36, 55, 73
p. 622   62
p. 649   36, 55, 73
p. 651   59
p. 659   57
p. 661   38
p. 672   27, 46
p. 676   97, 105
pp. 689ff.   7
p. 690   21

De ecclesia et de autoritate verbi Dei
(St.A. I)
p. 326   88
pp. 327f.   75, 92

p. 327	89, 91
p. 332	33, 41, 53, 54
p. 335	38
p. 336	87
p. 337	70, 75, 79, 93
p. 338	8
p. 339	88
pp. 340ff.	10
p. 345	74
p. 346	74, 76, 77
p. 347	76, 77f.
p. 349	79, 93
pp. 350f.	53
p. 350	8, 52
p. 351	53, 54
pp. 353f.	41
p. 353	40, 45
p. 354	61
pp. 355f.	48
p. 355	46, 49, 57
p. 356	32, 34, 48, 49
p. 357	31, 32, 70, 72
p. 358	71, 72, 73
pp. 359f.	24
p. 362	10
pp. 363f.	27
p. 365	22
p. 369	8
p. 376	10, 28, 85

Enaratio libri II. Ethicorum Aristotelis
(CR 10)

| p. 328 | 40 |
| p. 330 | 27, 40, 46 |

Enarratio Symboli Nicaeni
(CR 23)

p. 200	9
p. 214	131
p. 220	58, 64
pp. 221f.	43
p. 221	42
p. 222	43
p. 228	118
p. 229	5
p. 235	44, 58
p. 249	132
pp. 255f.	29
p. 260	94
p. 266	46
p. 282	46
p. 283	104
p. 285	27
pp. 288f.	26
p. 289	71
pp. 338f.	94
p. 338	114

p. 340	35, 36
p. 341	56
pp. 342f.	112
p. 342	75

Epistola de Lipsica disputatione
(St.A. I)

p. 6	59, 84
p. 7	95
p. 8	91
p. 9	10

Epistulae (Praefationes, Consilia, Iudicia, Schedae Academicae)
(CR 1)

p. 73	124
p. 159	74
p. 195	72
pp. 273ff.	6
p. 430	66
p. 547	33, 39
p. 840	107
p. 946	136
pp. 1083f.	39

(CR 2)

p. 209	107
p. 230	97, 107
p. 459	28
p. 472	14
pp. 614f.	50
p. 630	120
p. 640	67
p. 660	67
p. 816	7
pp. 851f.	7
p. 877	57
p. 921	56, 100
p. 926	6

(CR 3)

p. 69	17
p. 257	89
p. 275	91
p. 277	86, 89, 90, 92
p. 317	10
p. 329	57
p. 443	11
p. 629	11
p. 682	14
p. 746	92
p. 749	64, 67, 79
p. 750	5
p. 879	64

(CR 4)

p. 38	28, 33, 38, 58
p. 41	25, 26
p. 42	24, 26

p. 350	78
p. 351	91
p. 361	47
p. 572	107
(CR 5)	
p. 45	57
p. 57	61
p. 109	40
p. 234	28, 33, 96, 97
p. 804	24
p. 805	97, 105
(CR 6)	
p. 159	14
pp. 166f.	78
p. 167	99
p. 168	104, 107
p. 426	60
p. 452	144
p. 538	60
p. 783	40
p. 830	67
p. 892	60
(CR 7)	
p. 75	67
p. 105	67
p. 106	60
p. 348	65
p. 391	65
p. 489	74
p. 582	67
p. 622	50
pp. 684f.	129
p. 854	74
pp. 884f.	100, 101
p. 1057	20, 37, 62
p. 1068	62
pp. 1079f.	92
p. 1093	68
p. 1134	100
p. 1148	100
p. 1149	20, 37
p. 1165	46, 69
(CR 8)	
p. 2	64
p. 9	50, 76
p. 10	50
p. 30	94
p. 59	58
p. 60	57
p. 68	112
p. 117	50
p. 132	50
p. 191	20, 37, 62
p. 234	68
p. 362	62

p. 544	48
p. 620	50, 51
p. 658	50
pp. 667f.	37
p. 711	22, 95
pp. 731f.	50, 51
p. 739	107
p. 863	57
p. 925	20
(CR 9)	
p. 129	50
p. 147	50
p. 186	50
pp. 190f.	50
p. 190	50
p. 194	51
p. 434	50, 51
p. 436	50, 51
p. 442	40, 41
p. 460	57
p. 535	92
p. 666	50
p. 670	59
p. 719	50, 51
p. 803	50, 51
p. 922	58
p. 1024	57
p. 1045	80
p. 1055	80
p. 1083	58

De Erasmo et Luthero elogion, Ratio discendi, et quo iudicio Augustinus, Ambrosius, Origenes ac reliqui doctores legendi sint
(CR 20)	
p. 704	72
pp. 704f.	74, 136
p. 705	23, 33, 52

Erotemata Dialectices
(CR 13)	
p. 559	130
p. 656	85

Ethicae doctrinae elementa
(CR 16)	
p. 193	40, 46, 134
p. 240	40, 46, 134

Examen ordinandorum
(1552) (St.A. VI)	
p. 181	127

Examen ordinandorum
(CR 23)	
pp. 3f.	116
p. 4	37

p. 5	56
p. 6	73, 112
p. 15	27, 46
p. 17	50

Explicatio Sententiarum Theognidis
(CR 19)

p. 57	85
p. 58	7
p. 131	27, 46

Explicatio Symboli Nicaeni
(CR 23)

p. 350	127
pp.355ff.	119
p. 356	7
p. 360	30, 42
p. 363	8f., 64, 68, 91
p. 366	43
p. 367	116
pp. 368f.	114
p. 369	36
p. 370	35, 94
p. 371	35, 68, 112
p. 373	55, 70, 82
p. 374	114
p. 375	68, 118
p. 379	43
pp. 380ff.	116
p. 380	44, 58, 64
p. 383	131
p. 386	127
pp. 387ff.	127
p. 398	131
pp. 399f.	29
p. 403	99
p. 432	128
pp. 435f.	134
p. 436	40
pp. 438f.	71
pp. 439ff.	26
p. 457	76, 107
p. 462	37
p. 492	22
pp. 496f.	7
p. 497	119
p. 500	21, 37, 116
p. 501	62
p. 503	68
p. 508	34, 35, 68, 112
p. 509	70, 112
p. 510	21, 31, 36, 55, 73
p. 511	118
p. 513	55
p. 515	62
p. 520	100

p. 524	37
p. 525	119
p. 527	64
p. 535	46, 134
p. 544	40, 46, 134
pp. 545ff.	71
p. 545	26
p. 583	94

Initia doctrinae physicae
(CR 13)

p. 191	127
p. 199	7
pp. 200f.	128
p. 205	127
p. 210	127
pp. 221f.	130
p. 369	130
p. 375	127
p. 377	130, 131
pp. 377ff.	130

Loci communes
(1521) (St.A. II)

pp. 4f.	33, 74
p. 4	6
p. 5	56, 100, 103
pp. 6f.	4, 109
p. 6	4, 100, 110
p. 7	4, 111, 123
p. 8	8, 9, 95, 133
pp. 12f.	133
p. 15	133
p. 17	95
p. 19	23
p. 36	24
p. 39	8
pp. 42f.	123
p. 43	4
p. 51	23
p. 58	109, 110
p. 61	8, 109
p. 63	14
pp. 70f.	106
p. 82	109
p. 87	101
p. 89	107
p. 99	124
p. 100	124
p. 114	107
p. 118	119
p. 124	124
p. 130	23, 28, 52
p. 134	23
p. 154	39, 41

Loci communes theologici
(1535) (CR 21)

p.333	56
pp. 355f.	42
p. 363	112
p. 370	129
p. 376	40, 46
p. 459	28

Loci praecipui theologici
(referred to as *Loci communes*)
(1559) (St.A. II)

pp. 175f.	119
p. 176	5, 7, 100
p. 186	42
p. 192	79
pp. 193f.	75
p. 193	67
pp. 194ff.	38, 122
p. 197	52
p. 198	68
p. 199	112
pp. 200f.	118
p. 203	68
p. 206	43
pp. 207f.	43
p. 209	44
p. 213	118
p. 214	126
pp. 214f.	126
p. 215	127
p. 216	128
pp. 219f.	128
p. 220	128
pp. 220ff.	128
p. 221	128
pp. 221f.	128f.
p. 222	129
p. 223	129, 130
pp. 236f.	134
p. 238	134
p. 240	134
p. 241	134
p. 243	134
p. 244	40, 46, 134, 135
p. 245	135
pp. 250ff.	71
p. 257	94
p. 258	97, 99
p. 262	103
p. 266	29
p. 306	11
p. 316	129
p. 353	117
pp. 368f.	40
p. 368	23, 27, 95

p. 380	107
p. 386	139
p. 436	96
p. 483	97
p. 484	41
p. 489	59
p. 514	53, 75
pp. 563f.	47
p. 574	47
pp. 598f.	134
p. 599	25
p. 602	135
p. 652	7
pp. 654f.	119
p. 657	104
p. 661	5
p. 714	60
p. 722	11
p. 745	14
pp. 765f.	28

In officia Ciceronis (*Praefatio*)
(St.A. III)

pp. 85f.	7

Orationes
(CR 10)

p. 961	35

Adversus furiosum Parrisiensium Theologastrorum decretum Phil. Melanchthonis pro Luthero apologia
(St.A. I)

p. 142	14
p. 144	14
pp. 147ff.	23, 28
p. 147	52
p. 148	8, 23, 31, 48, 66
p. 159	23

Philosophiae moralis epitomes libri duo
(St.A. III)

p. 153	129
pp. 157ff.	7
p. 165	59
p. 187	27
p. 241	89

Doctrina de poenitentia
(St.A. VI)

p. 439	47

Postilla Melanchthoniana
(CR 24)

p. 74	42, 43, 115
pp. 77f.	35
p. 77	20
p. 78	94

p. 79	94
pp. 81f.	118
p. 117	68
pp. 129f.	114
p. 131	36
p. 132	112
p. 202	59
p. 252	119
p. 316	46
pp. 351ff.	45
p. 357	45, 89
p. 358	41
p. 363	40
p. 364	27, 41
p. 390	25
p. 391	27, 46
p. 432	47
p. 463	80
p. 475	119
p. 503	80
p. 553	55
p. 560	36, 55, 56, 73
p. 561	112
p. 569	94
p. 578	94
p. 579	94
p. 621	94
p. 750	37
pp. 762f.	119
p. 774	80
p. 799	60
pp. 826f.	119
p. 838	104
p. 839	52
p. 861	36, 100, 101, 112
p. 867	79
p. 871	21, 116
pp. 874f.	117
p. 874	37
pp. 910f.	116
pp. 923f.	112

(CR 25)

pp. 15f.	119
p. 18	42, 62
p. 20	37
p. 60	46
pp. 74f.	104
p. 74	40
p. 80	105
p. 83	92
p. 187	47
p. 194	51
p. 205	58
p. 273	51
p. 320	33, 45

p. 342	40
p. 381	51
p. 382	98
p. 424	22
p. 425	28, 139
p. 451	47
p. 478	46, 59
p. 554	68
p. 609	105
p. 665	45
p. 718	60
p. 862	97, 105
p. 914	69

Propositiones de Missa
(St.A. I)

pp. 166f.	107

Quaestiones Academicae
(CR 10)

pp. 726f.	88
p. 726	89
p. 735	38
p. 849	20, 62
p. 860	52
p. 866	67
p. 872	59
p. 882	42, 62
p. 895	58

Refutatio erroris Serveti et Anabaptistarum
(St.A. VI)

pp. 369f.	79
p. 369	64
p. 370	67
p. 373	37, 62
p. 374	34, 35, 68, 70, 81
pp. 375f.	73
p. 375	55, 82

Responsio ad scriptum quorundam delectorum a Clero Secundario Colonia Agrippinae
(St.A. VI)

p. 402	58

Responsio Phil. Melanchthonis de contro-versiis Stancari (St.A. VI)

pp. 261ff.	112
p. 263	37, 82
p. 264	68
pp. 265f.	114
p. 265	55
p. 266	55, 73, 114
p. 267	55
p. 271	55
pp. 273f.	82

p. 273	45, 69, 114
p. 274	30, 54, 100

Responsio ad criminationes Staphyli
(St.A. VI)

p. 464	70
p. 465	64
p. 466	57

Responsiones ad articulos Bavaricae inquisitionis (St.A. VI)

p. 291	10, 33, 70
p. 308	5
p. 323	46, 59
p. 327	22, 40, 96
p. 337	52
p. 338	52

De restituendis scholis
(St.A. III)

p. 110	91
p. 113	28, 33, 45, 63, 66

De studiis adolescentum
(CR 11)

p. 181	11

Unterschidt zwischen weltlicher und christlicher Fromkeyt (St.A. I)

pp. 171ff.	6

Verlegung etlicher unchristlicher Artikel welche die Widerteuffer fügeben (St.A. I)

p. 319	53

WILLIAM OF OCCAM

In Sententiarum libros IV

I, dist. xvii	103
II, dist. xxvi U	103
IV, dist. ix	103
IV, dist. ix M	103

Quodlibeta

VI 1-4	103
VI 1	104
VI 4	104

ORIGEN

Commentarius in Matthaeum

12, 10	92
12, 11	92

Commentarius in Ad Romanos
(Migne PG 14)

943	78
953	77
955	76
963	76

965	77
981f.	77
989	76
1047	76
1076	77
1089f.	78
1094	78

Contra Celsum

3, 70	15
5, 23	15

De Principiis

Praefatio

4	75
1, 2, 2	75
2, 6, 6	75

PLATO

Philebus

22C	7

Politeia

379C	7
380B	7

SENECA

Epistulae

73, 16	128

J. TAULER

Predigten (ed. W. Lehmann)

I 108ff.	105
II 7ff.	105
II 85	105

TERTULLIAN

Ad Scapulam

2	129

Adversus Marcionem

1, 10	129
1, 10, 1	126
1, 13, 3	9
1, 22, 9	111
1, 27	127
2, 3, 1	126
2, 5ff.	15
2, 5, 3	125
2, 20	15
2, 27, 1	110
5, 16, 3	126

Adversus Praxean

2, 2	79, 92
7, 9	80

De anima
23, 5   9
58, 9   14

Apologeticum
17, 5-6   129
21, 10f.   80
21, 29   80

De paenitentia
4, 7   81

De patientia
` **15, 1**   81

De praescriptione haereticorum
16, 2   13
19, 1   13

De testimonio animae
2, 2   129

THEODORETUS

Dialogus II (Inconfusus)
(Migne PG 83)
185   81

Dialogus III, Impatibilis
(Migne PG 83)
277   82
284   68

THOMAS AQUINAS

Summa Theologica
I, qu. 2, art. 3   129, 131
I, qu. 27, art. 4   117
I, qu. 45, art. 3   123
I, qu. 46, art. 2   123, 130
II 1, qu. 63, art. 2 106
II 1, qu. 68, art. 2 107
II 1, qu. 82, art. 1 108
II 1, qu. 108, art. 1 106
II 2, qu. 32, art. 5 106
II 2, qu. 94, art. 1 107
III, qu. 3, art. 5   115
III, qu. 16, art. 5   112
III, qu. 49, art. 1   107
III, qu. 52, art. 8   107
III, qu. 75, art. 1   65

VIGILIUS

Contra Eutychem
IV 5   82
V 15   82f., 100f.

XENOPHON

Memorabilia
1, 4, 7   129
4, 4, 19ff.   129

INDEX OF SUBJECTS AND NAMES

adoption 63
Aeschylus 27, 46
allegory 33, 57, 74
Ambrose 10, 20, 30ff., 38, 45, 51, 54, 70, 74, 84, 86f., 96, 97, 103, 110, 113, 136
Anabaptists 6
Anselm 94f.
Antioch (synod at) 109
Aristotle 6, 7, 20, 127, 130
Ps.-Aristotle 129
Arius 38f., 118f.
ascetism 72
Athanasius 9, 12, 16, 34ff., 45, 58, 61, 89, 94, 103, 110, 111, 112, 115, 122, 126, 129, 139, 140
Augustin 8, 10, 13, 15, 20ff., 33f., 38, 42, 45, 46, 51, 52, 54, 62, 65, 70, 87f., 97, 100, 102, 110, 111, 113, 114, 115, 116, 117, 122, 123, 127, 130, 131, 134, 136, 139
Basil 12f., 33, 39ff., 54, 58, 62, 63, 84, 85, 88f., 96, 115, 116, 134, 139
being (essence) 4f., 114ff.
beneficia passim
Bernardus of Clairvaux 95ff., 99
biblicism 140
Bonaventura 65, 97f.
Calvin 46, 118
causae secundae 127
causes (of God's will) 5, 114ff.
celebacy 54, 72
Celsus 15
ceremonial law 23, 77
christology *passim*
Chrysostomus 8, 45ff., 51, 60, 84, 89f., 129, 134, 136, 139
Cicero 7, 128, 129, 130
Chrysippus 130
Clement of Alexandria 50f., 54, 60
communicatio idiomatum 112f.
confession (of sins) 47f.
consensus (of the Fathers) 10, 84f., 108, 139
counsels (and precepts) 23, 60, 66, 106
creation *passim*
Cruciger, C. 5, 9, 43, 44, 58, 64
curiosity (cf. speculation) 4f., 11f., 109ff., 141ff.
Cyprian 51ff., 90, 136
Cyril of Alexandria 15, 37, 54ff., 111

Demosthenes 45
Didymus of Alexandria 36
Duns Scotus 93, 104
Eck, J. 8, 20, 95, 135f.
Epicureans 127
Epiphanius 57ff., 96
Erasmus 14ff., 30, 34, 39, 45, 47, 48, 51, 54, 63f., 66f., 70, 79, 84, 91, 111, 135f.
eternal life 28
eternity 126, 131
Euripides 50f.
facultas se applicandi ad gratiam 135f.
fasting 33, 97
fides formata 107
forgiveness (of sins) 6
generation (of the Son) 12, 21, 42f., 61, 100, 115f.
grace *passim*
Gregory Nazianzen 45, 58, 59ff., 84, 115
Gregory of Neocaesarea 64, 89, 97
Hilary of Poitiers 9, 12f., 34, 65ff., 90, 102, 111, 118, 122, 126, 127, 140
Hugo of St. Victor 98f., 102
Ignatius 8
incarnation *passim*
infant baptism 24, 53, 74
Irenaeus 9, 12f., 15, 33, 54, 58, 63, 67ff., 90f., 97, 106, 110, 111, 112, 125, 126, 127, 140
Jerome 20, 30, 33, 34, 45, 51, 54, 58, 70ff., 74, 84, 91f., 113
John Chrysostomus 45ff.
John of Damascus 56, 112, 125
justification 6f.
Ps.-Justin 55, 73f.
Luther 14, 30, 34, 39, 45, 48, 54, 58, 63, 66, 70, 79, 84, 97, 98, 102, 105, 111, 112, 140
Marcion 91
monasticism 41
moralism 7
morality (natural) 6f.
mortal sins 106f.
necessity 26, 61, 100, 134
Neo Platonism 10f., 140, 143
Nicene Council 8, 109f.
Nicene Creed 8f., 109, 140
William of Occam 93, 103f.

Origen 8, 15, 33, 34, 45, 48, 57, 60, 74ff., 84, 92, 108, 140
novelty 11, 14, 142ff.
original sin 29, 74, 94, 97ff., 103, 108
Paul of Samosata 38, 64, 80, 109
penitence 24
Petrus Lombardus 21, 61, 65, 82, 99ff., 113, 114, 116
philosophy 5ff.
Plato 7, 9, 142
Plotinus 21, 142
Polycarpus 90f., 97
Pope (authority of) 86ff., 109f.
potentia absoluta 104
predestination 5
pre-existence (of Christ) 65, 67, 75, 79, 80, 109f.
procession (of the Holy Spirit) 116f., 122
Rimini (synod at) 38f., 61, 109f.
scepticism 1
sciences 6
Scripture (authority of) 2, 5ff., 86ff., 141ff.

Seneca 128
sensus communes 129
Servet 1, 64, 67, 79f., 113, 120
Sophocles 50f., 60
speculation (cf. curiosity) 1ff., 4ff., 109ff.
Stoa 26, 127, 134
Tauler, J. 99, 104f.
Tertullian 8, 9, 13, 15, 67, 79ff., 92f., 110, 111, 125, 126, 127, 129, 140
Theodoretus 58, 68, 73, 81f.
theophanies 31
Thomas Aquinas 48, 65, 93, 105ff., 112, 117, 123, 129, 130, 131
time 123, 126, 130f.
tradition 8f., 44, 142ff.
Trinity *passim*
unity (of God) 4, 6f.
vestigium trinitatis 29f.
Vigilius 82f., 100
will (of God) 4f., 61, 114ff.
will (human) 25f., 40f., 46f., 133ff.
wrath (of God) 35
Xenophon 7, 128, 129

INDEX OF MODERN AUTHORS

Armstrong, A. H. 143
Auer, J. 102, 104
Bailey, C. 85
Bakhuizen van den Brink, J. N. 8, 11, 15, 88, 120, 144
Barton, P. 111
Bauer, Cl. 6, 128
Béné, Ch. 30, 34
Bizer, E. 124, 133
Bornkamm, H. 133
Breen, Q. 6, 17
Bring, R. 134
Brink, J. A. B. van den 11
Brüls, A. 6, 124
Büttner, M. 127
Chadwick, H. 15
Dress, W. 14
Engelland, H. 1, 11, 47, 59, 106, 107, 119, 123, 124, 128, 133
Festugière, A. J. 127
Fraenkel, P. 1f., 10, 19, 25, 29, 40, 50, 57, 67, 84, 87, 88, 91, 92, 104, 108, 137, 138
Fredouille, J.-C. 13
Friedler, R. 9
Geyer, H.-G. 6, 25, 132
Gilson, E. 123
Green, L. C. 10, 135
Günther, H. O. 23, 95, 135
Haendler, K. 9, 10, 27, 40, 46, 59, 74, 85, 92, 109, 116, 124, 135, 136, 139
Harnack, Th. 7, 17, 107, 111, 112
Hausschild, W.-D. 9, 23
Heering, H. J. 143
Hoffmann, D. 136
Horn, H.-J. 128
Hübner, F. 119, 131
Iserloh, E. 103f.
Jürgens, H. 113
Kantzenbach, F. W. 10, 15, 85, 88

Knaake, I. K. F. 113
Lehman, W. 105
Maier, H. 4, 7, 138
Maurer, W. 1, 7, 9, 10f., 16, 31, 79, 136f., 143
May, G. 125
Meijering, E. P. 11, 61, 65, 66, 118, 122, 127, 131
Mühlenberg, E. 134
Oberman, H. A. 11, 14, 17, 22, 30, 71
Oyer, J. S. 16
Pauck, W. 11
Petersen, P. 7
Plate, H. 128
Posthumus Meyjes, G. H. M. 14
Ritschl, O. 5, 10, 112
Römer, H. 4, 5, 138
Schäfer, E. 30, 34, 39, 54, 58, 63, 70, 73, 74, 79, 97, 98, 103
Schäfer, R. 28, 76, 134
Schäfer, T. 111
Scharlemann, R. 132
Schenk, W. 141
Schirmer, A. 4
Schmitt, C. B. 7
Schwarzenau, P. 133
Seitz, O. 22, 26, 47, 91, 95, 135
Smulders, P. 63
Sperl, A. 9, 11, 39, 133, 138
Stead, G. C. 12
Stege, H. 4
Stupperich, R. 6, 133, 138
Tecklenburg Johns, C. 17
Tollin, H. 67, 113
Tracy, J. D. 39, 79
Waszink, J. H. 13, 85, 129
Wiedenhofer, S. 4, 10, 14, 28, 57, 88, 89, 109, 117f., 127, 139
Winden, J. C. M. van 65, 108, 127
Zeller, E. 130